PLANETS
IN
SYNASTRY

Astrologic Patterns
of Relationships

PLANETS
IN
SYNASTRY
Astrologic Patterns
of Relationships

E. W. Neville

1469 Morstein Road
West Chester, Pennsylvania 19380 USA

For Freya who guided me and, by doing so, made this book possible...
with special thanks to her handmaidens of the Brisingamen.

Planets in Synastry
by E. W. Neville

Library of Congress Card Number: 88-63393
International Standard Book Number: 0-924608-01-3

Manufactured in the United States of America

Published by Whitford Press,
A division of
Schiffer Publishing, Ltd.
1469 Morstein Road
West Chester, Pennsylvania 19380
Please write for a free catalog.
This book may be purchased from the publisher.
Please include $2.00 postage.
Try your bookstore first.

CONTENTS

Part I

THE ART
OF SYNASTRY

The innocent moon, which nothing
does but shine,
Moves all the laboring
urges of the world.

Francis Thompsom,
Sister Songs

At its simplest level, synastry is the examination of the interaction of two astrological charts. Since questions about the relationship are perhaps the ones most often asked of the astrologer, the art of synastry is a basic skill required to practice astrology at any but the most casual level. While the most common form of the art of synastry is the widely used "overlay" technique (i.e. placing the planets and houses of one chart literally on top of those of another chart and examining the interplay between them), properly done synastry requires a much broader application of all the basic astrological tools to truly reveal all the facets of a human relationship. We use this special branch of astrology to identify the hopes and motives, the fears and doubts, the reality and illusions of a relationship between two people. Because nothing so profoundly affects our lives as our contacts with others, this art must be approached with both compassion and a commitment to thoroughness. The individual personality as revealed by the birth chart is complex enough but when two charts are brought together, this complexity compounds exponentially. Incomplete analysis leaves many questions unanswered for the people involved. In truth, astrology can't provide "solutions" as such. It can only raise questions about things of which the involved persons may not be aware or willing to confront and help them understand the source of these problems.

The most sensible way to approach a problem in synastry is to deal with it exactly as a human relationship comes into being and develops. Each step of an evolving relationship is definable and particular astrological techniques are available to analyze these steps. In this book, the individual phases of a relationship are set out and a method for analysis of each phase described. This simple and logical approach assures a complete examination of all factors bearing on the relationship and, because it follows a real-life path closely approximating what people actually experience in a relationship, it is easily communicated and understood by the person(s) involved. Most astrologers would, I think, agree that usually it is not the analysis itself which is the most difficult but rather the translation of those insights gained from the analysis into meaningful and relevant images and conclusions for the untrained listener. For that reason, throughout this book emphasis is given to providing synastric results which have a "here and now" reality and application.

It is probably well to comment early on the relative need for precise calculations, fine delineations and concern over minor aspects in synastry. Over the centuries, and particularly since the advent of the computer, some very precise and elaborate techniques have been evolved to calculate house cusps, orbs and the like. For some esoteric and specialized applications, these techniques may be necessary and desirable, but fussing over a second or third decimal place is unproductive in synastry. Human personalities are fluid, ever-evolving things not made up of neatly separated and conveniently severable parts. They are acted on by a myriad of external factors which cause them to fluctuate up and down a range of tones and keys, rarely settling for long into the precise blueprint of the birth chart. When two such rippling and evolving personality profiles are placed side by side and we speculate how they will interact, this imprecision is compounded further. Aside from the simple fact that we are free to act on our responses as our will dictates (or at least to prevent ourselves from making complete fools of ourselves), too many external factors influence a relationship to allow the astrologer to achieve precise synastric results and forecasts. Some purists may be bothered by the rather broad brush approach of this book but, in truth, all we can do in synastry is identify the main thrusts and drives, the primary harmonics and discords and the broad outlines of what might be achieved if the people involved really want to work at creating a relationship. The intimate details of a relationship must be provided by the persons involved and, thank heaven, no amount of calculations will reveal those to the astrologer.

THE SYNASTRIC PROCESS

The Capacity to Relate

To state the obvious, individual humans do not have uniform capacities to form relationships nor do they seek the same things from partnerships. Equally obvious is that persons enter into relationships because those relationships promise to contain whatever rewards and advantages the individuals believe will fill their needs. By definition, a partnership is a give and take proposition, and the place to begin in synastry is to identify what each of the partners seeks from relationships in general and what capacity they have to give to a relationship. While it is unlikely any partnership involves an exactly identical or equal contribution from each party, or that each seeks precisely the same thing from the other, a reasonable match-up of what is offered and what is desired must exist for the partnership to succeed. If there is a definition of "irreconcilable differences," it usually relates to the inability of two individuals to provide for each other what each sought when they originally entered into the relationship.

In later chapters we will examine the presumptions in people's minds which lead them into attempting to initiate a relationship (attraction), the relative freedom for each partner to go on expressing their own personalities within the relationship without annoying or disappointing the other (compatibility) and ultimately to come together to create a successful working partnership (composites). At the outset, however, we need to consider how well matched are the levels of need for intimacy and cooperation in the two persons and how well the life goals, styles, and rhythms of the two personalities blend. Some rather basic common sense questions about the individual charts should be examined by the astrologer before the two charts are brought together for synastric analysis.

1. How comfortable is each with their biologic role and how well do these roles match up?

In general, the Sun and Moon in a chart tell us much about how persons relate to their own and the opposite sex. A well-aspected Sun without squares or oppositions from other planets generally indicates a person at ease with males and comfortable in playing the role which one's own gender is expected to play with regard to men. A lightly aspected or unaspected Sun usually indicates a person for whom males will not play a significant role in their lives, be they the father or subsequently the lover or mate. A Sun with hard aspects from other planets tends to find relations with males stressful and anxious and the demands of the society in relating to males difficult.

A similar line of logic applies to the Moon. A Moon with conjunctions, trines and sextiles relates easily and happily to females. A lightly aspected or unaspected Moon usually indicates a person for whom interaction with females is perfunctory and unimportant. Hard aspects to Moon indicate a person who finds female qualities irritating or demanding either in themselves or others.

In the more limited arena of romantic/sexual relationships, the same logic applies to Venus and Mars. A well-aspected Venus indicates a free and happy capacity to give of oneself, find beauty and value in others and to act in such a way that that feeling is communicated. Hard aspects limit the ability both to express love and to develop the sort of trust in and admiration for a person of the opposite sex required for a love commitment. If Mars, the indicator of what we seek sexually from partners, is well aspected then the sexual demands will be made openly and with grace. A badly aspected Mars interferes with the free flowing expression of sexual needs and results in a stressful or discordant sexual style.

Regardless of the signs and houses involved, the relative harmony of the aspects to Sun, Moon, Venus and Mars can tell us much about how well individuals can relate to their own and the opposite sex and how this capacity will carry over to a fully developed partnership. Persons who are at ease with the opposite sex will find it frustrating and puzzling if they try to form a relationship with a person who is not. Generally we assume other people function much as we do and such an assumption plants the seeds of friction and annoyance when we find they do not. The astrologer should then look carefully at how each of the partners copes with both the opposite sex and their own biological role as a preliminary step in synastric analysis. Later steps may reveal that the partnership either may flounder on these differing capacities or, just as often, provide a welcome exception for a person who otherwise has difficulty with the opposite sex. Either way, it is important to note early on that the partnership plays itself out within the boundaries established by these varying capacities to accept and play out the male or female role.

2. How well do the life goals, the limitations and the unconscious needs of individuals match up?

While Sun and Mars tell us *how* persons will go about trying to fulfill their goals, houses in which Moon and Venus fall give a good general guide to *what sort* of life will provide a sense of emotional fulfillment and joy of living for an individual. In the same sense, the house position of Saturn indicates what area will create that frustrating ambivalence of wanting and yet not wanting the life content associated with that house. Neptune's house position tells us what element of life will seemingly forever elude us in finding completeness and for which we will endlessly chase illusions and fulfillments with only limited success. Later, in the discussion of the role of houses in relationships, we will examine the meaning of houses in detail, but early in the synastric process, the astrologer needs to develop a clear understanding of what each person's chart indicates about life goals, definitions (conscious or unconscious) of satisfaction and fulfillment and the built-in limitations, frustrations and illusions of each chart. If these are not well matched, no amount of love, sexual attraction, worldly success or diligent effort will prevail against a simple mismatch of what each person defines as the good and satisfactory life content.

3. How important are relationships to the individuals and what level of relating energy exists in each chart?

In the later discussion of the role of signs in relationship, we will examine the style and tone each sign brings to a partnership, but early on it is necessary to access the overall tone and depth of the charts. We need to measure how the potential partnership is balanced in terms of relating strength and energy. While there is no inherent reason why two people with greatly differing levels of relating energy can't form a satisfactory partnership, if such is the case then each must know going in that their partner differs from themselves in this capacity and be prepared to accept that difference. If one partner naturally pours much emotionally and/or physically into the relationship, but the other is, by nature, much less emotionally or sexually energetic, this can be misinterpreted as disinterest or lack of commitment to the relationship. As we will remind ourselves throughout this book, we always use ourselves as a yardstick of "normal" to measure others despite the fact that life tells us over and over that each human is unique and different. Foreknowledge that there exists in a partnership a significant variance in relating energy can go a long way toward avoiding either a bad choice of partner or unwarranted resentment about the level of partner's responses.

In general, the signs give us good general clues about the relating qualities of a chart, particularly those in which the inner planets and the cusps of the houses associated with partnerships fall. Water signs tend to bring the most emotional energy to partnerships, Fire signs the most physical energy. Earth signs, while bringing stability and durability to partnerships, have a more limited emotional range and energy. Air signs bring great companionability and intellectual stimulus to partnership but perhaps the least of all emotional energy and physical responsiveness. One must, however, be cautious in applying these generalities for two reasons: (1) most charts are made up of a combination of sign groups with each sign making its mark only on the particular planet in which it falls and (2) to the person whose chart is being examined, *their own* emotional and physical responsiveness is "normal" and not at all deficient or limited. Try telling a person with an Air sign Moon that they are "unemotional" and they will almost certainly reject that observation. They feel emotions, are moved by sexual desire and act to fulfill these drives just like everyone else. These generalities are then *relative* only. In fact, persons with Water sign Moons *are* more emotionally motivated and directed than those with Air sign Moons, but each sees the other's actions in terms of themselves. To the Water sign person, the Air sign person is overly controlled and remote, but the Air sign person sees the Water sign person as emotionally unstable and too driven by unthinking emotional responses. Each perceives themselves to be "normal" and the other to be "odd."

There is an axiom in the business of interviewing and hiring people that we are all vulnerable to the proposition that "if someone dresses like me, thinks like me and talks like me, they can't be all bad!" Certainly this human tendency prevails in evaluating another person as a potential partner. Yet as we will see later, there is no automatic linkage between attraction, compatibility, or the ability to form and sustain a successful partnership. These elements of a relationship function wholly independently of each other, and it is only randomness that brings them all together in a favorable mix to make a successful relationship. As most of us learn, we can be intensely attracted to a person with whom we are wholly incompatible, be compatible with a person with whom we cannot form a love relationship or any other combination of these three independent functions. Because of that, people of greatly differing relating energy can be powerfully drawn to each other...and then have to deal with the sort of frustrating differences described above.

4. Where are the two individuals in the great life cycles of the outer planets and how well do their life agendas mesh?

The relative timing of the movement of the outer planets through the houses, especially the transits of Saturn, affect the ability of the partnership to sustain itself in the face of change and maturation. At the beginning of the analysis, however, it is sensible to identify to what point in these long cycles each of the people currently involved find themselves. Saturn, the great timeclock of our lives, focuses us on a sequence of life areas about which, at any given time, we are reassessing and rewriting our life scenario. Inevitably, during such reassessment we focus on that portion of our life (as represented by the house through which Saturn is transiting) and are seeking fulfillment of that aspect of our life. It is not uncommon for relationships to begin when each of the individuals is at a point in these cycles where what they most seek appears likely to be obtained via the partnership. Knowing at the outset what focal points are most strongly present in the evolving charts of the two people helps the astrologer distinguish between genuine and durable compatibility and just the simple but transient coincidence of meshing desires. This sort of "timing" is comparable to someone perched on a stool in a singles bar. We can safely assume that they (like us at that moment) are there because they are seeking some sort of "connection." If, however, we were to meet that same person in a grocery store, we could only assume they are there to buy groceries. The fact that we both happen to find ourselves at the same place with the same objective at the same time tells us only that our cycles happen to coincide; it tells us nothing about any potential success for a relationship. Yet, relationships often get much of their original impetus from the simple fact that the two people happen to be open to and looking for a relationship at the same time. There may or may not be elements present which will sustain the relationship after this cycle evolves to another point, and it is the astrologer's job to sort out the contribution of coincident cycles from those more durable ingredients of the relationship.

In general, we are most focused on partnerships as the outer planets transit the 5th, 7th and 8th houses, but we can be equally attracted to the idea of cranking one up at the 4th (because we are unusually stimulated to establish a home and family) or at the 10th (to establish our identity within the sub-culture in which we wish to gain recognition). The astrologer should identify early the current focal points of each person's life script and consider how these relate to each other; whether, in fact, what each one is trying to bring about in their life either blends well or conflicts...and if both parties recognize what the other is trying to achieve via the partnership.

The writer Ernest Hemingway once described his lifelong, but unconsummated, love affair with the actress Marlene Dietrich as a matter of unsynchronized lust. Relationships which linger but never come together because of one or the other of the people is always prevented in some way from entering into it, almost always result from such a problem of mismatched cycles. Identifying this sort of cycle matching early in the analysis again provides a broad parameter within which the partnership will have to operate, regardless of its other ingredients.

In summary then, the astrologer must become acquainted with the entire environment within which the relationship (existent or potential) is operating. The basic personalities of the individuals and their degree of comfort with their biologic roles, life goals and limits, the level of relating energy each brings to the relationship and the point of personal focus and development of each create the stage on which this little playlet will be acted out....and set limits which cannot be crossed. Within those broad boundaries, the individual motivating and functioning ingredients of the relationship can be isolated using the synastric techniques described in the following sections and the right questions brought before the persons involved in the relationship; but always within the context of these broad boundaries which ultimately define the outer ranges of any relationship.

Attraction: The Person You Seem To Be

The poet Robert Browning once quite correctly observed, "Who ere loved but loved at first sight." Of course, he was talking about *romantic* love; that marvelous response to the beauty and sexual desirability of the other person. Since we feel this response to another almost instantaneously, it clearly has nothing to do with what sort of human being the other person is nor is it based on how their personality and ours will harmonize. It is "love" only in the sense that the person somehow seems to embody whatever paradigm of beauty and desirability we have stored in our mind and/or heart. Of course, it is *not* "love" in the way we come to trust and admire a person who has been a friend and ally through tough times or who finds ways to reassure and support us, to be a haven from an unfriendly and disinterested world and to give us both their bodies and their squeals of pleasure to gratify our physical needs. But, that first attraction is a potent force and, despite the tendency to downgrade its ultimate importance, that explosion of romantic/sexual response is amazingly durable and, in all probability, necessary for love relationships. Without its initial and powerful presence we may develop all sorts of positive feelings about the other person but, probably those will never include romantic love. But where in the world does such a powerful force originate before we know anything at all about the person who inspires it and long before we test the waters of spending any time with them? And even worse, why are our feelings so often not reciprocated, leaving us to suffer the pains of not fulfilling that surge of love/sex need?

Obviously it is the physical presence of the other person, but it is more than that. All of us project to the world around us a complex persona that goes beyond just our physical appearance. We project a whole self to which those persons who come in contact with us react and, of course, they all do the same. We are constantly "judging a book by its cover" in terms of what, if any, role that person should play in our life. The great mass of people who brush by us in the course of living make no penetration at all and remain, for all practical purposes, invisible. A few do somehow penetrate our own self-preoccupation and "attract" us, and the first, the very first, thing we do is cast them in our own live scenario (friend, lover, bed partner, etc., etc.) long before we know very much about them at all. Every action which follows the first exposure is conditioned by that impulse casting; how we approach them, what we try tentatively to offer them of ourselves and what we probe to find out about in their reaction to us. We all do this and we are all equally guilty of what seems to be quite foolish and irrational behavior; casting a person in some important role in our life before we have even had a chance to see them perform. Further, we will persist in trying to persuade them to play out that role well past the time that we should have recognized that they cannot or do not wish to do so, even well past the time that an obvious discordance exists between us and that we are not at all compatible or harmonious souls. Over a lifetime we come to learn that, more often that not, the projected persona is not at all what we find after we get to know the person and that we often "fall in love" with a phantom and pay all the penalties for doing so. Why does this happen and where does that projected persona come from? Do people deliberately project a false image of themselves, intentionally misleading us, or is this persona to whom we are immediately attracted, in fact, a natural and unconscious refraction of the inner person which is often unintentionally deceptive?

Another poet, Robert Burns, once opined that it would be a great gift if God would give us the power to see ourselves as others see us. He was commenting on this phantom persona we project to others and the extraordinary misinterpretations and misjudgments others make about us because of it. Burns knew that others typically see a different person than we really are inside and that this causes a great deal of misunderstanding and grief in our lives; something which could be much reduced if we could just see what others see when they look at us. "Attraction" then is based on this projected (if often misleading) self and, despite its potency, is undoubtedly the largest contributor to unhappy love affairs of all the factors in human relationships. Astrology fortunately does offer some insight into this refracted identity, this projected persona. The tool for "seeing ourselves as others see us" is the venerable but currently somewhat neglected solar chart.

The solar chart (sometimes called "Parts" i.e. the Part of Fortune, Part of Love, etc.) has a long and distinguished history, dating back at least to Arab astrologers of the 11th century and probably earlier. It has a prominent role in Eastern horary astrology and in some forms of Chinese astrology yet, for some reason, it did not enjoy much favor in the revival of interest in astrology in the West in the 19th and 20th centuries. This may be because it is an abstract construct rather than a literal statement of astronomic fact much as transits (literal fact drawn from an astronomic ephemeris) differ from progressions (arithmetic artifices based on abstract concepts such as "one degree per year" or "a year for a day"). The value of the solar chart seems unduly ignored in contemporary astrology, in particular as it relates to the projected persona to which others respond. Perhaps this reflects our Western commitment to "reason" and cautiousness about mysticism. Natal charts are astronomic "facts." Solar charts cannot claim this.

The logic behind the solar chart is straightforward enough. At the moment of birth, our natal chart is a complete and unmodified image of our personal astrological inheritance. From that moment through the rest of our lives, that birth potential is being acted upon and modified by our own life experience and the interpretations we give to those experiences. At birth, the Ascendant is the unqualified statement of the "I AM" and is the pivot point of our world view as symbolized by the circle of houses which proceeds from it. Where and how the various functions of our chart fit into that world view is determined initially by how the planets fall in the signs and houses. The role of the Sun from birth is to act as a great double convex lens, drawing in the experiences which surround us, distributing these to various relevant elements of our chart then regathering them to focus and project them outward to the world as our unique expression of ourselves. This function of the Sun is why it is possible to generalize about members of the same Sun sign...as long as the generality is limited to the *style* of self-expression and does not extend to generalities about the specific inner motives and contents. In the same way that we could listen to a random group of records or tapes and agree that one is classical and others are country or rock or whatever (but never conclude that all classical compositions are identical) it is possible to generalize about Sun signs; a recognizable *style* of expression makes each category identifiable. This focusing and expression function of the Sun is very powerful and that shaping power is the underlying rationale of the solar chart.

Eastern astrologers envisioned the Ascendant as a source of light and the Sun as a lens through which this light passes. If the Ascendant and Sun are closely aligned (as would be the case if a person is born very near sunrise) then the "light" of the Ascendant (the "I AM" of the personality) passes through the lens of the Sun without significant bending or refraction and the image presented to the outer world is an accurate image of the inner person. This close alignment of Ascendant and Sun is, of course, rather uncommon, and most natal charts contain considerable angular separation between these two points. This results in the inner self being refracted in its passage through the lens of the Sun, presenting the same sort of misleading image as a fish swimming in water does to the observer above the water. The fish isn't where it looks like it is and so it is with most humans. What you see ain't necessarily what you get!

To relate this refraction to the actual inner person, the solar chart realigns the natal chart to present that refracted image as seen from the outside; to allow us to see ourselves (or anyone else) as others see us. The formula is simple enough and many will recognize it as the same one used to calculate the various "Parts" favored by Hindu astrologers. The effect of the formula is mathematically quite rational (remember, the Arabs were great pioneers in mathematics) in that the array of planets remains constant, the aspects between them do not change, but planets do assume new sign and house positions based on the angular relationship between the Ascendant and Sun in the natal chart. Only two basic steps are necessary to construct a solar chart:

1.*The Ascendant and Sun exchange their natal roles.* The natal Ascendant becomes the solar "Sun" position and the natal Sun becomes the solar "Ascendant" providing the cusp of the 1st house from which all the remainder of the house cusps can be derived.

2.*The remaining planetary positions are calculated as follows:*

Ascendant + Moon – Sun = Solar Moon position
Ascendant + Mercury – Sun = Solar Mercury position
Ascendant + Venus – Sun = Solar Venus position
Ascendant + Mars – Sun = Solar Mars position
Ascendant + Jupiter – Sun = Solar Jupiter position
Ascendant + Saturn – Sun = Solar Saturn position
Ascendant + Uranus – Sun = Solar Uranus position
Ascendant + Neptune – Sun = Solar Neptune position
Ascendant + Pluto – Sun = Solar Pluto position

A chart set up from these new solar-based planetary positions, using the old Sun/ new "Ascendant" to establish house cusps then presents an image of what we project to others as our basic persona and goes a long way toward explaining why others so often misread us, misunderstand our objectives and motives and simply believe we are something quite different than we know, deep down inside, that we really are.

This projected solar personality has a much greater effect than is often recognized. It frequently dictates much of the course of our lives in the world in which we must function because, in many situations, our life direction is dictated by others and their appraisal of us. A person who is perceived to be ambitious is dealt with in those terms; a person who is perceived as a leader is given leadership roles; a person who is perceived as aggressive and determined is given tasks requiring these qualities...even if those perceptions are not accurate. We face a choice in life of either responding to these perceptions and trying to function as others believe we can or refusing the roles which we feel do not suit us. Of course, if we refuse too often, others then conclude we are lazy or fearful and that can spell real trouble for us in our careers. We usually then try to be what others perceive us to be, even if we know deep down that we are not really that person. As the psychologist Kraft-Ebbing demonstrated a half century ago, if we play a role long enough and with enough effort, we "become" that role in a very real sense. So it is with the solar chart. As we mature and the Sun molds and modifies our natal potential we gradually do begin to "become" the solar personality. It seems probable that by the time Saturn completes its first cycle around our 28th-29th year, we are as much the solar projected personality as we are our natal personality simply because the world around us has forced us to play that role. Certainly by the time Saturn completes its second cycle around our 56th-58th year, we no longer outwardly show many of our natal characteristics. The natal chart characteristics are, of course, still there deep inside us. If we were born shy persons then, inside we still are, but if our solar projected persona does not allow us that characteristic, we will have learned so well how to conceal our shyness that, for all practical purposes, we are no longer shy in a functional sense.

In synastry the solar chart then plays some important roles in initiating a relationship. First, it is the projected solar chart personality to which others initially respond: the "across a crowded room" reaction characterized as love at first sight. Predictably, if we subsequently discover that the inner natal personality which actually governs the behavior of the person to whom we are so strongly attracted is substantially different than the projected solar personality, we are confused and disappointed. Secondly, while we will see later in this book that comparisons of natal charts can produce elements of compatibility which are *mutually* felt, when we respond to the illusory solar image of another, there is no reason to assume that the natal personality behind that refracted image will feel any response to us. We are initially responding to their *solar* chart image because of what is in our *natal* chart, but they are also initially responding (attracted or not attracted) by our *solar* image, based, of course, on what is in their *natal* chart. At the initial contact stage, the whole business of attraction is a muddle of illusions and presumptions. No wonder that most attractions are one-way or dead end and fail to open the door to exploring whether there is any basis for pursuing the relationship. It is arithmetically just pure chance when two people are mutually attracted and even more serendipitous when they find behind that initial attraction any true compatibility. This solar chart phenomenon goes a long way toward explaining why so few really satisfactory relationships occur in most of our lives. The initial attraction is, in fact, something of an illusion, yet it must exist to hook us and hold us or we won't even bother to find out if there is some substance behind it....and even if there isn't, we cling to the power of that illusion well beyond the time we should, proving that truly "love is blind"--blinded by the solar chart image.

An interesting sidelight on this phenomenon relates to the point made earlier that because of the constant feedback we receive based on what people perceive us to be (our solar image), we ultimately play that role to the point that we may well "become" that person. There is some indication that, as Saturn completes its first "cycle of maturation" (beginning at pubescence and ending in our early 40's), we have so taken on the coloration of our solar personality that the solar personality becomes the basis for our responses to others rather than our natal chart. This might account for why people tend to have much better luck in putting together relationships which work well after they have matured a bit. If people do, in fact, take in and profitably absorb their life experience (the Sun functioning effectively as a great lens), then they learn to sort out the illusions from the reality and make better choices of partners. If, on the other hand, they fail to mature and later in life try to recapture the fantasies of youth rooted in the unmodified natal chart, they continue to fail in finding good partners. This latter situation is a rather sadly common phenomenon. We have all seen persons who seem to endlessly recreate the same ill-advised relationship, even to the point of continuing choosing persons who actually look like clones of the same person. They may well be persons who refuse to evolve toward their mature solar personalities and cling to the adolescent preferences of their unmodified natal chart. This is not to say, of course, that the deep inner qualities of the natal chart ever truly disappear. Those natal qualities remain with us always as inner needs which must ultimately be met, but experience eventually teaches us that we must modify our interpretations of the world and our self-expression of those to cope with how the world responds to us; to learn to use our solar personality profitably and successfully. That is, after all, a reasonable definition of "maturing."

Secondly, since we gradually evolve outwardly away from our natal personality toward our solar personality under the pressures from the world around us, the solar charts of two persons in a synastry problem give a long range view of what sort of track individual maturation of the people will take. It may be that they will mature in nice parallel paths, retaining the initial compatibility which convinced them at the outset to attempt a marriage. Regrettably, the paths of maturation sometimes gradually move the persons apart, and they will, over time, slowly evolve mature solar personalities which are no longer complementary. This is why the angular relationships between the Sun in one chart and the Ascendant in another are given so much weight in synastry. In the later section on the role of aspects in relationships, these will be discussed in detail, but it should be clear that such aspects are clues to the durability of the relationship as partners evolve toward their mature solar personalities.

Thirdly, the understanding and use of the solar chart in appraising a relationship gives us a valuable tool in distinguishing between real compatibility and the vital but less concrete quality of attraction. If we find that the relationship is based mostly on attraction but has little to suggest true harmony of inner selves, the right questions can be raised to reveal the essential incompatibilities..hopefully before an over-large investment has been made in the relationship. This same process also can uncover the origins of frictions which seem to be leading to a possible break-up of a relationship and help us distinguish between the passing perturbations of transits and more deeply rooted differences between the persons.

In summary then, the solar chart helps to explain powerful attractions which do not seem to be supported by compatible personality elements and reveals the source of much of the magic which draws us to another person. With the solar chart we can usually tell whether we have a true love potion leading to a happy ending or a wicked spell filled with illusions and fantasies. That insight alone may well make the use of astrology worth the effort in relationships.

Compatibility: Harmony and Discord

Compatibility is much less the *presence* of something than it is the *absence* of friction, discord, irritation and the like. Like a musical chord, a thematic note will have a number of harmonic partner notes which can be played simultaneously with varying but pleasing results. It will also have some lousy partner notes which, if played simultaneously, produce discordant, irritating and unpleasant results. In synastric analysis we are looking at the chords produced by the combining of two charts, each playing their own melody simultaneously, to find whether the themes unique to each will blend with pleasing results. The technique is simple enough. A thematic note such as the Sun (self-expression) is chosen from one chart and compared to the primary themes of the other chart such as Moon (emotional responses), Venus (the giving, creative force) or Mars (the energy released as the questing force). This comparison is achieved by examining the aspects formed by the thematic notes from one chart to those of the other chart. A simple aspect grid which contains the planetary positions from both charts reveals these angular relationships and the harmonies and discords between the two. What we are comparing are two complex compositions being played simultaneously and how they will blend. In the end, what we are seeing is simply whether the two people will bug each other so much that this irritation outweighs the power of the attraction which brought them together initially.

A second part of the overlay procedure (literally placing one chart on top of another) is to examine where the planets from one chart fall in the houses of the other. This reveals the role or function the planet from one chart will play in the life segment of the other. Hence, if Venus from one chart falls in the 8th house of the other chart, one can conclude that the romantic, giving qualities of the first chart will impact the sexual activity (among other things) of the second chart.

This overlay analysis examines not only fundamental harmonies and discords, but also the *qualities* of those relationships by distinguishing between the types of aspects formed. Where sextiles and trines occur, the two planetary functions will flow easily and harmoniously but without any great energizing force. If conjunctions occur, one can expect a powerful release of energy between the planets and very evident and observable results. Squares between planets of the two charts produce stress and a kind of functional mismatch like the grinding of gears in a transmission. The interaction of two planets in square will certainly get the people's attention but it is more like a grating, irritating noise than a harmonious playing out of the functions of the planets. Oppositions produce a strong magnetism between the planets because the opposition is symbolic of the mirrored image of the function; the astrologic equivalent of the physics law stating that for every action there is an equal and opposite reaction. With the exception of the 150° quincunx, minor aspects generally are only occasional grace notes in the performance with minimal importance. The enigmatic quincunx can play a significant role if the aspect is formed between major inner planets because this aspect always suggests a quality of non-simultaneity; that is, the two themes cannot be played at the same time but, if expressed in a sort of alternating, action/response pattern, can blend successfully. Perhaps the best way to envision the quincunx is to remind oneself of the quincunxial relationship between the 1st house and the 6th and 8th houses. In sexual relationships, the partners rarely function with simultaneity. One "takes" as the other "gives," then the roles are reversed for a time. The 1st house (ME!) first "demands" (8th) then "serves" (6th) in an alternating and complementary pattern. This absence of simultaneity doesn't seem to interfere with the sex life of most partners because it appears to be the natural order of things. In analyzing compatibility then, we need to raise the question with a quincunx whether such an alternating pattern of function between the planets involved is a natural expression of these functions or whether such an action/response interplay will cause resentment or irritation.

In developing this part of the synastric analysis, we need to keep a number of ideas in mind:

1. Most such comparisons contain both positive and negative aspects. What we are looking for is an on-balance, holistic appraisal of the interaction.

2. The absence of aspects between planets is as often meaningful as their presence since, if the major inner planets are not aspected, the conclusion must be that that particular function of the relationship will be largely absent also. When one listens to the complaints made by a partner in an unsatisfactory relationship, the list of things the other partner *fails* to do is usually much longer than any list of objectionable actions (i.e. "he never talks to me," "she takes no interest in my work," etc.).

3. The planetary overlay from one chart onto the houses of the other indicates the primary role the planet person looks to the other to play in their life. It is always well to look carefully at the roles each partner expects the other to play since, as noted several times before, we tend to think other people are responding to a situation as we are. Very often this failure to understand why and for what purpose one partner chose the other is the root cause of discord in relationships.

4. This overlay step in synastric analysis is a sort of midpoint between initial attraction and the ultimate forming of a partnership. It does not reveal nearly as much about attraction and role casting as does a comparison of the *natal* chart of one person with the *solar* chart of the other nor does it forecast the ability of two people to form and maintain a partnership as well as the composite chart. What it tells us is how each of the partners can play out the complex melodies of their individual and unique personalities in the presence of the themes of the other while retaining their own clearly defined identities. A harmonic interaction allows each person to be themselves and express themselves freely without clashing with the other. Too many discords between the charts at this stage result in the partners constantly being forced to sublimate elements of themselves to prevent some sort of upset or annoyance.

5. It is always important to remember that "attraction" and "compatibility" operate entirely independently of each other. Two people can be strongly mutually attracted yet be quite incompatible in the sense that they cannot be in an intimate and continuing association without irritating and annoying each other. Sometimes the attraction is so strong that people labor to find ways to stay together despite fundamental incompatibility. Such situations inevitably turn out badly for the two persons involved. Raising questions which reveal this situation, however, needs to be done, even if doing so brings some short-term pain into the life of the individuals.

Composite Charts: The Partnership

In a true partnership, the individuals so thoroughly blend their personalities that a new and separate entity emerges: something distinct and often different than either of the complex assemblies that each contributed. At its best, such a partnership is an operative example of the curious process in which a total product is greater than the sum of its parts. A successful partnership allows its participants to express and accomplish things which alone they could not and to find whole new qualities in themselves which lay dormant before the partnership was formed. Central to the idea of partnership is the concept that it exists as a *third* and *distinct* entity apart from the individuals and has properties which may well not be present in either of the individuals. The composite chart is the synastric technique best suited for analysis of this new and unique product of two persons coming together in such a blended way.

The procedure for producing a composite chart relies on midpoints which have a long and well established history in astrology but, like the solar chart, were somewhat neglected until the mid-1970s when Robert Hand published his definitive book. The wide acceptance of composites since that time has brought this valuable technique back to its proper place as a major element of synastric analysis. The logic behind the composite is, as in all good methodology, simple and rational. The presumption is that when two people undertake a partnership, they blend the qualities of each of the elements of their own natal charts into a new expression of these elements. This new function for each planet is presumed to be the midpoint between the two natal planets. Once these midpoints are found, a new chart is erected using the midpoint/blended functions. This new chart is a symbolic image of that new third entity, the partnership, which the two natal charts can produce.

Again it is necessary to emphasize that the composite chart and the partnership it visualizes operates entirely independently of both attraction and compatibility. It may seem contradictory at first, but it is true that highly compatible people often cannot form and maintain successful partnerships. Even more bizarre in its own way is that people who may not be all that compatible can, nonetheless, create some remarkably successful and fulfilling partnerships. On the surface, this may seem a contradiction in terms, but it really is not. We have all seen highly successful marriages which are sustained by people who seem to have little in common, just as we have been surprised to hear of the break-up of marriages between people who seemed ideally suited to each other. The only explanation for this is that when we enter into a partnership, it changes us, alters our fundamental personalities, because the personality qualities contributed by the other person mix with ours to produce something new and different. We, of course, remain much as we have always been outside of the partnership, and this transformation functions only within the confines of the relationship. Yet such changes are real. A generally self-centered person can be transformed by the partnership into a genuinely kind and sensitive person in the presence of the other partner. Of course, sometimes the transformations are not positive and the partnership catalyzes qualities in us which are not only unattractive but are not manifested outside the partnership. The alchemy of human relationships is a marvelous and enigmatic process but, fortunately, we have the composite chart to give us some insight into that mysterious process.

As with the solar chart, we are constructing an abstract image, an arithmetical artifice, from two factually based natal charts. It is important to remember that distinction with both the solar and composite charts. We are looking not at an unalterable, lifetime enduring construct but rather a *product* of a temporary interplay of forces. As such, they are both much more open to evolutionary change and to being somewhat ephemeral. Unlike the natal chart which is a life-long package of potentials within which the individual must inevitably function, the composite chart is a representation of only one set of potentials: those of a partnership formed with one other unique individual. It is rather like comparing our genetic inheritance with the many career paths we may take. One is fairly well set for life, but the other is open to our exercise of choice, wise or unwise.

The relevance of the composite chart in synastry comes at the point when we find both strong initial attraction and adequate compatibility to want to seriously consider a long-term commitment to another person. Clearly without the initial attraction, the relationship would have never gotten started in the first place. Without a modicum of compatibility, we would have tired of the stresses and irritations of being together no matter how strong the attraction. When these fall into place, however, there comes a time when we are persuaded that we have found a true partner and want to act to formalize that realization. It is at that point the we can, using the composite chart, speculate and raise relevant questions about the results of such a commitment.

The specific methods and procedures for constructing a composite chart are outlined in Part III of this book as are the steps for all elements of the synastric process. In this introductory section, however, it is sufficient to understand the place composite charts have in the synastric process and what it reveals. The basic thing to remember is that, while it reveals little about attraction or even compatibility, it tells much about both the transformations the partnership will work upon the two persons involved in the relationship and the main thrusts and themes of the relationship once the two persons commit themselves to it. The results are often surprising and frequently quite different than we might anticipate. It is not easy to accept, early in a relationship, that the coming together will produce new and unexpected priorities and goals, yet such partnerships often change the course of our life entirely. Still, we can accept that marriage impacts our lives more profoundly than about anything else we might undertake, and this impact is reflected in the composite chart.

Perhaps the most persuasive quality of the composite chart is that, unlike the other steps in the synastric process, it compares charts in a holistic way. Behind the mechanics of calculating midpoints and composite ascendants is the heart of the composite process; the comparing of the two charts *structurally* as whole entities. This becomes evident when one notes what becomes of the aspects which appear in the two natal charts when they are blended into midpoints. If both have a conjunction between Sun and Mars, for example, then that conjunction appears in the composite. If one chart, however, has a Sun/Mars square and the other has a 75° non-aspect between these planets, it can produce a quite unexpected conjunction given the right planetary alignments. In the first chart, the harshness of the square is softened within the boundaries of the partnership and, in the other chart, the natally inactive Sun/Mars combination is brought to life by the partnership. Similarly, an opposition in one chart and a trine in the other involving the same planets can sometimes produce a productive sextile, yet at other times a stressful square. It is the overall structural profiles of both charts that are being related in a way which reveals the effect the partnership will have on the behavior of the individuals when they join. New themes emerge and stresses in the natal charts soften under the alchemy of the partnership. New houses are activated which are not areas of high activity in either of the natal charts. All in all, the composite chart is full of surprises and revelations as it blends the two personalities and shows us what they can create.

The Evolving Relationship

The final step in the synastric process is the examination of the relationship unfolding over time. This is best done by examining (1) where the individuals are now in terms of the cycles of the outer planets as these influence the decisions and feelings about the relationship, (2) how well synchronized the two individuals are as the cycles continue to redirect their personal priorities and focuses, and (3) as noted earlier, depending on the ages of the individuals, the influence of the maturation toward the solar chart personalities on their continuing ability to enjoy the initial compatibility which brought them together.

Transits, particularly of Saturn, influence the state of mind of individuals as they relate to the world in which they find themselves. Outer planet transits over the angles of the chart (Ascendant, Nadir, Descendant and Midheaven) are the great refocusing points in our lives, changing the emphasis we give to various elements of our self-image. At the Ascendant, we are dealing with our own relationship with ourselves and are prompted during the period which follows to redefine our self-image and ego identity. At the Nadir we begin a period when we reexamine and redefine our relationship with our personal environment, accepting or rejecting elements of our inherited life script regarding family, marriage, children and how we establish our personal value to the world. At the Descendant, we begin a reappraisal of the externally provided criteria under which we have been living with regard to one-to-one relationships, romantic love, sex and ultimately the philosophic base for our relations with other humans. At the Midheaven, our focus begins to shift to establishing our formal identity in the wider world in which we find ourselves, striving for career recognition, seeking the particular subculture with which we wish to be identified and finally pulling back into ourselves to weigh all the life experience we have absorbed preparatory for again confronting the transit of the Ascendant and our own self-redefinition. Obviously, these great cycles strongly influence what priorities have the greatest meaning to us at any given time and, in a partnership, ideally these cycles are in harmonic relationship.

In appraising compatibility of personalities, as we will see later, the aspects formed by the *same* planets and ascendants in the two charts (i.e. one Sun's aspect to the other Sun) are usually considered less important than the aspects between *different* planets (i.e. Sun in one chart to Venus in the other). In examining the evolving relationship, however, these "same planet" aspects are important because the aspects between the two Suns or two Ascendants or any other two planets tells in what rhythm and sequence the individuals will experience transits. The general rules for aspects apply here and planets in favorable aspect indicate that the two people will generally be experiencing outer planet transits in combinations which do not cause difficulties or stresses in the relationship. Conjunctions between the same planets, of course, mean that the two people will be experiencing these transits more or less at the same time, bringing considerable turbulence to those periods, but since the two people are struggling with the same issues, there is good reason to assume that they can and will communicate about the matters which are occupying their minds and get past these critical points coopera- tively. Sextiles and trines between the same planets suggest a rhythm of transits where the partners are grappling with areas of the individual lives which are harmonious and do not conflict with each other's concerns. Squares, oppositions or quincunxes between the same planets indicate that at times during the course of the relationship, the partners will have such different life priorities and concerns that the potential for stress, conflict and a breakdown in the relationship exists. Aspects formed by the two Ascendants tell us much the same thing as they relate to the transit of outer planets through the houses and the house-related issues which occupy both partners. The absence of aspects between the same planets and the two Ascendants is not necessarily an indication of insurmountable difficulty but rather of a relationship where the partners will find one is usually in a relatively tranquil period at the time the other is struggling with some question energized by a transit of an outer planet. As long as the partners understand this absence of synchronicity and don't become upset with one another because of it, this absence of aspects causes no great problem.

While virtually all modern astrologers recognize the importance of transits, agree- ment on the significance and even the validity of progressions is not so widely present. As early as the 1930's, pioneer astrologers like Grant Lewi rejected progressions as artifices without much significance. Those who use progressions, both primary and secondary ("one degree per year" and "day for a year"), generally see them as influencing our relationship with the world around us as opposed to the transit's effect on our inner state of mind. Progressions of importance occur rather infrequently in our lives and each of us will have to decide for ourselves whether they are important enough to be brought into the synastric process. On balance, it seems prudent to calculate at least those likely to influence the relationship (progressions involving Sun and Venus or the ruler of the seventh house) as background information. It is probably also wise to keep in mind that while planet-to-planet transits are short-term perturbations which occupy us for a few weeks or months but largely fade away and allow us to return to our basic life path, progressions are usually seen by those who use them as making rather lasting changes, redirecting the basic course of our lives. Since the interplay of progressions in the charts of partners is, to a large degree, a reflection of the structural similarities of the charts, it can be argued that the composite chart reveals much of the same insights as a plotting of progressions might. In the end, any debate over what weight progressions are given in the synastric process falls into the same category as arguments over house systems, the significance of nodes or a dozen other issues over which astrologers love to discourse. Ultimately the wise old axiom, "use the system which gives you the best results," seems to apply. Astrology is, after all, more an art than a science and there rightly should be room for a number of variations in methods used to suit the widely varying skills and aptitudes of the individual.

In summary then, we need to look at the partnership in light of any transits (and possibly progressions) which may be currently affecting decisions about it and look carefully at how well the two individuals are synchronized in their future encounters with important transits of outer planets. Finally, look at the two solar personalities as long-range points on the horizon toward which the two individuals are gradually moving (particularly if the partners are relatively young) and ask if these mature personalities will share the same compatibilities as those which initially brought the partners together.

One final question may occur to the thoughtful reader: "since the composite chart represents the third entity of the partnership separate and distinct from the two individuals, is there any evidence that transits of the outer planets over composite chart positions have any effect?" In his definitive book on composites, Robert Hand conceded that he was uncertain whether the signs which result from midpoint calculations have any significance or were just arithmetical abstracts. Since this seems to remain unresolved, due largely to the relative recency of the wide use of composite charts, the question remains unsettled. Perhaps, as the wider use of composites gives us a greater and greater body of experience, this question can be answered in the way all astrological questions ultimately must be: empirically. Until that time, it is probably best not to include transits of the composite chart in the synastric process.

CHART ELEMENTS
AND THEIR
ROLE IN RELATIONSHIPS

The Ascendant and Houses

The Ascendant is our central vantage point, our base reference, in developing our world view. We have all experienced the phenomenon of seeing a particular event or situation, drawing our interpretations and conclusions, then being dumfounded that someone else viewing the same event reaches entirely different conclusions and interpretations. From such experiences we come to understand the meaning of the term "point of view" and how that dictates what we see and how we interpret the world around us. Our Ascendant plays the same role in the evolution of our personality. It and the houses which proceed from it create our personal perspective in dealing with any of the matters associated with individual houses.

The great circle of houses has a number of levels of meaning: a cycle of maturation, the shifting focus of our life efforts, the focal points of our greatest natal energies, etc. In the realm of relationships, the houses function principally as reference points in assigning roles to the people we encounter. Based on our perception of other humans and what they project about themselves, we "cast" them in our own life script. As we come to know them, we adjust that casting as their inner qualities become more apparent, but rarely does the original casting undergo much fundamental change. This role casting is communicated to others as we deal with them. They either accept the role we have assigned them, let us know they would prefer some other role or just tell us to bug off and leave them out of our script entirely. And, of course, they are going through the same process as they deal with us.

In synastric analysis we look to the interplay of houses between two charts to understand in what role (actually amalgam of roles) the individuals have "cast" each other with regard to the planets involved. If a substantial number of the other person's inner planets fall in the houses of our natal chart associated with partnerships and love relationships, we cast them in that role and proceed to try to make that scenario a reality. They, of course, are casting us too, but not necessarily in a similar role. The coming together of this role casting, with a more or less harmonious agreement on the scenario, establishes the basis for any relationship. Unfortunately, it is rare that two individuals in the throes of early romantic/sexual excitement sit down and carefully explain to each other just exactly what role they expect the other to play. Obviously the roles are seldom, if ever, precisely the same and yet we are always inclined to proceed on the premise that the other person wants substantially what we want from the relationship. Aren't we, after all, the center of the universe and all things function as a by-product of us? Which is, of course, just another way of saying that we tend to assume that our point of view (our Ascendant) is the point of view of the whole Universe. Time eventually teaches us that this is not always true, but we probably never really accept that there are an infinite number of points of view, none more "right" than any other. More likely we subconsciously live all our lives privately considering those which differ from ours to be wrong-headed.

In relationships then, we doggedly try to get the other person to act out the role in which we have cast them; and they, of course, do the same to us. If we are lucky, this role casting in a relationship is mutually tolerable, and we manage to satisfy each other enough to persist in the partnership. Regrettably, this is not always the case, even in partnerships with strong mutual attraction and compatibility. This lack of understanding of the roles in which partners cast each other is often the origin of discontent and resentment of the sort which causes relationships to break down. In the synastric process then it is necessary to define and describe the roles which the individuals wish the other person to play and identify any significant discrepancies.

The general rule in defining these roles is that we want the particular function symbolized by the other person's planet to respond to us in terms of the house of our chart in which it falls. For example, if another person's Venus falls in our 5th house, we want them to respond to us romantically and find in us the sort of attractiveness which stimulates them to give love and admiration. If their Venus falls in our 8th house, we cast them as potential bed partners who will respond to our advances. This is fine as long as they are casting us in compatible roles. If some of our relevant planets fall in the houses of their chart which suggest some sort of intimate partnership (i.e., 1st, 5th, 7th or 8th) everything works out fine. If not, we wind up in something of a stalemate coping with seemingly inane responses like "Can't we just be friends?" We get mad or frustrated and they ask dumb questions like "What made you think I would do *that*?" Mismatched roles;

and we throw up our hands and walk away swearing never again to get involved with someone like that!

As we will see later, this role casting based on our houses remains abstract and passive unless there are some significant aspects between planets to energize us in trying to bring the scenario to life; but even without aspects, it continues to function. If we encounter someone who lays a salvo of their planets on our 5th house, we respond to them as romantically attractive, often even beautiful or something similar, but we will do nothing much to act on the response except stand off and admire unless planet-to-planet aspects motivate us. Our "point of view" defines such people as beautiful or lovable. Nothing so clearly illustrates the function of this "point of view" as when we discover that an individual we find so overwhelmingly gorgeous is not seen at all the same way by friends in which we confide our response. Every individual has a base reference point (the Ascendant) and, unless we share that with another person, we perceive the world differently. There are, of course, universals as far as defining beauty or sexiness or admirability or companionability, and our friends may well agree that the person who so moves us does, in the abstract, possess some of these universals ("Oh, he's cute but he's just not my type"). Unless, however, our friends share our Ascendant-based criteria for role-casting, they remain unmoved while we turn to jelly. This is, of course, why blind dates never work.

In synastry, at both the attraction/compatibility level and in composite charts, houses have a unique property of polar linkage. In general astrology, the houses below the horizon (1st through 6th) represent the internal self-oriented areas of our life: our self-image, possessions, personal environment, home and family, creativity and pleasure and sense of value and utility. Houses above the horizon (7th through the 12th) generally deal with our interaction with the world around us: one-to-one relationships, the possessions of others (or the "possession" of another in a sexual sense), our philosophic orientation to our society, career, subcultures we are a part of and our metaphysical perspective. In general astrology, each of the twelve houses has a distinct orientation and, while opposing houses reflect the mirror image of the same fundamental idea (i.e., the 2nd relates to our personal material possessions, the 8th to property in the abstract, such as money or credit), each has clearly different meanings for the planets which fall in them. In synastry, however, this distinction is not nearly as clear between opposing houses. *All* elements of relationships are essentially self-oriented and acutely personal with the result that, in one sense, all house functions in synastry are "below the horizon." This has the effect of blurring the distinction between opposing houses and in many ways makes their function identical.

This polar linkage of opposing houses in synastry may be better understood if you consider the opposing houses as manifestations of the same underlying relationship need:

The **1st and 7th** both generate role casting based on a quality of sameness, of a shared cosmic identity. We respond this way because we perceive the person to be made of the same stuff we are and, as result, feel we can be ourselves and receive acceptance from them.

The **2nd and 8th** both engender an urge to possess, to "have" the other person as an instrument to fulfill our needs. As such, we cast them in a sexual role because sex, standing alone, is a very self-oriented, taking urge.

The **3rd and 9th** both cause us to see the other person as one with whom we can share ideas, world views and interpretations and anticipate that they will agree with us because their point of view is similar to ours.

The **4th and 10th** both encourage us to cast the other person as one who will help us establish our place and our formal identity in the world, whether that be home, family, career or simply social acceptance. These are persons who aid us in completing the sentence "I am _____" and are perceived as an instrument to generate our place in society.

The **5th and 11th** make us see the person as one with whom we can share a common subculture and recreational preferences. We cast them as friends and companions with whom we want to share our pleasure hours and anticipate they will find the same things exciting, interesting and rewarding as we do.

The **6th and 12th** create a metaphysical linkage in which we feel we should abandon self-interest and ego games to reach for more esoteric goals. They stimulate our urge to serve others and deny ourselves and to extend ourselves beyond our material world and physical needs to some higher plane of existence.

This bipolarity of houses is most evident in composite charts. The composite chart is created from midpoints between planets but planets actually have *two* midpoints. The conventions of this particular method of synastric analysis dictate that the midpoint between the acute angular relationship of the planet (i.e. that point midway between the closest angle formed by the planets) be used in constructing the composite chart. The midpoint of the corollary obtuse angle is not used although, because of the relative movements of Sun and Venus, the acute Venus midpoint is often more or less opposed to Sun; an astrological impossibility. In his book on composites, Hand quite reasonably suggests that the obtuse Venus midpoint be used in this case so that the composite chart is credible astronomically. The obtuse planetary midpoints are equally valid within the concept of the composite chart but, if those obtuse midpoints were used to erect the chart, the houses would then be inverted. The chart itself would essentially have the same meaning but the planets would fall in houses opposing those in the conventional chart.

While there are subtle distinctions in the interpretation of opposing houses in synastry, one usually can assume that the people involved in the relationship are not particularly aware of these. A sexual urge is a sexual urge and minor subtleties such as who is the dominant partner and winds up "possessing" the other more often than the other way around is usually lost among the hormone secretions. These distinctions may later become relevant if problems arise in the relationship because of a clashing of roles (i.e. if the 1st house is dominant in both partners' role casting, a question of whose self-realization should get top priority might arise) but, at least at the beginning of a relationship, the distinctions between opposing houses seem not to be nearly as important as they are in general astrology.

The Planets

Astrology, being a special algorithmic process for calculating subjective behavioral and personality qualities, always loses something in translation. If it were possible to fully express these qualities in everyday language we wouldn't need astrology. In the same sense that there are certain ideas which can be expressed clearly and precisely in mathematical terms but cannot be fully explained or understood if translated into a narrative, defining the function of planets (or any other element of astrology, for that matter) leaves us struggling for an adequate translation. The best we can do is to suggest some core ideas associated with the astrological element we are discussing and hope that the reader will, by repeated analysis of many charts, eventually come to a fuller understanding than can be verbalized.

With that disclaimer, then the role of planets in synastry can be generally defined as symbols of the potentially active and motivated forces of the personality. Houses establish a point of view and a sequence of life focuses, signs impart stylistic and tonal qualities, and aspects are the synapses which link active elements of the chart and allow the flow of motivating energy; but planets are the "doing/feeling/reacting" core of the chart. Without planets we have a stage, a script and lighting but no actors. The role of planets in synastry then is to establish the form and quality of behavior, the action/reaction elements of the relationship; in short, what the partners are likely to *do* about the relationship.

While individual personalities obviously function as an integrated whole and individual human responses and reactions do not function separately, we are forced to subdivide these functions into convenient and hopefully comprehensible components to achieve some initial understanding of the individual roles of planets. Try at all times to hold in your mind, however, the idea of holistic personality functioning as a single integrated entity when considering planet functions. It isn't always easy to do so, but if you fail to keep that idea central to synastric analysis, you will come out with a jumbled mosaic of reactions and responses which will not provide a clear picture of the relationship. Elements of relationship, like the individual natal charts themselves, blend and combine as do colors or musical notes to produce a single complex but integrated harmonic of distinctive and unique tone. Love, sex, affection or friendship are not compartmentalized elements of relationship. They blend into something which, while it may have stronger overtones of one than the other, nonetheless is a blended whole. If the relationship is without one or more of these elements, it is then a less complex, less complete entity and serves an equally limited purpose in the lives of the individuals. The role of the planets is then to reveal to us what components are activated and functioning in the relationship to achieve the final blended result.

There are a number of good basic astrology texts which provide thorough descriptions of the functions of the planets and this is not the place to repeat that fundamental information. In the synastric process planets, of course, retain their essential functions but these operate within the context of a relationship and must be interpreted as they influence a one-to-one relationship. Briefly, the planetary roles within partnerships are:

Sun The Sun is the integrative force of any natal chart, gathering up and interpreting one's life experience. It then returns the results of that integration, molded by the rest of the chart, to the world as an expression of the personality, attitudes, perceptions and values. The Sun is a broadly based statement of what sort of person we are and, in relationships, the way one person responds to another in a generalized way is revealed by the planetary interactions and house placements. In and of itself, the Sun has no specific partnership connotations and its role is largely to establish a general ambience within which more personal and specific responses can be expressed. It is possible, of course, to feel strong affectional romantic or sexual responses to a person whom we do not especially admire or approve of, but such a pattern of response limits the scope and depth of the relationship. If synastric analysis indicates a negative or even unactivated response to Sun, it is then probable that the relationship will not be able to evolve into something durable and complete and will be limited to a one-dimensional interaction. Positive and harmonious responses to Sun create an atmosphere of friendship, approval and basic agreement and, as such, are a vital sustaining ingredient in any lasting relationship.

Moon The Moon in a natal chart always tells us much about the emotional qualities, depth and stability of the individual. In particular, the Moon indicates what sorts of things are required in a person's life to feel content fulfilled and secure. In synastry, Moon placement in houses and aspects which link it to the partner's chart indicate in what form and how successful the partner is likely to be in meeting these non-intellectual needs. Emotionally motivated behavior such as affection, generosity and sensitivity to the partner's needs can be anticipated in this lunar synastric analysis. Of course, the negative counterparts of these such as anger, insecurity and emotional insensitivity or just the general absence of a meaningful emotional response can be inferred from Moon interaction with the partner's chart. Again a limited form of compatibility of romantic or sexual responses can exist in the absence of this emotional warmth or even when harsh contacts with Moon engender emotional intensity of a negative and counter-productive form. We can be at ease with, romantically enthralled or sexually obsessed by another person without feeling much in the way of real generosity or warmth toward them. When this occurs, however, our acts of giving become self-serving and manipulative and lack genuineness. Moon then, like Sun, establishes the general emotional environment within which the relationship will function and is an equally important element in bringing honest concern, kindness and sensitivity to a partnership.

Venus In natal charts, Venus indicates how we define our own particular images of beauty, joy and pleasure and in what way we will express them in response to those people, experiences or events in our life which fulfill these images. When we encounter anything which conforms to our inner paradigm of beauty, value (in a pleasure-giving sense) or which stimulates a feeling of joy and happiness in us, we are flooded with such ideas as "priceless," "perfect," "exquisite." Our knees buckle, our common sense turns to jelly and we find ourselves paying nearly any price to be in the presence of such magic. This is why paintings by the masters command prices in the millions, why we create and preserve places of great and unique scenic beauty...and, of course, why we "fall in love." In synastry, Venus interactions tell us much about this sort of mind-scrambling response and in what way the partner stimulates romantic love in us. If one is cynical about human relationships, this could be seen as a form of fantasy fulfillment and, therefore, fraught with potentials of disillusionment. Of course, love *is* blind in this sense and when we encounter someone who fulfills our romantic paradigms, we do become more than a little impractical. Nonetheless, no partnership can fully realize itself unless we feel some considerable amount of this response. It insulates from the little annoyances of sharing space with another, lets us ignore their little flaws and lapses and provides us with a constant source of pleasure and enjoyment. Venus placement then tells us in what form and to what degree this response is stimulated by the partner; in short, what role romantic love plays in the relationship.

Mars Mars focuses our energies and efforts and points us toward that which we seek in life to achieve a sense of accomplishment. In the natal chart, the level of such life energy and the objectives toward which they are directed is defined by Mars. In synastric analysis, Mars contacts indicate the degree to which the partner is perceived worthy of our efforts, how we will seek to acquire their participation in our life and for what purpose. The vitality and aggressiveness of interaction and how those are expressed within the relationship is revealed by Mars contacts with planets and houses in the partner's chart. In these contacts we see the demands, objectives and outlines of what we want to take from the partnership. Unlike Venus which indicates what and how much we are willing to offer to the partnership, Mars suggests what rewards and satisfaction we hope to derive from it. While this may seem an essentially selfish response, without significant contacts with Mars the relationship remains passive and inert. The best relationships contain both the motivation to give and the satisfaction of receiving and Mars provides that latter quality. Harsh contacts create an unfeeling and greedy sort of demand from the partnership and the absence of contacts indicates we just won't expend much energy in creating and sustaining the relationship. With more positive contacts, however, the demands made on the partner will be expressed in a comfortable and acceptable way and provide the necessary counterbalance to what is being offered. Because of the self-gratifying nature of Mars, it has strong sexual overtones if other contacts and house placements support this. In synastry then, Mars indicates how strongly we are motivated to "acquire" the other person for a partnership, how we will go about achieving this and to what end or purpose we seek them.

The remaining planets play lesser but still important roles in partnerships, romantic and otherwise. Briefly, their contributions are:

Mercury Linkages with Mercury contribute to the capacity (or limitations) of the partners to communicate and to arrive at some agreement on the sort of personal environment and daily life style to be shared. The way individuals respond to and interpret the everyday events of their lives and go about solving the ongoing problems in making their way through this routine is conditioned by the natal Mercury placement. Positive and harmonious Mercury contacts between the charts of partners ease this process and bring stability and continuity to any shared activity. Harsh contacts suggest a pattern of disagreements over dealing with the process of living and functioning in the greater world and a divergence of preferred ways to deal with problems. The absence of contacts, while not debilitating in a relationship, does suggest that each will have their own way of doing things and some accommodation to this diversity of approach will be required.

Jupiter Our capacity for growth and development as humans and the environments in which this is most easily achieved is indicated by Jupiter's placement in the natal chart. Contacts between the charts of partners involving Jupiter suggest what stimulus and encouragement the partners will offer each other in this continuing process. Positive contacts indicate the partnership itself will contribute to the personal growth and evolution of the persons. Support, encouragement and faith in each other's ability to reach whatever goals are set grow out of positive Jupiter contacts. Jupiter's house placement indicates in what environment and toward what sort of goals the partnership will stimulate the individuals to grow. Negative contacts introduce a quality of excess and over-indulgence triggered by the partnership. Absence of contacts may only mean that the two individuals will rely principally on their own inner resources for personal growth and do not turn to the partnership itself for stimulus or support in achieving this.

Saturn Despite its bad reputation, Saturn is actually Jupiter's partner in evolution and growth of the personality. It provides the structural rigidity, the skeleton, upon which the personality can support itself as it develops. In the natal chart, a good balance between Jupiter and Saturn allows the individual to evolve as a human being without becoming disorganized or erratic. Saturn's function in synastry is much the same. Its house placement and contacts indicate the structural soundness of the relationship and how well it might survive the erosions of time and intimacy. Positive contacts augur well for the underlying strength and endurance of the partnership. House placements suggest the fulcrum point on which the relationship relies for stability. Harsh contacts indicate over-rigidity and areas of frustration and lack of flexibility in the partnership. Absence of meaningful contacts indicate that the outlines and purpose of the partnership may not be as clearly defined by the individuals and will probably require reassessment and redefinition periodically to keep the partners secure in their relationship.

The role of the last three outer planets is somewhat less predictable than those discussed above. These less easily defined functions root in the fact that astrology is an empiric craft based on an accumulation of observations over thousands of years. With the outer planets, we have had a much shorter time to deposit these myriad observations, like corals making a reef, and erect a large and certain edifice of consensus. The three outer planets appear to have their impact principally on the unconscious and, as a result, the personality qualities and their behavioral manifestations are expressed indirectly and in somewhat difficult to penetrate disguises. To the degree the function of these planets is definable, their roles are:

Uranus This planet appears to be the source of those impulses and compulsions which originate deep within us and drive us to behavior which, at a rational level, is difficult to interpret or account for in terms of cause/effect. Certainly in natal charts, the house position of Uranus seems to indicate the sort of behavior or self-expression we are compelled to act out regardless of whether there is an immediate external stimulus for that behavior. Uranus' association with revolutionary or eccentric behavior derives from the fact that when we observe such actions, we are frequently at a loss to understand or rationalize the impulses which engender it. In synastry then, Uranus placement and contacts suggest the sort of impulsive, even compulsive behavior stimulated in the partners by their contact with each other. Often the origins and causes of this behavior are not readily apparent or understood by either the person who is acting or the other partner. The house placements suggest the objectives of this compulsive behavior and contacts between Uranus and other planets indicate unconscious drives which are being impulsively acted upon. With positive contacts, such behavior will not disturb the relationship and may well introduce a delightful quality of unpredictability and serendipity. Harsh contacts, however, may engender compulsive actions which grate on, puzzle or upset the other partner. To the degree it can be predicted, Uranus then tells us in what form and with what objective sudden, unaccountable compulsions are stimulated by the partnership and how well they can be dealt with without injuring the relationship.

Neptune In natal charts, Neptune's house placement suggests that area of our lives in which we are forever chasing uncatchable rainbows, pursuing unachievable fantasies and are most vulnerable to disillusionment and disappointment. The effect of Neptune seems to be to melt away any structure we try to built within the confines of the house in which it falls. In synastry, Neptune's role appears to indicate the areas of the partnership which will be built on less than stable foundations of fantasy and illusion. The presence of such amorphous elements in a relationship is not, in itself, inherently inappropriate. After all, we often successfully turn to other humans as instruments through which we can fulfill our fantasies. The Neptune house placements then appear to indicate what illusions the partnership creates and sustains. With positive contacts between the charts, these lovely fantasies will probably persist and give us much happiness and pleasure (i.e. the husband who, after 40 years of marriage, still believes his wife is the most beautiful woman on earth). With harsh contacts, however, there is a clear suggestion that the fantasies stimulated by the partnership may cause the individuals to build their relationship on an unreal perception of its purpose and value.

Pluto This remote planet's function is the least clearly understood, largely because we have had only as few decades to observe its effects and because its effects seem to be buried deep in the unconsciousness. Astrologers have associated it with violence, crime and the sort of blasting away of old structures to make room for the new which is associated with turbulent revolutions. At a personal level, it appears to have this dichotomous function, being both destructive and regenerative. It appears to be the source of obsessive, even mindless behavior which drives individuals to persist in aspirations and goals despite all sorts of resistance and failures. As such, its function is no more inherently worrisome than any of the other planets. Much depends on Pluto's house placement and especially its contacts with other planets. In synastry, it appears to indicate if and in what form any such behavior or action may be triggered by the partnership. Because of the violent qualities associated with Pluto, it has some dark sexual connotations, tapping the deep animal urges in us if it is so activated by contacts between the charts. In some instances, it may indicate the quality of mindless lust or obsessive questing in a sexual response, but more commonly it suggests what life-altering, revolutionary effects the partnership might stimulate. Whether these upheavals result in positive regeneration and growth or a precipitous and cataclysmic breakdown in one's life structure depends largely on the nature of the contacts and the form and content of the relationship as a whole. Despite its dark and remote nature and potential for damage, its effect in synastry is deep, subtle but seldom major. If, however, Pluto appears to be the central element in the interplay between charts, it can result in a relationship filled with revolutionary changes, major upheavals and elements of self-destructiveness.

The Signs

Signs are principally stylistic in their function, coloring and modifying *how* people respond to their life experience. They also give particular qualities and tonal values to the way in which the planetary activity is expressed to the world. Sometimes signs are incorrectly perceived as having motivational qualities (i.e. "Leos want to be leaders"). A more accurate description of the function of signs is that they serve as discriminators in filtering the raw energy of the planetary functions, modifying them to conform to the particular qualities associated with the sign. They are like color filters through which untinted energy of that light is passed to give it a particular tone and hue. In synastry then, we are considering the behavioral and response qualities of the signs as they influence the way two individuals respond to each other. Since signs determine the style and form within which people behave and express themselves, we are attempting to measure how this externalizing of an individual's feelings and thoughts will blend with those of another person. In the same sense, we are examining the effect of the signs on the interpretation of life experiences to determine if two people respond to the same experience in similar or different ways.

In many ways, the circle of zodiacal signs resembles a color wheel, as if someone had held up a prism to the aggregate expressions of the human race and split that aggregation into a color spectrum. As with colors, it is possible to blend any combination of sub-divisions of this spectrum, but the results vary in clarity, luminescence and tonal values. Some combine to create rich, powerful variations; other combinations seem to cancel the best qualities of both and result in muddy, muted or lack-luster results. In considering the impact of links between signs in two charts, it is well to remember a basic axiom of astrology: each sign contains primary qualities which are largely rejections of and inimicable with the primarily qualities of the preceding sign. Adjacent signs, then, tend to produce the least attractive combinations, neutralizing and deadening the strongest qualities of both.

In classical astrology, blending of signs from the same Triplicities (i.e. Fire, Earth, Air and Water) produce the most true and brilliant combinations. Such combinations, however, do lack subtlety and nuance and when two charts are linked entirely by signs within the same triplicity, the relationship will lack both the stimulus of variety and the energy created by dynamic tension between signs: in short, a rather one-dimensional interaction lacking in subtlety.

Classical astrology also recognizes the kinship between the Fire/Air groups and the Earth/Water groups (essentially a sextile interplay). If two charts are linked by such combinations, the partners are enough alike to be comfortable with the responses and behavior of each other, but different enough to stimulate growth, expansion of horizons and widening of perspectives. Such combinations are efficient and productive, indicating the partners functional well together, and stimulate the partnership to reach out for whatever shared goals exist. The styles of the individuals blend well and, as a result, such linkages often result in worldly success for the partnership. The downside of this combination is that it may be so efficient and harmonious that it lacks energy and vitality; neat but rather unexciting.

A release of "energy" always results from the coming together of combustible and volatile elements and this is certainly true in sign combinations. We must not forget, in our quest for "compatibility," that seemingly inimical signs do share a particular kinship represented by the Quadraplicities (Cardinal, Fixed and Mutable). The sequence of these signs in the zodiac is that of the square and their interplay is dynamic and volatile. While it is likely that two charts linked primarily by such combinations of the Quadraplicities would be just too violently clashing in style and tone to function well together, the presence of some linkages of this sort between individual planets provides the spring tension, the dynamic content of the partnership which makes things happen. Opposing signs have this sort of interplay and, as a result, are highly energetic and volatile, but more fundamentally blendable than the combinations which represent a square interplay.

Of course, planets linked by the same sign share so much in the quality of their responses and behavior that it is the most harmonious linkage between planets. The weakness is that if the entire linkage between charts involves the same signs, the individuals tend to lose their individual identities in the interaction. There are no sparks flying off rough edges to enliven the relationship, no demand to grow and adapt and become more than you were when you entered the partnership. It is a linkage based on sameness rather than magnetism or complementary qualities; powerful and gripping but, if overdone, more like power and grip of paralysis.

The most enigmatic combinations of signs involve those which fall in a quincunxial sequence on the zodiac (150°). While they have the underlying quality of non-simultaneity and do not combine easily, they introduce a sort of exoticness to the planetary linkage. The responses and behavior of the partners may seem strange and foreign to each other but there is the intriguing quality about such linkages that is much like that we feel toward other cultures and mores; a sort of strange and mysterious magnetism. We mustn't forget that this is the relative position of the 8th house and its associations with the deep and mysterious forces of sex, magic and the arcane. In small doses, it adds a quality of fascination with the unknown and foreign to a partnership. A significant number of such sign combinations would, however, create such a sense of oddness and lack of common ground that the individuals cannot identify with each other.

In considering the synastric blending of signs, then, the ideal interplay would contain a variety of combinations. Except for adjacent signs, it is probably reasonable to say there are no "good" or "bad" synastric linkages between signs; just different forms each with its own qualities. In synastric analysis we are probing for the main themes of these sign linkages to identify how the styles and qualities of response and behavior of the individuals impact and influence each other.

The principal function of signs is to modify and shape the quality of planetary expression. A brilliant spotlight (planetary energy) passed through a pink filter and shown onto a landscape results in a tranquil, sunset warmth. The same light passed through the same filter and played on an exotic dancer creates an erotic and impassioned ambience. The general qualities of the sign do not change but the effect of those qualities varies over a wide range as the situation changes. This is why it is possible to speculate about what sort of work or recreation or personal environment is most suitable for individual signs. Each sign has circumstances and environments in which its qualities are most relevant and appropriate. In synastry, when we are considering the interaction between the charts of two individuals, the underlying question is how well they blend and harmonize; in short, how do the partners react to each other's behavioral style?

Within the narrow concerns of synastry, the main tonal qualities of the signs are briefly as follows:

Aries The great vitality, physical energy and predisposition for self-gratification without regard for consequences colors any planetary energy expressed through Aries. The fundamental optimism, impulsiveness and hair-trigger qualities work best with the other signs which can cope with the high risks and turbulence such behavior can create. Signs which need stability and predictability to be at their best are disoriented and threatened by the "hell-for-leather" quality Aries imparts to any planetary function.

Taurus The real world, no-nonsense effect of Taurus on planets stabilizes and focuses the energy expressed, brushing off the whimsical or impractical. This persisting single-minded dedication to the here-and-now imparted by Taurus works well with signs which measure their life satisfaction in tangible and utilitarian terms. Signs which are stimulated by high-flying imaginative exploration and the exciting interplay of intellectual and emotional stimuli on the personality are restricted by Taurus's limited capacity for light-hearted detours and play.

Gemini This sign imparts a grace and delicacy to the expressed energy of any planet, filtering out any qualities of crudeness or runaway passions. There is a certain fragility and lack of staying power in Gemini behavior which does not create a problem for other signs which rely primarily on intellectual and abstract rewards for life satisfaction. Signs which, however, need the powerful resonance of deeply felt emotions and the warmth of physical contact and intimacy find Gemini's light touch and flit-away qualities too ethereal and insubstantial.

Cancer Despite its reputation for sensitivity and self-protectiveness, Cancer is a Cardinal sign of considerable power. The over-riding tone of Cancer is parental and, in that sense, protective and nurturing. Signs which seek secure and sheltered life situations and clear evidence of a partner's commitment respond well to Cancer. For signs which need a large measure of freedom and action and an active involvement with the world at large, Cancer's over-protective, confining qualities are resented and rejected; a response which is the primary cause of Cancer's predisposition for martyrdom and self-protectiveness.

Leo Planetary energy molded by this sign is expressed with exuberance and theatricality, the very dynamism of which is calculated to capture and hold an attentive audience. This dramatic and assertive force intrigues and pleases signs which seek active and vital involvement with the world and are not compelled to hide their light behind false modesty or unctuousness. More inward-looking signs which depend on their own self-appraisal more than the feedback they receive from others are discomforted and distressed by Leo's "star quality" and self-projecting assertiveness.

Virgo A deep sense of obligation and need for recognition of its utilitarian value pervades any planet which must filter its expression through Virgo. Virgo's reputation for criticality roots in the conviction that, like the faithful butler, life's chores are most efficiently performed within a pattern of well-tested routines. This enduring faithfulness to a task and sense of order reassures other signs which need stability and a tranquil prospect of the future. Virgo's concept of order, however, is seen as unimaginative drudgery lacking in both style and elegance by signs which require a more lively and gratifying quality of life.

Libra This sign gives a lovely quality of graciousness and style to the expressed energy of the planet, the root of which is an acute awareness of how others will respond to such expressions. The capacity to see through the eyes of others and anticipate reactions impresses and enchants other signs for whom the interplay with society and sub-cultural behavioral modes are important. For more self-oriented signs which look first to their own fulfillment for life satisfaction, however, these qualities are seen as cloying and lacking in genuineness and depth.

Scorpio This sign seems to function like a magnifying lens, giving any planetary energy passing through a sharply focused, penetrating intensity. The predisposition to act on emotional responses and an undertone of obsessional commitment to a goal is exciting and magnetic for signs which rely on emotional gratification for life satisfaction. For more outward-looking signs, these qualities engender suspicion about motives and raise questions about Scorpio's willingness to be open and aboveboard about their objectives. No other sign seems to give planetary energy such deeply colored force yet creates such anxiety and fearfulness in others.

Sagittarius There is a questing, exploratory quality to any planetary expression passing through this sign; an adventurousness and speculative quality which seems to be reaching for higher planes and insights. The most intellectually oriented of the Fire signs, Sagittarius lifts the energies associated with the group to a philosophic plane, finding its rewards in activities which feed the soul and elevate the spirit. For those signs which find their goals and satisfactions in the complex workings of the society around them, the bottomless curiosity and openness to life experience of this sign are stimulating and companionable. For the quieter, more private signs, these qualities only raise fears about the reliability and capacity for long-term human commitment of Sagittarius.

Capricorn This sign gives a kind of structural sharpness and angular regularity to the planetary energy passing through it. The expression of energy follows straight lines to its goals with no quixotic detours or looping inconsistencies. For signs who are needful of a predictable and objective-oriented future and a sharply etched pattern within which to fashion their lives, the sturdy consistency and geometric predictability of Capricorn is comfortable and reassuring. For signs which thrive on change and fluidity and need the stimulus of responding to new and unexpected turns in the road, Capricorn only appears to be in danger of dying of dullness.

Aquarius Any energy passing through Aquarius seems to acquire a diffusion which lights up large expanses but is without a sharply focused center. There is a sort of sweeping, probing quality to the energy which reaches into remote corners to uncover new and revealing insights but rarely remains sharply focused on a single point. The reputation for detachment and dislike for entangling commitments which this sign has earned roots not so much in its indifference as in its tolerance for a wide range of behavior. For signs which appreciate a non-confining, amiable environment in which to function, these qualities are welcome and rewarding. If a sign needs to believe itself the center of a partner's universe and to have the reassurance demonstrated without ambivalence, this detachment of Aquarius creates uncertainty and a feeling of vulnerability.

Pisces Planetary energy touched by Pisces is softened and gentled in its tone and when it touches others it has a placating and non-threatening effect. The self-abnegating nature of this sign roots in need to achieve the spiritual fulfillment which sacrifice and abandonment of ego can produce. Molding itself to contours of less compassionate and empathetic signs, Piscean energy flows around and with the thrust of any force it contacts. For signs which need the warmth and gentleness of a partner who will stimulate them to express their own humanity, this curious combination of supportiveness and chameleon-like willingness to assume whatever identity the partner imposes is both therapeutic and erotic. The more self-assertive and hard-shelled signs find Piscean passivity and diffused outlines too flimsy and malleable to trust.

As a final comment on signs in synastry, the reader should always remind themselves that (1) individual charts contain a variety of signs which blend qualities described above to produce something different in tonal values than any single sign's colorations, (2) the qualities of a sign relate only to the planet which must express its energy via that sign and often the more assertive planets such as Sun and Mars mask the expression of the signs in which the less aggressive planets such as Moon or Venus fall except in intimate and secure partnership situations, and (3) as noted above, the qualities of signs are very situational and more or less strongly expressed as the circumstances surrounding the individual require. Situations which require assertiveness will draw on whatever resources the chart has to meet that demand, just as a close relationship will tap capacities for intimacies not usually expressed in daily life.

The Aspects

Aspects, the angular relationship between planets, are the synaptic link through which the energy of the planets flows and is exchanged. In natal charts, aspects bring together the energy of the two planets with the result of certain predictable expressions of the combined forces of the linked planets. In synastry, the aspect plays a similar role, connecting a planet from one chart to a planet in another, activating the energy in both and providing the fuel for acting out the responses created by the role-casting described above. Without these inter-chart aspects, the roles into which we cast people and the way in which we respond to their own particular form of expressing themselves remains inert and unacted upon. We may find ourselves with all sorts of responses and feeling judgements prompted by our contact with the other person, but we will not likely *act* to bring that scenario to life without significant aspects between our planets and theirs.

In considering aspects between charts there are several generalities worth keeping in mind. In a natal chart, the energies of the two aspected planets blend to produce a resulting expression in the individual personality. When, however, a planet in our chart is linked and activated by a planet in another person's chart, the active quality of the energy released in us is limited to that *single* planet in our chart. If, for example, our Moon is aspected by another person's Mars, it is our Moon behavioral mode through which we will express our response to that person; and they, obviously, will express their response to us via their Mars action mode. When this sort of linkage occurs, we are both likely to *do* something: to actively express our response to the other person. The aspect has triggered the behavioral mode of our Moon and their Mars. Obviously, the particular quality of each planets natural mode of behavior reveals itself and, if they are harmonious, we get a result which contributes positively to the relationship. If, however, these behavioral modes clash with each other, what results is a discordant interaction.

There is sometimes a misconception that aspects function with an independent and different force of their own apart from interactions between signs and houses. Actually, all they do is measure "proximity," indicating whether the particular elements in a natal chart or in the linkage between two charts come close enough together to spark a reaction. It is rather like two people who are strongly sexually attracted to each other but, for whatever reason, decide they should not allow their attraction to draw them into an intimate relationship. To avoid the temptations of such a situation, they do their best to keep a safe distance. Proximity or closeness creates a "critical mass" and the two people, knowing this, maintain the distance to keep this from happening. Such are aspects; indications that things are within a range which will trigger action, but only "action" pure and simple. The aspect itself is only a symbolic representation of the general harmony or discord between the forms of actions natural to the signs and houses in which the linked planets fall. It is regrettable that aspects are sometimes discussed as if they function independent of the remainder of the chart. What, in fact, they tell us in synastry is whether the two persons involved are likely to *act* on any responses they feel to each other or just pass in the night without acting on responses they feel. As in natal charts, many close aspects between charts in synastry indicate a complex and multi-dimensional *interaction* (as opposed to an unacted-upon response) between the people involved and whether expressions of the natal personalities will be harmonious or discordant.

In considering aspects in synastry, then, we are not just speculating in the abstract about what the general properties of two charts may be and how blendable they are. With aspects, we are confronting the likelihood that the individuals will test this interaction by *doing* something about the "feelings" they release in each other. This typically is a much more narrow focus in analysis of charts. With the interplay of signs and houses, we consider the general harmony of the personalities. Within that general picture, aspects tell us what the *active, connective* elements of the interplay may be. Clearly we can find all sorts of combinations: general personalities which do not mesh well but with a few highly energetic aspects which may cause the individuals to try to make it work anyway. We may find broadly compatible charts which are unaspected (hence no real effort to "relate") or with disharmonious aspects which make it difficult to translate the general compatibility into a functioning partnership. Whatever the general qualities of compatibility or discord may be, the aspects tell us in what active way the individuals will try to connect with each other and with what probable results.

Within the general understanding of aspects outlined above, the qualities of the principal linkages between planets are as follows:

Conjunction This aspect brings two like forms of planetary energy together and, as a result, has a greatly amplifying effect on each. Whatever the innate properties of the planet's energy, filtered through the quality of the sign in which it falls, this sort of contact will increase its intensity even to a point of exaggerating these qualities. One can expect not only a high level of motivation to act but also that the action will be almost an archetypical expression of the qualities of the planets and signs involved.

Sextile This comfortable and harmonious aspect brings planetary energies into contact which are complementary and, to a degree, compensatory. The two energies tend to provide a nice counterbalance for the strengths and weakness inherent in each with the result that the two planets and signs act together with ease and success in achieving whatever end is indicated. Of all the aspects, it is the most likely to produce a durable and satisfying blending of energies; not necessarily electric or exciting, but with lasting satisfaction.

Square The square brings into contact two forms of planetary energy with very different properties. These energies are not truly blendable and, as a result, they create tension and stress when they connect. Each struggles for dominance in the interaction rather than flow together. The result often is a negative exaggeration of the basic qualities of the planets and signs involved, producing extreme and heated behavioral responses which seem to feed on each other. Clearly this is not an easy interaction but, in some linking of planets, it generates a very compelling and exciting pattern of response. The tolerability of this overheated linkage within a relationship depends entirely on which planets are involved and within what sort of a general pattern of compatibility it occurs.

Trine Trine aspects bring into contact two forms of the same planetary energy, like two octaves of the same musical note. Clearly they are harmonious but equally obviously, this sort of blending is without complementary harmonics to give the interaction a transformative quality. The two energies flow together so easily that neither individual is required to expend much energy or do much more than continue being as they always have been. Despite the clear compatibility of this combination, it contains the risk of boredom and repetition. Within the larger context of a multi-dimensional and complex relationship, it lends a welcome tranquility and absence of stress, but such planetary contacts need more energizing aspects elsewhere in the charts to avoid slipping over from "tranquil" to "tranquilizer."

Quincunx Although usually considered a minor aspect with a very small 1° to 2° orb, the quincunx can have a measurable impact on the release of planetary energies if it is within this small orb. It brings together forms of energy which not only do not blend easily but which cannot even be expressed simultaneously. While one is active, the other must remain passive and silent until its turn comes. When two planets have this sort of linkage, the effect is analogous to what a composer seeks in using both notes and pauses or silences between them to create a dramatic effect. This interplay between dominance and passivity, with the alternating of roles, has a contentious and potentially stimulating effect in the same way that competition can enliven a relationship. Whether this is a friendly rivalry or a grudge match depends on the rest of the synastric interplay.

Opposition In this aspect, the reverse images of the same energy form are brought into contact. Much like magnets, the result can be a powerful combination of attraction/repulsion depending on which polarity is rotated to link the planets. It is the highly dramatic love-hate form of energy flow in which we are confronted with mirrored images of ourselves, in the other person's mode of expression. It contains the fascination of narcissism but the anxiety of confronting our own flaws and weaknesses. The effect of this aspect is deep and powerful, and sometimes disturbing and destabilizing. While its antonym, the conjunction, amplifies the qualities of the planets and signs involved, the opposition sets up a circuitry which has the potential of either a crackling collision of energy or a short circuit which locks the relationship into stalemate and confrontation. It is this aspect which inspires the conviction that, in some forms, the line between love and hate is a thin one.

In synastric analysis, then, the important things to keep uppermost in your mind are that (1) they link planets closely enough that the natal energies of the planets involved will actively test their ability to function together, and (2) that we are dealing with two *different* sorts of energy being activated in the individuals. To put it another way, aspects result in the individuals acting out two different urges or feelings. They have two different objectives, two separate goals, two scenarios, each related to the activated planet in their own chart. These individual aspect links then must be put into the context of the overall role casting and script writing each has consciously or unconsciously done as they enter the relationship. This is not an easy thing for us to analyze and describe, yet synastry is like all other forms of astrology; requiring us to develop a holistic synthesizing overview of the chart(s) to achieve an "on-balance" judgement. In the end, we come back to where we started in discussing synastry. We can only raise questions and suggest ideas. Synastry in particular should be a non-predictive form of astrology, since only the individuals within a relationship can ultimately decide whether the "bottom line" of the interaction is worth the investment of themselves. If astrology can contribute to the understanding of the forces and drives which brought the individuals together and the factors which bear on their ability to function harmoniously, then synastry has made its valid contribution.

SUMMARY OF THE SYNASTRIC WORK METHOD

Not every question about relationships requires a full synastric analysis; however, once the work method has become familiar and a basic worksheet developed, even a full analysis is not time-consuming to prepare. As in all other branches of astrology, interpretation and translation are the truly demanding part of the analysis, not the mechanical preparation. In the second part of this book, some guides for interpretation are offered. A summary of the preparation steps of synastric analysis is then as follows:

1. Prepare the natal charts of the individuals and become familiar with the primary qualities of each. Give particular attention to:

A. Aspects to Sun and Moon as they reveal how the persons relate to their own and the opposite sex. Are they comfortable with their own biologic role? What role do they expect the opposite sex to play in their lives? Since aspects to Sun and Moon often reveal the quality of the relationship the individual has had with their own parents, probe a little to see if there are some carry-over stresses, doubts or angers from childhood experiences which might influence their adult relationships.

If possible, discuss with the individuals their parent-child experiences, particularly with the parent of the opposite sex if such stresses are indicated. Parent/child experiences strongly influence our adult images of relationships and the "appropriate" roles for the sexes to play. Be especially alert to hard aspects from the outer planets to the Sun or Moon as these relate to the person's perceptions of how they accept their own biologic role in partnerships. Relationships frequently contain strong elements of compensatory behavior when such aspects occur, with the person rebelling against or compensating for their childhood experiences with regard to male/female relations. Is the current relationship attractive because of such compensatory behavior? Is it an attempt to create a positive adult experience, to realize an unfulfilled expectation of the parent of the opposite sex?

B. Develop a good general image of what sort of life content each individual perceives as likely to be satisfying and rewarding. The signs and houses in which Moon and Venus fall provide good general outlines for such an image. Are the hopes and goals of the two people in general harmony? Can the life content desired by both be achieved without requiring major compromises and sacrifices of each other? Where are the likely areas of disagreement, if any, and what is the sort of compromise which will be required?

Look at the house positions of Saturn and Neptune and at any hard aspects made to these planets by Sun and Moon to isolate areas of the individuals' lives where frustrations and disappointments are likely to emerge. Saturn's house gives a good clue to what areas of life the individuals are likely to have difficulty in achieving their goals and where ambivalent social and professional attitudes will arise. Can the partners accept the limits they will place on their relationship because of these difficulties of social and professional uncertainties and frustrations? Do the Saturn houses function well together or do they suggest divergent attitudes toward the sub-culture in which the two persons operate?

Neptune's house indicates the illusions and fantasies which will persist in the personalities of the partners. How will these influence the relationship and what, if any, influence does the hope of realizing these dreams and hopes have on the willingness to enter the partnership?

C. Form a general sense of the strength of the relating capabilities of the partners, the way in which they will express themselves in close relationships and how well these aggregate elements blend. Do the Sun/Moon and Venus/Mars linkages involve blendable forms of planetary energy or do they set up difficult adjustments for the persons? Assess how strong the need for close relationships is in the lives of each person. Are you looking at well-matched partnership needs or is there a substantial difference in the level of need each has for close relationships? The relative interplay of signs in which the inner planets fall and the number and kind of aspects to Sun and Moon provide a good general guide to the relative strength of relating capacity and need for intimate partnerships.

D. Note the current transiting position of the outer planets, particularly Saturn and Uranus, to focus on what life area each of the persons is most stimulated to examine and alter. Is this life focus contributing to the willingness of either to form a partnership at this time?

Before going on to the mechanics of synastric analysis, it is important to lay this foundation of insight into the individuals and how their general personality qualities blend. While the synastric process itself reveals much of this detail, the general overview prevents us from focusing too strongly on specific interactions in the chart interplay. It is easy to lose sight of the fact that, just as individual personalities are holistic amalgams of the natal chart content, partnerships are similarly aggregations of all the synastric interplay. The insights revealed by the synastric process are not, as they sometimes appear to be, separate and distinct pieces of a mosaic. They are rather ingredients which will be stirred into the pot of the relationship and lose their individual identity. What we get in the end may be a gourmet's delight or mud, a smooth mixture without lumps or a grating compound of unblendable aggregates. This initial overview of the relationship helps maintain a perspective in synthesizing these ingredients in the abstract and in speculating on what sort of end result they will produce.

2. Calculate the solar charts using the method outlined in Part III. With this calculation, we then have the inner natal personalities which form the basis for responses and the projected refractions of these inner personalities as initially perceived by others. Using simple aspect grids (as shown in Part III), first compare the *natal* chart of one person with the *solar* chart of the other to isolate the perceived qualities which attracted the natal person to the solar person. Reverse the procedure with another grid, noting the "attraction" felt by the other person. These two grids reveal the expectations, role casting and assumptions each of the partners had about each other at the time they initially came together. Even if considerable time has transpired since the relationship began, these initial responses will persist and influence the evolution of the relationship.

3. Prepare a third aspect grid using the *natal* chart positions of the partners. This will reveal the compatibility of the individuals as they attempt to spend time together and their inner personalities reveal themselves. Compare the natal/solar grids with the natal/natal grids to isolate where the expectations of the initial attraction are being realized and where these hopes are likely not to be fulfilled. If the question before us involves unfulfilled hopes by one or both of the partners or anxieties about the future course of the relationship, it is likely that any significant divergence between what the other partner is perceived to be (and why, therefore, is "attractive") and what they ultimately reveal themselves to be is the source of the concern.

4. Prepare a composite chart using the natal charts of the individuals as a base (as shown in Part III). This chart will reveal the probable result of any attempt by the partners to move beyond a social relationship to a full blending of personalities into a third and durable entity: a true partnership.

5. Examine aspects formed by the *same* planets and the two ascendants to gain a sense of timing of future transits as these affect the individuals. Harmonious aspects between the same planets (i.e. Sun to Sun) and the ascendants generally indicate these future transits will be handled by the partnership without difficulty. Hard aspects between the same planets indicate that transits will occur in a sequence which will make it difficult for the partners to be supportive and understanding as these perturbations occur in the lives of the individuals. Absence of aspects between the same planets suggests that the partners need to anticipate that one member will be experiencing these crisis points in their states of mind and life focus while the other is relatively content and comfortably settled in a life pattern. Knowing this, each should be prepared to accept these short periods of turbulence in the other even if they seem unwarranted by the condition of the partnership at the time.

If progressions are used, note these as they will emerge in the future and affect the partnership. In distinguishing between the effects of transits and progressions, it might be useful to remember that transits are most felt as an internal welling up of concerns or anxieties and have their principal influence on the state of mind of the individual. They pass rather quickly and usually allow us to return to our basic life path without a significant change in course. Progressions have a much longer duration and seem to have more of an external quality, influencing our interaction with the world around us. They can and often do cause fundamental and permanent changes in our life paths. Transits primarily affect our inner relationship with ourselves and our ego-image. Progressions affect our interaction with our society and our efforts to alter that role.

PART II
SYNASTRIC AND COMPOSITE CHART INTERPRETATION

Clouds come from time to time
and bring to men a chance to rest
from looking at the moon.

Matsuo Basho (1644-1694)
Clouds

SYNASTRIC INTERPRETATION

No one ever said that creating and sustaining a relationship was simple or easy. Any mathematician will tell you that, considering all the random variables involved, the chances are a thousand to one that any relationship will work successfully. Consider what we are up against. We begin with two highly complex and essentially unique personalities, each with their own hopes and dreams, flaws and foibles. When these two people come into initial contact, they almost immediately begin casting each other in rather complex roles. They begin writing a script for the relationship, but it is based almost entirely on the projected solar personalities which are probably *not* very accurate images of the true qualities that each personality contains. Assuming that the script and role-casting each person does add up to something like "well, let's give it a try," then they settle into testing whether the real qualities which they possess can continue to function without driving each other up the wall again, an entirely random possibility unrelated to the initial attraction. If, by some miracle of chance, the two people find they can enjoy being together and are not periodically overcome with the desire to strangle each other, they go on to the well nigh impossible task of combining their hopes and dreams and quirks and fantasies into a workable, sharing partnership. By any rational measurement, such a statistically improbable sequence of convergence is so remote that the human race should have died off several million years ago. It did not; a tribute to the extremely powerful forces which act on us to *make* a relationship work in spite of its flaws and deficiencies.

Those forces are, of course, the procreative drives which exist to assure that the species doesn't die off. These forces are, equally obviously, rooted in the sexual/reproductive urge, but they are much broader than just hormones. Over the millions of years of the evolution of higher life forms, we have "learned" (not actually "learned" in an intellectual sense, but rather selectively evolved responses) which tell us that people are safe, happier, more likely to have enough food and shelter and warmth on cold nights if they pair up and make the necessary compromises to remain paired. While the modern, technologically elaborate world has made such pairing for security less necessary as a survival mechanism, we are still the product of millions of years of selective evolution and no amount of labor-saving devices, work specialization or societal supports is, in a few decades, going to overcome this ancient and profound drive to relate. It's built into our genes and you can put all the bumper stickers you want on your car saying "Happiness is Being Single," and it isn't going to have the slightest impact on that genetic heritage. Individuals have varying capacities to relate, varying needs to fill and varying luck in finding partners, but there are no real "loners" in the world, just varying degrees of ability to create and sustain partnerships.

In synastric analysis, then, two central ideas need to be kept ever-present in examining the interplay of two charts, (1) *everybody* has the need for relationships at some level of urgency, and (2) *nobody* responds to another person exactly as that person responds to them. We must see all interactions within the context of the natal chart potentials of the individuals and we must sort out the individual responses the people feel toward each other and see if these different and unrelated responses harmonize or conflict. Perhaps someday we will get clever enough with our genetic engineering to manage to have people born with an easily read and understood sign on their forehead like those which are stencilled on trucks "Maximum Capacity 40,000 lbs, or one husband and two children." Until then, the natal charts and synastric analysis will have to suffice.

Elements of Synastric Interpretation

In this second section we will examine the two mechanisms which operate in a relationship: (1) the *house* links which create the outlines of a scenario and cause us to cast ourselves and others in roles in this hoped-for outcome and (2) the *aspects* which provide the impetus to act on this role casting and script and try to bring it to life. These mechanisms work at two levels, each operating quite independently of the other: (1) *synastric*, in which the overlay of the two charts on each other causes two individuals to respond in terms of the role each hopes the other will play, and (2) *composite*, in which the two charts blend energies and structure into a possible partnership. This interplay of chart elements and structures then establishes the process humans go through in reaching out for and exploring potential relationships; a sequence of responses and reactions which, while almost entirely unconscious, we all pass through in developing a relationship. In broad terms, that process and the relevant synastric elements are:

1. The individuals respond to the projected personality (solar chart) primarily in terms of how *natal planets* in one chart are "captured" by the *solar houses* of the other. This initiates the early role casting and scenario each of the individuals creates. Analysis of natal planets as they fall in the projected solar houses gives us insight into that early response.

2. If the relationship moves past that initial step, the aspects formed between planets of the two charts indicate the motivation to act on the initial responses of the individuals. (Note that the aspects formed between planets of the two charts remain the same in both the solar and natal charts, even though signs and houses are usually significantly different in the solar and natal charts of the individuals.)

3. If both adequate attraction and motivation is present, the individuals will go on to explore their ability to be together and express their own personalities in each other's company. The synastric fall of *natal planets* in the *natal houses* and planetary aspects of the overlaid charts tell us most about this level of compatibility.

4. As a final step in the evolution of a full relationship, the individuals attempt to blend their personalities into a true partnership in which on-going joint and interlocked activity of the individuals creates a third and new entity: the composite chart. The houses and aspects of the composite chart tells us how successfully these natal entities are likely to be in creating a full, working partnership.

Of course, all of this is going on quite unconsciously and certainly is not as analytically cold and rational as the above sequence suggests. All these responses and reactions bubble up and rattle around in us quickly and in a flowing, overlapping way. The rather common confusion and mental upset we all experience in the face of a strong response to another person is indicative of just how many things are happening at once and how hard it is initially to sort all of them out. One of the most useful applications of synastric analysis is to do just that: sort out and give some qualitative meaning to this rush of feelings and hopes. In preparing this analysis then there are some general guidelines to remember:

1. Individual responses generated by solar and natal house overlays are not inherently reciprocal. Role casting and script writing are processes going on in the mind of each individual without regard to whether the other person is writing a matching script. Just as often as not, the two independently created scripts don't match up and we have either two entirely different and unblendable plots for the relationship forming in the minds of the individuals or only one individual is doing any plotting at all while the other person is largely indifferent and unresponsive.

2. Despite the fact that it is the Ascendant and houses of an individual which play the largest role in generating a script, it is the person whose planets are "captured" by the net of another person's houses who most acutely feels the magnetism of the scenario in which they are being cast. In effect, it is the projected Ascendant and houses of another person which stimulates us to create our own little private scenario about them and the role they will play in our lives. The reason this occurs is that the Ascendant and circle of houses are not, in themselves, actively expressed qualities of the personality. Their function, as noted before, is a sort of "point of reference" from which one sees and responds to the world, a rather passive temperament or environment in which the personality functions. The planets, however, are the active, motivating forces in the personality and, when they are stimulated by an external source, they are impelled to express their particular form of energy. It really shouldn't surprise anyone that it is the *projected* qualities of another person which "turns us on": triggers our planetary responses to fantasize and dream. It is then easy to understand that it is the aggregated statement of "I AM" which flows out from another person's Ascendant and houses which causes us to respond to them.

3. Natal planet-to-planet synastric links are mutually felt, but only in terms of the planet within each chart which is activated by the aspect. If an aspect is formed between the Sun in one chart and the Moon in another, the Sun person will respond and act within the parameters of their Sun's natal qualities. The Moon person will, on the other hand, respond and act within the parameters of the natal qualities of their Moon. This "complementary" interaction, the stimulus to respond to another in terms which are different but complementary is why aspects formed between *different* planets are much more potent than those formed between the *same* planets in two charts. An aspect between the two Suns may be pleasant (if it is a harmonious one), but all it means is that we can go on being who we are without getting on each other's nerves. A Sun/Moon aspect, however, permits each to give to the other person something unique and different and, therefore, is pleasant and welcome in the same way that exchanging gifts can be.

4. The insights offered by synastric links between charts are equally valid in both solar/natal overlays and natal/natal overlays as long as the distinction is made between

qualitative nature of the responses. In solar house/natal planet overlays, we are looking at the responses of the natal person to the *perceived personality* of the solar person, a perception very likely not to be accurate in terms of the true inner personality. In natal house/natal planet overlays we are, of course, seeing the real, long-term interplay of planets and houses. As noted before, however, that initial perception of the projected solar person is truly "attraction" and, while it may be based on only a partial truth, it nonetheless is powerful and enduring.

5. Interpretations of the linkages between charts must always be made within the confines of the basic natal personalities involved, within the innate qualities of planetary energies as they fall in houses and signs in the two natal charts and are activated by natal aspects. Relationships do not "change" people in any fundamental way. The stimuli of synastric linkages only bring to life, energize or diminish, sharpen or blunt the basic qualities of the two natal charts. Those who believe that, through a relationship, they will "make a new person" of their partner or significantly deflect them from a basic pattern of behavior established before the relationship existed are deluding themselves. The fundamental keys to the individual personality are in the natal chart. The clues to the course of the relationship are in the synastric and composite links which must function within those basic natal parameters.

6. In one sense, a planet in a natal chart acts as if it were its own Ascendant or 1st house cusp, casting out its net of "houses" within the limited meaning of that planet's function. For example, if Mars falls natally at Aries 10°, that marks the "cusp of the 1st house" as it relates to the Martian function of channeling of one's energy to take from the world what is desired and needed. Another person with Venus in the opposing sign of Libra will, even if planets do not form a synastric opposition aspect, nonetheless tend to respond to the "I take" quality of Mars with a Venusian "I give" role-response. Without a synastric aspect between the two planets, this will likely remain an unacted upon role-response (unless strong synastric aspects occur between other planets which lead to a romantic relationship), but the basic tone of script-response will be present. The key element to remember here is that, as a natal planetary position acts as its own "cusp of the 1st house," the projected function is limited to that planet's basic meaning. With the true houses radiating from the natal chart's Ascendant, we are looking at a broad, all-pervasive statement flowing outward defining holistically "I AM." With the pseudo-houses which radiate from a particular planet's natal position, we are seeing a much more limited statement of functional identity. In the above example, the Mars projection is "I AM....at least as far as how I'm going to reach out aggressively to get what I want from life; however, as far as other things are concerned, I will probably act in different ways and if you

want to see what those might be, look at the rest of my chart....assuming you have any interest in me, and you are not otherwise engaged or have plans for the weekend."

7. As a final thought, do not be disheartened if this is a new discipline you are learning and you become a bit overwhelmed by the initial complexity of the subject. Human relationships *are* complex, and multi-dimensional and synastry is, unavoidably, similarly so. Still, despite all the currents and cross-currents in a relationship, all the contradictions and improbabilities, there is that powerful force working which we noted earlier: the force that has kept the human race alive and burgeoning. Given a core of strong attraction, a modicum of compatibility (actually, the absence of any really devastating discordance) and a reasonable capacity to relate, virtually any combination of personality elements can function together successfully.

Synastry can, then, if properly applied, help identify the real human needs which exist within individuals and the potentials of another person in meeting a fair number of those needs. It can, perhaps even more importantly, help isolate those pseudo-needs which have accumulated in our minds from all sorts of external sources: what Mom and Dad said we were supposed to want, what our early peers and teachers pressed us to accept as "correct" and what the ever-present, ever-manipulative mass media has pounded into our skulls. In the end, the primary goal of synastry is to raise the questions which help an individual distinguish between real and illusory needs and help that person assess whether a potential partner might fill some of these true relationship needs. Approached at that simple, human level, synastry is no more complex than a thorough inventory of one's hopes and dreams.....followed by a much needed inventory clearance sale.

The Relative Impact of Synastric Links

The discussion of the synastric interpretations in the following section is presented in a sequence which may not be one with which readers in astrology are accustomed. Typically, this sort of material is presented in a traditional combination of egocentric and heliocentric order with the Sun and Moon in egocentric primacy (because of their greater influence on the natal chart), then in a strict marching order as the planets array themselves outwardly from the Sun. In addition, there sometimes is a tendency to give "equal billing" to each planet. While there is nothing inherently wrong with this established tradition, it does risk suggesting that (1) the sequence of the discussion, in some subtle way, reflects the relative importance and impact of the planet and (2) the amount of space devoted to the individual planets, if largely equal, somehow indicates that their impact on the personality is also equal in weight. We know this isn't true, but this sequence is an old tradition, and it is a handy way to organize and present material.

The purpose of this discussion of synastry is, however, to help the reader to assess the interplay between charts and, to achieve that, one must not just interpret the interplay, but also weight the *significance* of all the ingredients of that interplay to find the substance of the synastric analysis. As Robert Hand comments in his book on composite charts, the core of the partnership is nearly always revealed in the Sun and Moon house positions and aspects. For this reason, and to assist the reader, this discussion of planets in synastry is presented *in the order of their impact and importance*, even if that departs from the egocentric/heliocentric traditional sequence. In addition, where some of these synastric interplays are subtle, slight and ancillary, hopefully this is made clear. This prioritizing of considerations is intended to add to our understanding of how these complex elements combine. Giving proper weight to each element will result in a better balanced, more holistically valid analysis; easier to communicate and not cluttered by minor background noise. The material then is presented in the following order which reflects the impact and importance of the influences in relationships:

Primary group The *Ascendent* (as it creates the house/planet overlays and composite houses), *Sun* and *Moon*. This group establishes the fundamental gridwork of the relationship within which all other influences must and will be contained in their function.

Secondary group *Venus, Mars* and *Uranus*. This group introduces the masculine/feminine element into the relationship. The question is not whether a given relationship contains this polarity; *all* relationships do, regardless of the gender, age or relative circumstances of the individuals. The question is how, within the confines of the relationship created by the primary group, this polarity will manifest itself and whether this will express itself positively, negatively or not at all.

Uranus belongs in this group because of its catalytic effect on a relationship. Humans are, both by instinct and social conditioning, remarkably guarded in dealing with a stranger; probably an inheritance from the million years of human existence in small hunter/gatherer groups which competed violently with other clans for sustenance. Because of this, we still unconsciously deal with strangers, no matter how attractive, as possible threats who might be dangerous to us. Linkages involving Uranus, however, trigger strong subconscious impulses to overcome this guardedness in the face of a response to another human and indicate the mode of expression we will use to bridge the gap between ourselves and an attractive stranger. This method will not only emerge in initiating the relationship, but also will persist as long as the relationship continues as a recurring impulse in reaching out for contact with the other person.

Tertiary group The remaining planets play a lesser role in synastry, in part because they operate primarily at the unconscious level and in part because their influence is typically felt only in a subtle way as any relationship evolves into an on-going routine. *Saturn, Jupiter* and *Mercury* establish the tone of daily processes of the relationship, how we are likely to deal with ordinary requirements of surviving together in the world in which the relationship is operating. The impact of *Neptune* and *Pluto* is subtle and ephemeral, like herbs in a bouillabaisse, contributing a pungency and bouquet to the partnership, but adding only a faint piquancy to the primary ingredients. Their role is interesting but minor. Like herbs and spices, no dish can be made of them alone, but without them, the subtle complexities and surprises in a relationship would be missing.

THE PRIMARY GROUP

Sun in the Houses

The Sun is the integrative force in the personality, gathering up life experience and distributing it throughout the rest of the chart for interpretation, then collecting this understanding of our experiences and expressing it to the world around us. As these myriad quanta of experience and expression pass through this great instrument, they are inevitably colored and modified by the particular qualities of the sign in which the Sun falls. In synastry, the Sun performs this function in the more limited arena of appraising other humans and assessing where they might fit into our lives. When we meet another person and the full weight of that person's apparent qualities reach us, it is the Sun which captures and filters that projection and, as it does, selectively routes the various elements of the perceived personality to the other components of the chart for interpretation. The Sun is not, however, a neutral objective receiver. It filters and discriminates based on the predilections of the natal sign and house in which it falls. If it detects qualities which are not harmonious with our inner self, it rejects them; turns them back almost as if we are saying to ourselves that no one with *those* qualities is even going to get past our first level of discrimination. What does pass through this initial filtering reaches other parts of our chart for response and reaction and, when that is done, the Sun gathers up those responses and relays them to the person we have met; again in the style and form dictated by the Sun's natal sign and house. The Sun then is our first and primary assessor of other human beings and our channel for telling them where, in a general sense, they may fit into our life.

Sun in the 1st House
Synastric A sense of kinship and essential similarity of world view is produced by this overlay. We find ourselves approving of this person; their style, appearance and

apparent approach to life. There is usually a sense that we can communicate with them; and they will, being so much like us, generally agree with our perceptions and appraisals of the world which we share. There is little feeling that we must be guarded in our self-expression or cautious in revealing some part of our personality. We assume they will respond well to us and allow us to be open and candid in what we say and do. The 1st house person senses this quality of harmony we feel about them and, on the basis that "anyone who likes me can't be all bad," will typically respond positively. Everyone enjoys being approved of and noted by others, and when such approval is forthcoming, they are usually willing to at least open the door to some exploratory testing of whether a more profound level of relationship is possible and desirable.

The primary tone then of this 1st house overlay is a broadly based, shared response to the world and harmonious ways of responding to and coping with life. Given other supportive houses and aspects, it offers a comfortable and non-stressful general environment within which a companionable and open relationship can develop. It is quite common for marriage partners to have this overlay; more often with the man's Sun being overlaid by the woman's 1st house than the reverse. It seems that women, in particular, bask in this sort of general approval from their mate, and men, conditioned by the society to see all things associated with them as extended expressions of themselves, tend to choose wives about whom they feel this general sense of approval and "rightness." All in all, this overlay does good things for both persons' egos and self-images.

Composite This blending of energies in the composite 1st house indicates much agreement on lifestyle, goals and directions for the partnership. There will be an unspoken but clearly felt ambience that the partners seek the same results from the partnership and, perhaps most important, that the partnership itself is the reward, the fundamental purpose for coming together. The relationship itself may be somewhat self-contained and inward looking with the people relying almost entirely on each other for companionship and entertainment. This can sometimes result in a rather stultifying atmosphere after a time; a feeling that life does not contain the variety of experiences and happy surprises that it might if the partners were less interdependent. As close and binding as this composite house position may be, it does not always contain the ingredients for stimulating growth and maturation in the partners. They may well find that, after a time, the partnership has not adjusted and grown parallel to their own individual maturation. Hopefully, other elements of the partnership are less inward oriented, but a composite Sun in this house is powerfully placed and the partners will have to consciously guard against becoming so isolated from their individual worlds behind the sheltering bond of the partnership that they have no other avenues open should the partnership falter or circumstances change.

Sun in the 2nd House

Synastric This overlay has an undertone of a "means to an end" in which the response is colored by a feeling that the other person may be an instrument to obtain what one wants. What that objective might be is entirely a matter of the remainder of the synastric linkages, but generally the perception is that there might be a practical, often acquisitive benefit to any subsequent relationship. It is not an especially warm or personal response, but it can be a good general environment for material or utilitarian activities. Assuming the house person has some similar objective, this matter-of-fact feedback will be accepted as useful and potentially profitable. No one, however, really enjoys the feeling that they are a "tool" and there will remain a distance between the persons; a business-like quality which often is productive but not truly intimate.

If other linkages indicate a strong sexual/romantic attraction, this overlay can suggest that the house person is the object to be acquired; a vehicle for sexual gratification or, through sex, to obtain material needs. The overlay seems to retain its real-world, objective oriented tone even if a close romantic/sexual relationship evolves. While it may become highly beneficial in a practical way, it will probably never entirely lose its "means-to-an-end" undertone. The Sun person does not really perceive the other person as one with whom a peer relationship can be established. The house person may fall victim to the Yuppie disease: seeing the relationship in "goal-oriented" terms and one in which any personal investment is made against a yardstick of probable return.

Composite This house position suggests that the partners will at least share a common value system with regard to their combined resources. The priorities in using joint resources, in acquiring possessions or making investments and setting financial goals will not be areas of disagreement or discord on the partnership. While not an especially intimate or personal interaction, it has the advantage of easy teamwork in achieving real-world goals. It is an excellent position for business-related activity where the two persons must work together closely in the handling of resources, particularly if the main focus of the partnership is on tangible, "hands-on" type of assets such as property or inventories.

It is not quite so favorable when the jointly held resource is an abstract asset like money or credit or a jointly undertaken creative activity. When dealing with objective, material goals, the communication is clear and without confusion. If the partnership becomes involved in more subjective matters, the absence of intellectual or emotional linkage can produce some lack of mutual understanding, particularly if some considerable sacrifice may be required of the partnership to reach their goals. There are shared material hopes, but there may be an absence of underlying agreement of how to convert any material achievement into a mutually satisfying lifestyle; an absence of a common definition of emotional and intellectual fulfillment or a shared philosophical criterion of "success." This composite position is excellent for material achievement but, without other composite indications of emotional and intellectual harmony, may produce a rather unemotional and pragmatic interaction.

Sun in the 3rd House

Synastric With this overlay, there is a perception that the way in which the other person deals with everyday living and responds to the ups and downs of life is sensible and agreeable. It seems possible to share all the routine and rather uneventful happenings of living with the house person without constantly being distracted by irrational or unjustified responses. There is, of course, the element of "communication" associated with this house, but it is not so much verbal linkage as it is harmony of reaction in how the people cope. The planet person finds that their own interpretation of a given circumstances or event is harmonious with the house person's appraisal and, as a result, it is easy and comfortable for the two persons to function together in a real-world environment.

The planet person will see the house person as having "common sense" and being, therefore, predictable in the way they go about their life; perhaps not a highly emotionally exciting response, but one which is very welcome in a world full of scary surprises and anxiety. Perhaps the most attractive quality of this position is the feeling that one can just be oneself without much role playing or compromise and not jeopardize the relationship. This largely stress- and artifice-free response is, of course, a fine ambience for any interaction which requires continuing close contact. In itself, it does not suggest much of an emotional interaction nor does it necessarily have any romantic/sexual qualities, but should other linkages create these more intimate responses, it can be an excellent synastric link in keeping the interaction free of hassles and upheavals. In such a relaxed and comfortable interaction, a lot can be accomplished, both at a personal and worldly sense, because the interaction is not being constantly drained by little discords and angers. More divorces are caused by an accumulation of such little, repressed angers than by any single large flap, and this house link goes a long way toward preventing this sort of gradual encrustation of petty grievances.

Composite Perhaps the best way to envision the result of a combining of planetary energies in a composite 3rd house is as a fundamental harmony of lifestyle and daily living. "Lifestyle" in a partnership is, travel magazines and TV ads to the contrary, mostly a matter of simple, uneventful shared hours. This composite blending allows the individuals to go about their ordinary and necessary activities with a kind of unspoken concord, getting the car washed and the shopping done without tripping over each other's priorities. The life rhythms seem to flow along at a compatible pace and a hundred little things which either need to be done or which provide the small daily pleasures of living come easily to the partnership. The timing of urges and impulses is good and, as a result, there is a sort of continuing, happy spontaneity in the partnership. Nothing is so subtly abrasive in a relationship as a pattern of small disagreements over what movie to see or when to visit the relatives. This house placement seems to minimize such conflicts in priorities and makes for a friendly tandem of activity.

If there is a downside to this composite house position, it lies in this very lack of positive tension. As comfortable as it may be, it requires little of the partners in stretching out their potentials or in the sort of compromises which other persons can force upon us through their divergent interests. One of the great benefits of a close partnership is that it drags us, kicking and protesting, into new areas and interests...and we grow and develop because of this. With this composite house, the partners can slip into routines and ruts which, while tranquil and unstressed, may in time result in a gathering of dust and moss on the relationship. The partners should guard against this phenomenon, hopefully by tapping other linkages to shake each other up occasionally with some off-the-wall idea or project. There is a truism in relationships that the longer you know someone, the more unexpected qualities you find. With this position, the partners need to continue to probe for those new nooks and crannies to keep the relationship alive and interesting.

Sun in the 4th House

Synastric One of the strongest forces in the human personality, perhaps exceeded only by the procreative drive itself, is the "tribal" or group/clan bond. In the 4th house we see the power of this bond revealed; the sense of linkage with a particular, if ill-defined, segment of the larger society. While we tend to think of clan bonds or identification with a particular "tribal" group as largely a matter of blood-ties, this same identification can root in a shared cultural perception or deep sense of where primordial "truth" lies. It is kinship at its most profound and mysterious level; that base-of-the-spine sensation which we feel when we encounter someone with whom we seem to share an intuitive feeling of "place" in the larger society. With this overlay, the planet person responds as our more ancient predecessors did when they recognized the distinctive marking of a member of a related group; almost a sub-specie response. The traditional association of the 4th house with home and family is relevant here, but in the greatly extended sense of those ideas.

When we experience this overlay, we anticipate that we will be accepted by the other person in a societal way; be allowed to enter into the restricted world of trusted allies. We feel a quality of "us-against-them" in our reaction to the other person and, as a result, reveal our attitudes and evaluations of the society in which we find ourselves. It seems clear that if push comes to shove, we'll be on the same side, struggling to preserve the same things and warding off the intrusions of "foreign" things. It is easy to envision such a person sharing a base of operations, the same shelter and cultural values. The house person typically accepts this identity, feeding back the reinforcement of cultural priorities the planet person elicits. The kinship quality of this overlay sometimes reveals itself in the evolving of a surrogate familial role; a person dealing with the other as a stand-in or substitute parent or sibling. The response this overlay engenders is largely then a feeling of belonging to the same "family," the same order, and we proceed with the trust and security of kinship in our interaction.

Composite This is a strong and deeply intuitive composite placement since it directs the energies of the two planets toward establishing a communal shelter and defense. It is parental and domestic in its focus, making it natural and almost "fated" that the partners in some way combine to reinforce their clan bond needs. The relationship fills a basic need in us to ally ourselves with like-minded and motivated persons for the common welfare and success; an alliance for both safety and perpetuation of what we feel really matters in our world. The partnership is much more likely to express itself in traditional ways than in eccentric or unconventional forms, with the combining of energies to achieve something which provides a stable and secure center from which the two persons go forth to deal with a more hostile, less allied world. Obviously, it is an excellent blending for any partnership form which has a mutual support and confrontational alliance objective. Its power and depth should not be underrated simply because it is not traditionally associated with romantic/sexual interaction. The modern world is a threatening place, seemingly more and more ready to swallow us in an impersonal, metallic gulp of overpopulation, deteriorating environment and violence. The kinship tone of this composite placement can be a deeply reassuring support in such a world and, as a result, can combine planetary energies most successfully.

Sun in the 5th House

Synastric Some years ago, the drama critic and author Walter Kerr devoted an entire book, *The Decline of Pleasure*, to the subject of our modern obsessive pursuit of enjoyment. His theme was a simple one: "pleasure" cannot be hunted down like a trophy or planned and scheduled to occur precisely in synchronization with our two-week cruise vacation. "Pleasure" is a spontaneous happenstance, a happy convergence of randoms. All we can do is remain open to it, welcome it when it comes and accept that, as with the butterfly analogy Kerr used, it is a rather infrequent event. The 5th house overlay is such convergence in synastry; that delightful discovery that another person somehow carries with them the substance of pleasure, enjoyment and delight. Pleasure comes, of course, in many forms: recreation, shared creativity or interests, exchanges of sensual experiences like seeing a movie or dining together and, quite obviously, sex. This overlay triggers a role casting by the planet person which defines the house person as someone with whom enjoyment can be derived and shared.

In synastry, the concept of "beauty" often is associated with this overlay. Some things we gather in with our senses give us pleasure and enjoyment simply because of what they are; some mysterious amalgam of symmetry, balance and grace which pleases us. We can feel this in the presence of a work of art or nature, even for a mundane product such as an automobile or piece of furniture. Beauty defies analysis because it touches our sensory perceptions and seems to proceed directly to the right brain, intuitive storehouse. As a bit of music, the whiff of flowers or the feel of grass on our bare feet pleases us, another person can engender this sensory response. We enjoy their presence because they please our senses; we find them "beautiful." Despite the delight we may feel, however, this overlay is not, in itself, a solid base for a partnership in the full sense. It is, of course, fun to be seen in such a way and the house person will be "pleased" too; being admired or adored is a very rewarding sort of feedback. But this response is, as noted, a sensory one which functions independently of any other capacity to share space or harmonize personalities. While it contributes a lovely romanticism (or at least, a sort of tender blindness) to any relationship, it can so overwhelm the senses that other, more basic discordancies may be ignored or sublimated; discordancies that can eventually break through the fog of fantasy and cause any relationship to erode away into disappointment and bitterness. With this overlay, it is always wise to look to see if such underlying incompatibilities are being temporarily ignored.

Composite With a composite 5th house Sun, the focus of the interaction will tend to be on coming together for the welcome release from daily pressures which shared enjoyment brings. The partners will find it easy and natural to plan joint recreational activities, spend much time in relaxed, idle pleasure and usually do not tire of each other's company....as long as the activity remains ancillary to the primary focus of the individual's life. In one sense, this composite position suggests almost an *alternative* to a full partnership; allowing each person to go on with their individual lives, but to come together away from the mundane routines of living for sensory and intellectual fulfillment. It is much like a "dating" relationship in which the partners see each other under the most pleasurable, responsibility-free circumstances and at their physical best....but go on their individual courses afterwards.

If other linkages provide a more substantial basis for the interaction, this can be a happy composite placement, allowing the individuals to conduct the partnership as if it were, itself, an element of play. It certainly indicates that the relationship will not fall victim to boredom or routine. There must be, however, more solid bases for the relationship elsewhere in the composite chart to give the partnership dimension and durability. Without these, the partnership will remain one-dimensional and somewhat superficial, without shared life goals beyond fun and games and unlikely to draw a full commitment from the individuals to a true combining of efforts and dreams.

Sun in the 6th House

Synastric The subordination of one's ego needs in the interests of some communal or joint endeavor has always been the keystone of a successful group enterprise. The 6th house has traditionally been associated with "service" in this sense; the sacrifice of individual reward for some collective end. This overlay has such a tone of combining for an objective, and the planet person will tend to see the house person as one to whom they can give this sort of support and cooperation. The role-casting created by this overlay is not of peers, but rather the acceptance of the role of subordinate or sustainer; one person assuming a leadership role and the other surrendering some of the control over their own life as a means of achieving some joint objective. Typically, it is the planet person who yields in this overlay and the house person who takes charge to frame the purpose of the interaction and provide the initiative in moving it toward its goal. Obviously, this overlay is more useful and appropriate when the element of "work" is a major thrust of the relationship; when some chore or burden confronts the two individuals, and they must combine their energies to meet this demand.

This overlay is not inherently inimicable to a generally balanced and satisfactory relationship, given other linkages, but it will tend to retain a major element of this leader/ follower quality. It is as if one person recognizes that certain abilities and strengths are necessary to cope with the situation in which the persons find themselves and, seeing this, yields to the other person who appears to possess these qualities. Confronted with a problem to solve and unsure we have the resources to deal with that problem, we often turn to someone whom we believe can cover the gaps in our own arts and skills. It doesn't do much for our self-images or egos, but we tend to accept this diminution in our own self-interest. In a complex and demanding world, this sort of interaction is not entirely unwelcome. It always, however, carries the potential of resentment and ultimately the eroding of self-esteem which can be tolerated only by rather passive personalities whose sense of vulnerability exceeds their need for independence.

Composite The logic of composite chart lies in its revealing of the structural interplay between natal charts. When the composite chart discloses a 6th house overlay, there is always the quality of dependence; of imbalance and the playing off of strengths and weaknesses in a noncompensatory way. Wherever planetary energies combine to produce a 6th house composite, a tone of sacrifice and burden tends to emerge, and when this involves a composite Sun, it is rare even that individuals relate well enough that a composite chart is ever drawn. Partnerships are attractive to us because of some objective they help us reach; something personal we seek which appears achievable through the partnership. The effect of the 6th house composite Sun is so leaden and burdensome that one might almost be suspicious if an intimate relationship had developed between the two persons. Normally such an interaction can function satisfactorily only at an impersonal level where tasks are confronted by the individuals and they form an alliance to cope with those tasks. If a more personal and intimate relationship exists, then there is a strong suggestion of a deliberately out-of-balance relationship, perhaps one in which a very dominant personality is responding to an equally passive or submissive one and the partners are finding in the partnership a way to act out these qualities.

Of course, the other possibility in such relationships is that the partnership is an illusory cover for self-interested objectives. Arrangements between persons in which one person's material needs are met in exchange for whatever gratification the other realizes from forming the partnership are sometimes a product of this composite. Behind the arrangement, each sees the partnership as a burden, but accepts the load out of self-interest, need or simple venality. In general, however, this composite position works well only in a work or task-related environment and even then only if the individuals accept the imbalance of the relationship as not too high a price to pay for the solutions it provides.

Sun in the 7th House

Synastric This overlay evokes perhaps the most clearly felt and deeply moving response of any. We are seeking not a twin of ourselves, but rather an intriguing reverse image; a polar opposite of the integrative force which binds our personality into a whole. The magnetism of such an overlay is that of two pieces of a jigsaw puzzle; normally irregular and unable to match with the other floating fragments which pass in life, but suddenly snapping into lock fit as if the two psyches were once one. The planet person is pulled by the projected essence of the house person into this complex union of disparate parts; the house person welcomes the bonding as one might the snug closing of a door against the cold. The underlying mechanism of this overlay is a sense of reuniting fragments to recreate a cosmic whole. Because of this, the partnership which can emerge from this overlay is truly a uniting, not simply a pairing up of harmonious but still separate parts.

The concern is, of course, that in this union the outlines of each of the individual personalities are blurred, the individual identities potentially lost. Often this results in an equally powerful and rebellious reaction as the two personalities struggle to regain individuality. The entire nature of this overlay is built on a dynamic attraction/repulsion tension and is not an easy or relaxed interaction. The tension of the relationship often drives each personality to more extreme expressions of their unique qualities, heightening the contrasts within each. A personality with latent dominating tendencies will, in such an interaction, tend to reveal this quality, behaving more high-handedly than outside the relationship. A personality which is normally only quiet and introspective might be pressed to an extreme of passivity and muteness. The 7th house is associated with partnerships, but also with intense forms of enmity; the sort of violent response which is kindled by a pressing intrusion into our most private and guarded self. This sort of tension is much more easily released when a fully evolved, intimate relationship exists and many levels of expression are available. In a more restricted circumstances of a work or purely social interaction, the tension of this overlay has difficulty finding acceptable ways to release the pressures it creates. It is an electric interplay for romantic/sexual relationships, but often a stressful one in less intimate involvements. The individuals are seeing themselves in a mirror and seem to respond as the old axiom observes...that "we" are our own worst enemy.

Composite By definition, the composite chart exposes the results of an attempt to blend planetary energies. Most of the time we are seeing two forms of planetary energy coalesce in a sort of lamination with each still retaining its original properties, but uniting with each other for various purposes and with differing degrees of success. With the 7th house composite Sun, however, we are seeing a unique sort of alchemy. The planetary energies bond much like linking molecules to create new properties and, very often, the individual identities disappear within the confines of the relationship. This sort of linkage is transformative and, as long as the partnership functions, the persons actually do alter their behavior, their style and expression. We have all witnessed occasional relationships which seem to truly change people, at least in terms of how they go about life, align their priorities and reach out for goals. Most often such metamorphic encounters are the product of this composite linkage.

As in all 7th house linkages, a significant amount of tension is generated. With this composite, the stress is a by-product of the personality altering catalyzed by this blending. Prior to the relationship, the personalities had established a more or less well-defined identity and life mode. Under the influence of the partnership commitment, however, these modus operandi undergo substantial change, at least within the range of activities which impinge on the partnership. Some of the old worldly identity, of course, remains as the individuals continue to function in their work or other relationships. Typically, then, some stress or conflict is generated by the partnership as the individuals attempt to play out these alternating roles: one within the partnership which is new and one outside the partnership which has been around as the familiar old person. Despite the strength and magnetism of this linkage, it is not an intrinsically harmonious one. It has great potential for a combining of energies to create something together which could not be achieved individually, but the price tag for this highly productive interplay is a continuing gripping sort of tension. Much depends on the remainder of linkages in the composite chart and on the fundamental personality qualities within the two natal charts. Perhaps no other composite position for Sun requires as much generalized synastric assessment; digging back to the natal charts and the synastric overlays to determine whether this powerful composite linkage will result in a dynamic and successful partnership or an unendurable, stress-filled interaction.

Sun in the 8th House

Synastric No one would read this book if there wasn't a feeling that beneath the patina of knowledge the human race has acquired, there lies another reality not entirely reachable through logic, scientific method or laboratory measurement. We sense the presence and effect of cosmic forces and tides that influence the world in which we live, even reaching down occasionally to touch us individually, but these always seem just outside the span of our conscious minds, just over the horizon. Migratory birds and fish (and perhaps even the ancient Polynesian navigators) make journeys of enormous distances to places of which they have no direct knowledge. Part of our race memory, our race heritage, is this awareness of something important "over the horizon"; not knowable at the conscious and rational level, but nonetheless, "there." The 8th house overlay makes us try to see over that horizon, sensing some mystery, some deep and important discovery in another person. It intrigues and it frightens, draws us yet makes us tremble because deep in the back of this dark cave there may well be creatures of primordial violence and mindless ferocity; that part of us retained over millions of years of evolution from beast to self-aware human.

By definition, anything unknown is "mysterious" and that which is unknown and possibly unknowable is disturbing. Such things are abstract, undefined; driven by forces we can't reduce to formulas and equations. Money, sex, war, weather phenomena, violent behavior, seemingly supernatural experiences, and many other things which disturb and trouble our lives are like this; and individuals who capture our Sun in their 8th house affect us in this way. They unsettle us, make us less certain we can cope with them or anticipate their effect on us. Somehow they touch parts of us buried under millennia of frontal lobe evolution, back down where some part of us remains fearful of gods and mythical beasts. More often than not, we slip away from these reactions, unwilling to confront the deep turbulence we feel, but sometimes we cannot resist the pull. We remain, as we do in a horror movie or a gory boxing match, transfixed by the terror and blood lust. Probably we stay because only in confronting this dark response can we know ourselves, gain some sort of handle on what is, in fact, over the horizon of our consciousness. There are risks and perils, possibly of even finding things in ourselves which we might better not allow out into the light; but this overlay has its own sort of fascination. Perhaps these people will somehow teach us about ourselves, stir up something which will reveal our inner workings: disturbing, hard to be intimate with, but equally hard to draw away from. Not always a healthy or beneficial happenstance, this overlay, but necessary if we are ever to know and master the beasts within us.

Composite The combining of the energies of the two Suns in the composite 8th most commonly results in an element of disturbing yet magnetic fascination with the interaction. Often this blending seems to overpower logic or convention, bridging gaps between persons which normally might hold them apart. Cultural, educational or age differences which might otherwise argue against any profitable or meaningful interplay are often irrelevant. This composite position reaches deep below these societal measures to touch something basic in the persons and normal barriers lose their substance. Not uncommonly there is an element of guru/chela, of initiation and revelation in such partnerships in which each of the individuals is drawn into a deeper exploration of themselves by the partnership. This is an inherently unbalanced position, neither harmonious nor complementary. Nearly always one partner is leading the other, but equally commonly the roles can be alternated. Even the strangeness and an undertone of fear and mystery can motivate the individuals to sustain the relationship.

Venus never wanders far from the Sun and, in composite charts, the composite Venus is also never far away. If the composite Sun is in the 8th house, the composite Venus will fall somewhere in the adjacent houses, usually in the 7th, 8th or 9th. In speculating about what expression this combining of 8th house Sun energies will take in a partnership, the composite Venus house strongly influences how the ambience of this composite house will be translated. Regardless of the remainder of the composite positions, this position will have the effect of stirring up awarenesses, stimulating the probing of each partner's motivations and deep drives and drawing out some profound emotions. This can be as superficial and harmless as a shared interest in making money or exploring some facet of New Age phenomenon, as intriguing as sharing feelings and insights about the forces which drive the human race or even a willingness to reveal ones most private and troubling fears and fantasies. It can also produce less easy to deal with interplays: sexual obsessions, experimentation with self-destructive processes like drugs, "magic," repressed hates or venality or, in extreme situations and if the natal potentials exist in the individual charts, aberrant and violent behavior. Whatever form it does take, if the individuals do not flee their initial responses (not always a bad choice), then the relationship will bring about some deep changes in the partners; in their perception of themselves and in their life view. Whatever the ultimate impact, the effect of this composite position will not go unnoticed.

Sun in the 9th House

Synastric To say reality is relative is neither redundant or whimsical. Each society evolves a consensus reality, a shared perception of the appropriate way for its members to behave. Sometimes this is expressed in religious or mystical terms, sometimes as ethics and morals. Whatever form it takes, it represents the accumulated cultural wisdom and insight which is passed from generation to generation as a framework in which both the individual and society are obliged to function. The term "occult" describes that which is partially or wholly hidden from our full knowledge; the term "cult" that which is revealed and known, at least to those who are privy to this insight. A "culture" then is this shared body of wisdom and insight, and when we experience this 9th house overlay of Sun, we respond to the person as one with whom we share this perception of social, behavioral and ethical standards and value systems. It is essentially an intellectual bond, built on abstract concepts and values. As a result, we tend to find ourselves wanting to revalidate our own views, reinforce our own conclusions, by drawing from the 9th house person reassurances and agreements. Often the 9th house person, finding themselves cast as interpreter and articulator of the culture in which the individuals find themselves, will be stimulated to refine and clarify their own views. The effect is then to stimulate the intellectual and cultural awareness of the individuals and reinforce their sense of place in their society.

The dominant theme in this overlay is the exchange of ideas, interpretations and questions which occupy the minds of the individuals. Typically the relationship will stimulate extended exploratory exchanges, and the persons will seek each other out in times of uncertainty to reestablish confidence in their individual world perceptions. Not uncommonly, this interaction occurs in an environment in which the persons are attempting to alter or rectify some process within the shared culture. Depending on the natal charts, this may take the form of religious effort, political activism, judicial or litigative exercise or as a teaching/learning process. On the obviously valid premise that anyone who agrees with us is clearly a superior and worthwhile person, this overlay often produces durable friendships and strong intellectual bonds. Its shortcoming is, obviously, that the interaction is based on pre-formed world views and, therefore, is unlikely to do more than reinforce conclusions which each held before they met. Such harmony (and this is a classically harmonious interaction) is valuable in an intimate relationship because it tends to eliminate any fundamental discord at the philosophical or intellectual level. In itself, it is not likely to stimulate romantic or sexual responses, but if these urges are triggered by other linkages, at least these more emotionally satisfying activities will not be disturbed by the abrasive effect of trying to make love to someone who clearly is politically wrong-headed and philosophically confused.

Composite The composite position of Sun generally indicates the primary focus and objective of a partnership. If the composite Sun falls in the 9th house, the individuals may well not even define the relationship as a "partnership" or detect that one has actually formed. Because this position is so oriented toward abstract, intellectual issues and so essentially lacking in any sort of more personal orientation, it tends to fall outside the common definition of "partnership": the coming together for some mutually desirable purpose. Much more likely, the individuals will see the interaction as a friendship or pleasant interplay with a like-minded person with no particular objective other than to share ideas and observations. Each will freely admit that the relationship has reassured them, taught them and even perhaps caused them to adjust or clarify their world view. They may well describe the relationship in terms of valuable insights and interesting revelations, tend to say complimentary things about each other's intellectual powers and be neither stressed, threatened or very excited about the whole thing. The least likely term they will use to describe the interaction is "relationship"; largely because humans tend to reserve this term for interactions which involve emotional, romantic or sexual responses. Nonetheless, this composite does offer the opportunity for a true partnership of an altruistic, platonic sort; and these are often the ones we recall with warmth and pleasure much later in our life because they caused us no pain, suffering or disillusionment.

This is an excellent composite position if the primary objective of the relationship is learning and growing. It is equally positive if the individuals come together for some common enterprise which needs harmony of philosophic or ethical principles. It is the composite we believe we share with the political candidate we support, the charity to which we contribute and the religion we practice. Perhaps the only downside of this composite position is that, since it does indicate a shared focus on esoteric matters, it can be the basis for one of those painfully noble and self-sacrificing partnerships formed, not for the pleasure and benefit of the individuals, but rather for some abstract and ephemeral "good of humanity" cause or crusade. These involve people who have shallow relating capacities and weak emotional and sexual drives and who become attached to causes and "revealed truths" as outlets for their personal needs. For purely practical reasons they form partnerships with others to further their efforts on behalf of their crusade. Real partnerships don't truly interest them, but if they must have one to act out their self-prescribed missions, they might as well have it with a person who shares their world view. This is not a common phenomenon, but as often as not is the underlying motivation when an intimate partnership has this composite Sun position.

Sun in the 10th House
Synastric Every society has its "pecking order," its yardsticks and symbols for

individuals to establish themselves within the hierarchy of the structure. We seem unable to avoid arraying certain talents and achievements on a vertical scale and giving both recognition and reward to individuals in terms of these measures. Often this reflects some current or past appraisal of the true value of these talents and achievements in assuring the survival and prosperity of the group. Just as often, however, it only recognizes a sort of simple uniqueness without regard to any real contribution which might be made by the person who possesses this. Rational or not, we "recognize" individuals in terms of how they array themselves on this scale and award them not only symbols of their status in the form of privileges, costumes, paraphernalia and wealth, we more importantly award them "authority." We accept these persons as someone who should be attended to, followed if they yell "charge" and deferred to if they demand it. The 10th house overlay tends to kindle that sort of response in the planet person; the perception that the house person somehow deserves this status and recognition and is, perhaps, a vehicle for the planet person to share in that status. It is almost as if we have a paradigm for "leader" and, when we encounter such a person, and they capture our Sun in their 10th house, we assume they will fill that role.

Obviously, such an overlay can be a strong incentive to ally oneself with another. Everyone struggles through most of their life trying to find a suitable ending for the sentence, "I am a _____." We live in a society which, unlike older ones in which one's status was largely a function of clan links, tends to measure status and position in terms of job titles. About the first question a stranger asks after being introduced at a social gather is "What do you do?"...not "What kind of person are you?" or "What kind of ethics and morals do you have?" but, what is your job title, your official status? This overlay can create an entirely irrational, but nonetheless potent, perception that the house person either has or deserves such status. We accept them almost without thinking, as someone whom we are willing to follow, that they know their way better than we, and that if a disagreement occurs, it is more than likely that they, rather than we, are seeing things clearly. They fit our inner image of "authority" and we defer. This is not always a self-serving response since acceptance of authority and leadership is necessary if anything useful is to get done by a group. It is reassuring to be led by someone in whom one has confidence. Whether the response is simply filling this need or is that of a toady and hanger-on finding a hook on which to hang their ambitions requires a look at the individual natal charts. In almost all cases where this overlay occurs, however, the element of acceptance of the inherent authority and status of the house person plays a large role.

Composite This composite position for Sun suggests, at the very least, that the persons share a need for and a common interest in establishing themselves in the hierarchy of their society. This can take the form of a joint endeavor such as business partnership or it can be expressed simply as an ongoing exchange of ideas and inspirations on how the persons can achieve what they wish in terms of status and recognition. Often the focus of the interaction will be on work interests, on career and "getting ahead." Even if other linkages are more personally warm and affectional, there will remain a continuing focus on theses issues. It is likely that the partners will value each other either as means of achieving this sort of recognition or actually as ready-made instruments, the acquisition of which will assure that result. This can sound a bit cold and calculating, but it need not be. Many people need this sort of achievement to maintain their sense of self-worth and personal value. For such people, a partnership which is supportive to that, which brings a pleasing and rewarding "place" in society, is highly prized. "Successful partnerships" are always such because they meet the joint needs of the individuals. If a firm, well established position in the world is what is needed, then this composite is a likely vehicle.

The difficulty that can occur with this composite's focus is that often it is not the objective which initially attracted the individuals. As individuals, it is much more likely that they responded to each other on more personal and intimate levels. If these initial responses brought them together, but the partnership, once formed, is most amenable to a 10th house sort of focus, the partners may find worldly success in the union, but not the personal fulfillment they sought. This composite position, perhaps more than any other for Sun, is an example of how synastric and composite linkages can mismatch. This occurs because people attracted to each other and compatible at the synastric level for emotional, romantic or sexual reasons may well, with this composite Sun, manage a socially and materially successful partnership; one which may be very difficult to abandon even if the partnership proves to be less satisfactory at the personal level. With this composite position, an especially careful look needs to be taken at the individual synastric links to be sure they blend reasonably well with the probable partnership focus.

Sun in the 11th House

Synastric Just as there is a well-defined status structure in a society based on one's work or career identity, there is a parallel social gridwork of elective sub-cultures which define the individual's interests, recreational and pleasure preferences and, in the narrow sense of the word, "cultural" affinities. These are elective in that they are chosen based on both the interests of the individual and the desire to associate oneself with the other inhabitants of this sub-culture; to be in the company of and identified with persons with whom the individual has common enthusiasms and appreciations. With this overlay, the planet person senses that the house person will share these interests and pleasures and responds to that person as a potential comrade or co-enthusiast. This is, of course, the primary basis on which friendships evolve and why people turn to each other to share leisure hours. The house person, finding themselves cast in the role of friend and companion, is usually appreciative and responsive, since such a role is as free of price tags as any humans assume. Particularly with a measure of maturity, humans come to realize that companionable friendships are the most rewarding, least likely to disappoint and most hassle-free of all interactions.

Sometimes this interaction takes on a formal rigor with involvement in organizations, clubs, societies or the like, based on common concerns or interests. More often, the relationship is less formal, involving the simple sharing of every-day leisure hours and entertainments. Whatever the tone, there is a particularly relaxed and non-judgmental character to this linkage. There may be major differences in the "status" or career identities of the individuals, and they may not even share a common world view, but somehow these differences do not interfere with the interplay. The individuals accept each other as is, warts and all, and tolerate, without disapproval or discord, considerable divergence of behavior or attitude. Often the individuals feel free to share confidences, release private anxieties and distress and use each other as sounding boards when confronted with problems. The essence of this interaction is its tolerant, non-judging quality. Obviously, this is an excellent atmosphere for nearly any sort of relationship and, whatever the remainder of the linkages impel, it is likely to be a happy and welcome synastric connection.

Composite This blending of Sun energy may be the most comfortable and productive of any of the possible composite positions. Individuals tend to have fairly firmly held and strongly felt views about the world in which they live and, with those, some clear priorities and goals. Usually, such complex personal structures abrade others in some way or other, despite linkages which bring people together. As a result, most relationships involve a degree of unwilling tolerance of minor annoyances and frictions. This feeling of being forced to compromise with another's foibles, and mask some of one's own predilections, to keep the peace creates stress and tension in the typical partnership. With the composite Sun in the 11th house, this quality of imposed self-regulation is largely absent and the partnership is free from these minor frictions. It is not so much that the individuals are alike or go about their life in a similar way, as it is that somehow the little quirks and flaws in the partners do not seem to matter. Behavior or attitudes which might be unbearable or foreign in others can be tolerated in each other and even found amusing and entertaining. Indeed, it is the "refuge in a mad world" tone of such partnerships which offers the greatest attraction; a feeling that within the partnership, the insanities and maddening frustrations of the outside world can be escaped, laughed at and survived.

Perhaps the only difficulty with this interaction is its very tranquility and ease. Even if there are other linkages which generate romantic or sexual interplay, or one or both of the partners is motivated by synastric links to develop the relationship into a full, formal commitments, this composite still may not provide the urgency and incentive to form such a relationship. It often creates a situation where things are proceeding so smoothly and without stress that the partners almost fear complicating the partnership by deliberately adding new dimensions to it. As a result, the partnership can float along, providing a great deal of pleasure and acceptance for the partners, without taking any well-defined shape or purpose. Depending entirely on the natal charts of the individuals and what those charts suggest in terms of life goals, this situation can create a feeling that the individual is not fulfilling their own personal "destiny." It is a regrettable fact that humans evolve rather rigid prescriptions and scenarios for themselves early in life and, despite being in a comfortable and pleasant relationship, may feel a self-generated unhappiness because those scenarios aren't being realized. Romantic and sexual fantasies from youth can, in the environment of the 11th house composite position, run afoul of reality and maturity and erode away what ought to be one of the most successful forms of partnership.

Sun in the 12th House

Synastric The word "exotic" has, unfortunately, lost part of its original meaning, at least as this word is commonly used. Its original premise was that something can be striking and, therefore, fascinating because it is foreign; not native, not related or even of our world. There is a kind of attraction and awareness which is based more on apprehension and strangeness than on a sense of kinship. The 12th house overlay typically creates such a response when our Sun is captured in this position. The house person seems so unlike us, so propelled by processes foreign to us that we cannot help but stare and wonder. In the truest sense, they are a mystery. We don't feel we can "read them" or grasp what it is they are likely to do nor do we feel they understand and, therefore, might approve of us. All is hidden and unpredictable, motivations and responses incomprehensible and separated from us by a veil of non-kinship. The association of the 12th house with the unconscious is not so much, in synastry, a process in which we are impelled by half-understood urges as it is characteristic of interaction between persons experiencing this overlay. They simply do not understand each other and, as a result, have no conscious rationale for the other's behavior or response. To the degree that curiosity and a momentary urge to experience something totally outside our own familiar world can motivate, this overlay can intrigue and titillate. It is the dabbling in the arcane, the flirting with the unknown, which is often triggered by this response.

Obviously, this is neither a harmonious nor particularly stable response. The planet person, if linked by other aspects or overlays which cause the person to seem attractive, will find themselves propelled almost against their good judgement into trying to establish contact with the house person; but always with the underlying feeling that they are not quite sure who or what they are reaching out for. The house person will probably find the actions of the planet person difficult to interpret and somehow discordant. Almost inevitably there will be misunderstandings and confusion in the interplay and, even after time, there will be no sense that the two persons are developing some insights into what is motivating each other. Since humans tend to interpret the actions of others in terms of their own inner drives and motives, each will try to relate the actions of the other to their own personal base; roughly like two people speaking different languages trying to manage a conversation without an awareness that each gives different meanings to the same sounds. Try as they may, only the outlines of their meanings get across and no real comprehension of what each has on their mind is achieved. Almost certainly, they will eventually give up and go their own way, wondering why they even tried to bridge this gap.

Composite Because this composite position for Sun is often accompanied by either an 11th or 1st house Venus, it crops up in partnerships more often than one might anticipate. Given sufficient other synastric and composite links, it will not prevent a partnership from forming, but it will have some sort of eccentric quality, a pairing of two persons who seemingly don't have a great deal in common. The Sun energies really are not blendable, and the relationship must sustain itself on other foundations. Typically, the two persons pursue different life courses, have divergent objectives or opt for quite unrelated life styles: bound together not by blending of fundamental personality parallels, but rather by affection, romantic love, sex or other drives. Given the willing- ness of the individuals to accept such a regimen, the partnership can function success- fully, but it will always have the quality of a lid that doesn't quite fit the jar properly. It can seal the contents well enough for most situations, but some special handling and care will be needed to keep the contents from leaking away. More often than not, when other linkages do bring people together who have this composite Sun position, there is a lot of misunderstanding of motives and inability to maintain a durable life course. The partner who is forever complaining that their mate "doesn't understand" them may well be correct if the union has this composite Sun position.

Curiously, this composite position does work well enough when two individuals are caught up in careers which tend to separate them often or which must be pursued with considerable independence of action. In situations such as this, too great of a bonding quality is actually a nuisance, and the people do better utilizing the partnership as a retreat from which they can draw emotional and sexual pleasure without being otherwise involved at a more mundane level. Certainly one of the characteristics of this composite is its essential privacy and detachment from the world in general; a quality of hiddenness. There is not much in the way of intellectual or philosophic bonds in this sort of partnership, but the deeper, less conscious drives can be strong and compelling. Because it is based on these unconscious links, it can occasionally have a negative expression, tapping the weaknesses and flaws in the personalities and triggering some less-than-healthy behavior. It is always wise, with this composite position, to examine the potential for such behavior in the individuals and ask of oneself whether it is these unpretty qualities which, in fact, form the basis of the partnership. Partnerships which lack basic harmony in the Sun composite house position are always suspect, to some degree, of terms of filling some unconscious needs, needs which are not always healthy or productive.

Moon in the Houses

The familiar phrase "...in the hearts and minds of people..." recognizes that humans respond to the world around them at two distinct and independently functioning levels. At one level, our conscious, more or less rational mind sifts through what we encounter and arrives at conclusions which are, if not entirely logical, at least can be explained in what seems to be reasonable and justifiable terms. At an entirely different level, however, we respond with our "hearts": our intuitive, non-lineal and largely unconscious feelings. The modern pioneer astrologer, Dane Rudhyar, noted a half-century ago in his classic *Astrology of Personality*, that we are motivated in many areas of our lives by what he called "feeling judgements." In synastry, as in all other areas of astrology, these feeling judgements are a product of the interplay of our Moon with what (or who) we are responding to and how that object (or person) touches this inner, intuitive capacity. Actually, we probably make the majority of our personal decisions from this base. As rational as we would like to believe we are, in fact we support a candidate, choose a car or a new coat, play a record and select our friends and lovers with our hearts rather than our Sun-related minds.

The rational mind chooses based on what a theoretical mathematician might describe as the "elegant symmetry" of what we observe; the highly persuasive completeness and apparent flawlessness of the object, argument or, in synastry, personality. The intuitive side of us, however, responds to something quite different. It is as if we have stored in us an awareness of our imperfections and irregularities and, when we encounter an object, an idea or a person whose unique *asymmetry* seems to match with ours, we feel a cosmic kinship; a highly personal and non-rational, inexplicable bonding. This kind of response is why a handmade object commands a much higher price than a mechanically produced identical item. The mechanical item is at least as functionally useful, probably cheaper and certainly much more free of flaws and imperfections. Logically we should value it higher, yet we don't. When we encounter some object which, being handmade and largely unique, we sense the little, almost invisible imperfections and irregularities it contains. If those flaws somehow cause us to respond, we pay exorbitant prices for such items because it simply makes us "feel good." Unlike the conscious, rational response of Sun, this is an unconscious, unfathomable and highly personal response which defies logic, suspends judgement and moves us emotionally in a way no Sun-based response could ever do. It is the loyalist's unshakable support for the "cause," the devotion we feel for a long-time pet, the sacrifice we would make for an old friend and the attachment we have for that moth-eaten old sweater that has seen us through countless winters.

Despite its depth, this response is not truly "instinctive." It is a learned response based on what our senses have experienced and accumulated over time. One cannot feel homesickness without having experienced a home. Nostalgia, loneliness, friendship, kinship and the like are experientially based. When recollection is jogged by an encounter with an image, a sound, a smell, taste or feel, our senses recall some paradigmatic experience and our emotions surge, propelled by that memory. We need not have ever experienced sex to feel the instinctive sexual response nor do we have to experience eating to feel hunger or danger to feel the need to flee a loud noise. We seemingly are born with these instincts in our lower brains. Emotions, however, are learned responses based on our sensory experiences and Moon-based interplays are reflective of these. The line is not, of course, always precise between "emotions" and "instinct" (e.g. parental responses or tribal/clan bonds), but usually we are dealing with recollective, unconscious feeling judgements based on past experience when we are analyzing Moon responses. Our response to political parties, religions, music, and other humans for whom we feel a welling affection is rooted in our past experiences and what those have taught us about the sources of our life satisfaction.

Moon in the 1st House

Synastric With this overlay, the Moon person tends to assume that the house person feels the same emotions and responses when confronted with a given circumstance. The quality of affection felt by the Moon person is based on presumption of understanding and identification between the two persons. There usually is a willingness to reveal the emotional responses and preferences and to proceed on the premise that there will be a shared response by the house person which allows for mutual enjoyment of the same experiences. Whatever the Moon person cherishes and seeks out as a means of emotional satisfaction, the house person is assumed to value also. The house person usually responds to this openness and emotional candor and, given other linkages of a positive type, will welcome the unguarded attitudes and warmth of the Moon person's interaction.

Composite This composite position for the Moon indicates a very easy and almost "fated" sort of teaming up to achieve those things which the partnership might seek as emotionally satisfying and fulfilling experiences. The partnership itself might be perceived as the primary avenue for the individuals to find contentment and emotional fulfillment. Certainly, the partners will find little to disagree about when planning goals and activities which are aimed at deriving pleasure and satisfaction from life. With such a composite Moon, the partnership can become so self-absorbed and insulated from the rest of the world that a rather dangerous sort of emotional dependence evolves. So much of what each seeks in emotional satisfaction is rooted in the partnership that the capacity to relate to the rest of the world may atrophy over time. This may take the form of simply relying almost exclusively on each other for emotional sustenance or, in the extreme, to such emotional interdependence that any form of separation or perturbation can seriously threaten the individuals. This sort of closeness may seem ideal in a rather callous and indifferent world, but it can be carried to such an extreme that the partners lose their ability to function if not operating jointly. Career and general social interactions can sometimes be negatively affected by such a self-absorbed relationship and partners with this bond need to be aware that, despite the linkage, they should retain their connections with the rest of the world in their own emotional self-interest. It is this sort of linkage that creates partnerships in which, when one dies or leaves or otherwise severs the partnership, the other partner may well simply not be able to go on with their life.

Moon in the 2nd House

Synastric This overlay probably works best if the Moon person looks to the house person as a resource in achieving some sort of emotionally valuable material objective. If we are contemplating buying a new home, replacing our stereo or investing in government bonds, we might respond well to a house person with this overlay. This is obviously not a particularly intimate or personal reaction, but somehow we feel some confidence in the house person's ability to help us achieve this sort of objective. It seems comfortable to work for a boss with this overlay or to hire someone to remodel our bathroom who captures our Moon in their 2nd house because of the quality of soundness and practicality which we feel about them. We sense we can work with them to bring the object or project to material reality. If other linkages are more personally energizing, at least we feel we can share some harmony in our appreciation of those tangible things which we seek to acquire to give us emotional satisfaction. Often this overlay will be present when two persons share an interest in such avocational activities as model building, woodworking or other hands-on, materially oriented projects. This overlay then tends to work best when we look to the other person to help us achieve some real-world project rather than for a full emotional involvement. Look for this overlay when you're ready to replace your furniture and need someone to help with your interior decorating.

Composite This composite position for Moon is not, in itself, a strong incentive for forming a partnership. If it occurs in the context of a composite chart which is otherwise supportive to teaming up, it is likely the persons will find their strongest emotional bonds developing over the use of joint resources to bring to the partnership the sort of fulfillment found in a home or a car or some other jointly owned object. Typically, romantic/sexual partnerships with this Moon position will place great emphasis on establishing and enjoying a "nest": a sanctuary for the relationship which provides actual physical satisfaction and security. There is unlikely to be disagreement over use of joint resources and, given the large role the hassles over money can play in disrupting a partnership, this can contribute to a relationship. At the least, the partners will share interests in material objects and find pleasure in working together to get them. The composite then works well when the interaction is focused on material security and acquiring those things which the partners perceive will make their life more fulfilling. Certainly, every peddler of a product or service would like to see this sort of partnership come walking in the front door of their store.

Moon in the 3rd House

Synastric Probably the strongest response created by this overlay is a feeling of approval and admiration for the way the house person goes about their life. Most of us are often upset or distracted by people who seem to be frittering their time and resources on things which we find of little value or focusing on what seem to us irrelevant goals. With this overlay, the Moon person feels at ease with the apparent priorities and routines of the house person and, because of this, is supportive and encouraging. The house person, of course, enjoys having their efforts and methods applauded and usually will react to this tacit approval with a cooperative and friendly attitude. The personal environment created by this overlay is especially relaxed and productive, and it is an excellent combination for nearly any activity. The interplay is largely mental and down-to-earth, so this overlay, in itself, is not a particularly strong stimulant to close personal interaction. In the presence of other, more emotionally enlivening links, however, it is a fine combination for any relationship which requires continuing close contact. Many of the irritants which might accumulate in such constant interactions will not occur with this overlay because the people find their responses to daily problems are harmonious and easily coordinated.

Composite One of the most enjoyable and rewarding parts of any relationship is the ability to share responses, assessments and reactions to the events which impinge on the partnership. With this composite Moon position, the partners will find such openness and sharing not only easy and comfortable, but stimulating and entertaining. Typically, the partners will enjoy talking about everything from books and movies to current politics and spend many hours both jointly experiencing these ordinary things and rehashing and comparing notes about their feelings and appraisal. While other motivations may exist for bringing the individuals together, probably the strongest bond which will develop with this position is a highly companionable interaction. The individuals will find each other good company, especially in the more relaxed and mundane hours of the day and will seldom tire of each other's companionship. Often the partners will combine or develop shared intellectual interests and stimulate each other to pursue these in greater depth. The essential harmony of emotional responses to the world will find its expression in the way the partners choose to spend their time and mental energies. Disagreements over how to use leisure hours or on the relative value of various sorts of activities to amuse, entertain or learn will rarely occur with this position. It is likely that the effect of the partnership will be to stimulate each to a wider and more energetic range of interests, and the individuals will, with this stimulus, find new and rewarding things to see and do because of this interaction.

Moon in the 4th House

Synastric This overlay creates an ambivalent response not unlike the interaction between siblings. At one level there is a feeling of bonding which roots in belonging to a similar order or genre, a feeling of linking based on some deeply rooted but hard to define shared quality. At another level, however, there is a competitive, challenging sort of response and a tendency to contest with the individual to establish one's "place" or rank in the relationship. The familial tone of the Moon person's response is not so much that of "brotherly love" as it is that of members of the same team, working together for some common end, yet still competing with each other for preeminence. This is, then, not a tranquil or relaxed response, but it can be highly energetic and stimulating. The house person will sense this response and typically return the throwing down of the gauntlet with an "Okay, pal, let's go at it!" response. There is no inherent reason why this should not be a friendly and good-natured interplay, but it is not the sort one might choose for the quieter moments. There is too much tension and energy being released in this overlay for the persons to spend long, uninterrupted hours together. It works best when the individuals can come together for short periods of intense and highly active interplay, then go their own way to find relaxation and easy companionship elsewhere. If you are looking for a doubles partner or someone to go rafting with, this is a fine combination, but a four-week tour of the museums of Europe would probably end in a double murder.

Composite Despite the association of the 4th house with "home and family," this composite position is anything but a signal of domestic harmony. It has the high-tension, lock-horn quality of those couple who seem to scrap constantly even though they may be strongly bonded. At its best, there is a wry sort of interplay with the individuals clearly not always in accord, but because of their affection and dependence on each other at other levels, this tension is released with ironic humor and tolerance. At its worst, this can result in constant bickering and contesting with one another over inconsequential things and an endless struggle over who's steering the ship. Despite this emotional jousting, this can be a strong stimulus for the individuals in their personal growth and expansion. The relationship is less a place to retreat for rest and recreation than it is a source of recharging; a relief from the fundamental sameness and uneventfulness of life. The people challenge each other, and if this can find a positive outlet such as career or personal growth, it can be highly productive. Actually, this combination works better when the relationship is multi-dimensional and has many levels available for the partners to link, especially at the physical and emotional levels. When this composite occurs in more transient or casual interactions, its stressful qualities usually result in too much competition and pushing and shoving to allow an enduring partnership.

Moon in the 5th House

Synastric Now and then we meet someone and find ourselves saying to ourselves, "Now that's the way people are supposed to be!" Actually, with this overlay, it is not so much that the person behaves in such a winning way as it is the pleasure our senses take in their physical presence. The 5th house always, in one or the other, taps our pleasure responses, and when the Moon is captured by the 5th house, it is much like our unconscious reaction to a lovely scene or a moving melody. All the guards go down around our emotions and we find ways to be with the house person simply because their presence cheers us and surrounds us with a feeling of beauty and sweetness, an aura not all that common in a rather grimy and harsh world. Because of this emotional synapse, the Moon person is motivated to seek out the house person as a companion for any sort of activity which is intended to be fun and pleasure giving. The house person, flattered by this appreciation, will join in the fun if there are other linkages which cause them to respond to the Moon person. Most typically, this can be characterized as a "dating" response and, given any sort of other supports, often evolves into a very enjoyable social and recreational interplay. Whether the interaction evolves beyond this happy sensory level depends, of course, on the remainder of the links between the charts, but such an overlay rarely produces an unpleasant scenario.

Composite This is, of course, a classically happy blending for the composite Moon and, if there are sexual undertones in other links, it can produce the intense romanticism and dreamy pink cloud delight of an archetypical love affair. The emotional qualities of the partners blend so congenially that they float along on the emotional harmony of the relationship, falling often into staring into each other's eyes and looking a bit glazed and dazzled. In the wider context of a well-aspected partnership, this inserts an enduring romanticism in the partnership in which the individuals find endless beauty and delight in each other. Because this is an essentially sensory interplay, it provides strong impetus for physical intimacy; at the very least, a lot of hugging and squeezing. Even if the partnership is not fundamentally a romantic one (i.e. because of gender or age difference or whatever), there remains an urge to communicate at the sensory level. The difficulty with this composite Moon position is that it speaks only to the emotional blending of the two charts, but it is so potent that it can patch over other less harmonious interplay for a time. It may cause the individuals to persist in a relationship which, at its core, is not sound. Whenever this composite appears, it is particularly important to examine the fundamental harmony of the personalities to determine if it may be blinding the partners and setting up the relationship for an eventual disappointing failure.

Moon in the 6th House

Synastric This overlay creates a curiously ambivalent response in the Moon person: a sense of obligation to the house person, but an equally felt quality that, somehow, the interaction may impose a responsibility or burden. Often the house person will sense this interplay and almost unconsciously look to the Moon person for favors or concessions. The result is often a relationship in which one person tries endlessly to help the other, but wonders why they are so extending themselves and carrying this load. Much depends here on the essential integrity and character of the persons involved. If the individuals are not abnormally self-absorbed and grasping, this can be a useful and productive interplay with one person providing opportunities and support for the other. Not uncommonly, this overlay takes on the character of a master teaching an apprentice or one person putting their particular skills at the disposal of another without asking much of a reward for their efforts. If, however, one or both of the individuals is less than ethical or overly ambitious and demanding, this overlay can create almost a martyr role for the Moon, forcing considerable sacrifices for the house person in spite of the illogic of doing so. The house person may be drawn into an enterprise which demands efforts or actions which are resented but somehow seem able to inescapable. Given the essential self-orientation of most humans, this overlay usually does not stimulate a very pleasing interaction because of the demands it makes and the resentments it can create. If you are considering someone as a roommate, look out for this overlay. It won't work out well.

Composite This composite position comes about as close to being an unworkable blending as any for Moon. The individuals seem constantly to be making emotional demands on each other which are uncomfortable and unwelcome. There is a pattern of inequity and endless compromise in the interplay with both persons feeling that they are forever required to give in to the other. This usually degenerates into a bickering, argumentative interaction with an exaggeration of the nastiest critical faculties of each person. When this occurs in a romantic/sexual relationship (and, given the power of lust, it can), there is an undertone of anger and bitterness in the relationship. The partners do not truly make each other happy or fulfilled at an emotional level and, people being what they are, this will usually result in each blaming the other. In the extreme, this composite introduces an element of contesting for dominance in the relationship which may even reach an emotionally violent level. This sort of scrapping is not a healthy, "letting off steam" sort, but rather a periodic erupting of the repressed resentments and angers which may be tolerated at other times in the throes of passion or demands of survival. The inability to blend the emotional qualities of the partners may be, in the end, the greatest barrier to a successful relationship and this composite position certainly raises considerable doubt about this capacity.

Moon in the 7th House

Synastric The emotional response of the Moon person to this overlay is perhaps best characterized as familial with a quality of naturalness and security in the presence of the house person. It is as if the Moon person expects the same sort of unjudging acceptance as comes from a parent or close kin. It seems entirely natural to join together for even the most mundane activities and pleasures and the atmosphere is relaxed and open. while the 7th house can, in many situations, create a kind of dynamic tension, when the unconscious emotional qualities are involved, this tension usually remains at a low and comfortable level. This individuals appear to complement each other, filling out the blank spaces for each other without struggling for the same airspace. Often the house person takes on the role of an amused and tolerant surrogate elder sibling, aware of the quirks and peculiarities of the Moon person, but finding them nonintrusive and somehow agreeable. This is a natural bonding for joining in some partnership enterprise and, whether this is only a casual or transient effort or an on-going relationship, the tone is of mutual acceptance and noncompetitive interaction. Given other links which reinforce this overlay, the house person will be motivated to provide an atmosphere of shelter and reassurance for the Moon person and be an exceptionally loyal and reliable pal. This usually is not a highly charged interplay. More typically it is characterized by durability and sureness rather than electric excitement or overpowering emotions.

Composite With this composite Moon position and even the most modest supportive linkages elsewhere, the individuals will almost certainly form some sort of lasting bond. The blending of emotional qualities is so natural and free-flowing that this composite position can sustain a relationship of some sort almost by itself. What other elements may be introduced into the relationship will depend, of course, of the remainder of the synastric connections (most likely indicated by the composite Sun), but whatever evolves has great staying power. To be with someone with whom one feels a strong and enduring emotional bond and commonality of responses to the world is, regardless of other objectives, a deeply pleasurable and reassuring experience. This position offers such a potential, and usually the individuals will find ways to share warmth and companionability even in the face of problems such as geographic separation, cultural or age differences or circumstantial barriers. In the absence of romantic/sexual stimulus, it may appear to be only a warm friendship, but it is not really that. The individuals do not come together primarily for active companionship or shared experiences, but rather seek each other out for emotional reassurance and support. Often they share their most intimate anxieties and hopes, secure in the knowledge that these revelations will be understood and treated with gentle compassion. In the context of a multi-level relationship, this position is the best glue ever invented to bond individuals into an enduring, unshakable partnership. Even without these other links, it is these people who will remember your birthday, applaud your successes and stand by you when you world caves in. They truly "care."

Moon in the 8th House

Synastric This overlay is a vaguely troubling and disturbing one. Every human harbors some dark thoughts, some strange corners or some aberrant fantasies in their unconscious; forced into these recesses by the behavioral requirements of the society. The conscious mind can manage these urges and prevent them from being translated from arcane phantoms into actualizing, but there is no way we can prevent these unconscious emotional drives from giving birth to them.....no way, of course, except severe repression which leads to true madness. For most humans, this phenomenon is quite manageable and we experience only fleeting and very private break-outs of these drives. The 8th house overlay appears to trigger this sort of response in the Moon person, reaching into the deep emotions and stirring up these phantoms. The particular form in which these demons reveal themselves depends, of course, both on the natal potentials of the Moon person and the remainder of the links with the house person. We must look to the natal chart of the Moon person to see where any such drives root, where the potential for unacceptable social behavior may lie dormant and restrained. The house person may well sense this response and, should there be any incentive created by other linkages to the Moon person's chart, be motivated to capitalize on them. These responses are familiar enough: greed, possessiveness, power, sexual excess or any other of humanity's less attractive qualities. In general, this overlay tends to bring out the least positive of our potentials, and we are at least momentarily tempted to escape from the restraints of society in some way when we experience it.

Composite While not an easily blended combination of emotional qualities, this composite position can create a pervasive fascination between individuals. They tantalize each other and not uncommonly engender such troubling and upsetting responses that the behavior is more extreme and exaggerated than the normal patterns each follows. Given a generally positive and stress-free interplay between the individuals, this may only offer an opportunity for the individuals to release subconscious emotional drives harmlessly in a guilt-free and open relationship. This release from all of society's restraints and typical individual fears and doubts may get out of hand. Often this interplay touches too many sensitive and concealed parts of the personalities to be easily accepted. Compulsions, obsessions, guilt, anxiety and even occasionally anger and violence can emerge, all based on the undercurrents set off by the interaction. Any tendency toward suspicion or self-protectiveness in the natal charts will be activated, and the individuals will cope with each other in a guarded and untrusting way. At its best, this composite position can allow individuals to share their inner, darker selves and thereby relieve some of the stresses these very private qualities may create. Relatively harmless shared interests in the occult or similar, not-quite-mainstream subjects may provide an outlet for the drives which this composite triggers. At its worst, however, the composite creates such deep disturbances and anxieties that the two people come almost to fear and resent each other in a vague and unfocused way. Successful and enduring partnerships which deliver to the individuals what most seek in any sort of relationship are rather unlikely with this composite position. In an anxiety-ridden and troubled world, the last thing we need from a partnership is more of the same.

Moon in the 9th House

Synastric Along the way of living, we all evolve paradigms for concepts such as "heroic," "genius," or "admirable" and, of course, their antonyms. In time, we accumulate a rather large file of such social and cultural yardsticks and, as we encounter other humans, we apply them. With the 9th-house overlay, the Moon person may find in the house person qualities which conform to these measures; or at least feel that the house person will share similar standards. These paradigms are, of course, feeling judgements rather than nice, neat logical analyses. Ratiorally we may recognize the value and contribution of other individuals, but the really critical and important measures root in our own personally evolved and quite illogical emotional conclusions. At a superficial level, it is these judgements which make us "fans." At a more profound level, they are the root of our own highest aspirations. With the 9th house overlay, we find something to admire or respect in the house person and they, in turn, are usually more than pleased to be seen in this light and respond accordingly. Because of this positive intellectual interplay, it is quite likely the individuals will turn to each other to hone their own perceptions of the world and reinforce their own feeling judgements. Because these paradigms are emotionally rooted, they often are difficult to describe or defend in purely rational terms. We believe in them with great passion, but often collapse in an emotional tangle when we are called upon to defend them. Typically we then turn to like-minded individuals with whom we can stand, shoulder to shoulder, to "defend what is right!" It is in the interaction of the Moon and the 9th house where we find right-headed political thinkers, those who have seen the true word in religion and those wonderful people who have the proper attitudes about personal and social behavior. There is, after all, nothing so winning as a person who thinks like me, acts like me and agrees with me. As a result, this overlay, while not an intimate or personal one, is highly harmonic and very likely to get both persons to the same meeting, rally, fund raiser or cultural event. There are worse bases for a relationship.

Composite In some ways it is easier to talk about what is *not* present in a relationship when this composite Moon position occurs than what *is*, because the blending is so harmonic that it almost loses any identifiable features. The partners will have difficulty in finding anything on which to disagree in a fundamental way and will probably arrive at the conclusion after a while that bringing up any topic for debate is a waste of energy. The individuals are going to agree on just about any abstract idea which occurs to either and, in the end, all they do is wind up nodding and sharing "wish it were otherwise, but..." feelings. In the context of warmer, more personal linkages, this makes for such a tranquil interaction that it even risks being dull. We avoid falling into blind, unthinking conformity with social norms largely because of occasional jolts we receive from persons close to us. Because we care about them, we can't just ignore them when they confront us with some challenge to our perceptions of the world. We tend to associate rigid conformity with insular, closed personalities for this reason: they have blocked off the stimuli of other persons unless those persons share their perceptions. The "true believer" or "knee-jerk" reactor is a product of such blocking of stimuli. With this composite Moon position, as tranquil as it may be, the partners tend not to provide these stimuli for each other. The result can be a rather conventional, unimaginative interaction which can easily fall into routines and unchanging patterns of living. The stimulus for growth is so absent within the partnership that, without knowing it, the partnership begins to ossify and one day one or both look up and realize that life and the world has passed them by. This is not an inevitable consequence of this Moon position if there are other, more lively linkages, but the potential exists. We should look at the remainder of the composite chart to see if a little dash of some destabilizing or energizing interaction is present in the relationship to serve as an antidote for this stultifying effect. Given that little impish element, this Moon position can then be the basis for a very relaxed and satisfactory blending of emotional qualities.

Moon in the 10th House

Synastric The impact of this overlay depends greatly on the circumstances in which it occurs and the basic orientation of the individuals. It is a fundamentally discordant interaction largely because, in Moon responses, rational conscious appraisals of other humans are not the controlling factor in how we respond to them. In positive overlays to Moon, we experience affectional appreciation and a stimulus to be generous and open in dealing with the other person. With Moon in the 10th, there may well be sensible and productive reasons the Moon person should interact positively with the house person, but the inherent discordance and conflict of this overlay may make this difficult to do. Given other, more harmonious links and, perhaps most importantly, that the Moon person is strongly oriented natally toward achievement and worldly success, it can be a useful overlay in teaming up for mutual benefit. The house person may find value in the Moon person as a colleague and coworker, but more because the individuals bring different temperaments and capacities to a situation which may, in combination, benefit both, than because there is any strong affectional or emotional bond. This overlay is limited in the depth of feelings the individuals will have for each other and the range of goals toward which they can jointly work. Within the narrow range of career or shared tasks, they may well find a basis of accord, but the relationship will likely remain impersonal and not function outside that limited circumstance. In the end, the self-serving quality of this overlay is inimicable to the essence of Moon's emotional and empathetic nature and it is unlikely that any other than a pragmatic and utilitarian interaction will evolve.

Composite The impersonal nature of this composite position will, under most circumstances, cause the interaction to pass without any sense on the part of the individuals that a real "partnership" can be achieved. In the context of a composite chart with other, more intimate and warm links, it can suggest an undertone of agreement on where worldly success fits into the priorities of the individuals and perhaps even how they might work together to achieve this. In itself, it is not a barrier to a more personal and rewarding interaction, but its contribution to any close emotional bonding is minimal. No matter what other elements are present in the interaction, there will remain a rational and controlled quality to the way in which the persons deal with each other; a sort of double-entry bookkeeping system in which each person's investment in the partnership will have to produce a balancing return for the partners to be willing to sustain the relationship. Much depends here on the basic emotional qualities in the natal charts. If the individuals are rather objective, practical sorts with relatively low-order needs for emotional fulfillment (i.e. perhaps lightly aspected Moons in either Air or Earth signs) and are career and achievement oriented, they can blend their emotional qualities successfully without making what might be considered excessive emotional demands on each other. This sort of successful interplay, however, is likely to be the exception since virtually everyone hopes to find in a partnership some sort of warmth and emotional sustenance. This composite then is probably most useful when the partnership is limited in scope and is not the primary source for emotional reassurance and fulfillment in the lives of the individuals.

Moon in the 11th House

Synastric This is a very companionable and upbeat overlay. The Moon person will feel an almost immediate bond with the house person, perceiving them as approachable and worth the effort to initiate a relationship. There is an unconscious appraisal of the house person as someone with whom the Moon person can be at ease and find common ground. The house person typically will enjoy the easy, open reaching out for contact which comes from the Moon person and, even if there are not strong links elsewhere, will accept the exploratory actions of the Moon person. Perhaps the strongest element of this overlay is the absence of need for artifice and role playing the individuals feel and the atmosphere of relaxed interplay. Most human contacts create some degree of stress or anxiety at the emotional level largely because of the unknowns involved. With this overlay, the concern about how the individuals will respond to each other is greatly reduced. That rare but delightful feeling that you have known someone all your life even though you have just met usually roots in this overlay of Moon. In the context of romantic/sexual response from other links, this can be a marvelous foundation for a warm and enduring relationship. It seems to function as a calming and good-humored counterbalance for more heated response and can do much to keep a relationship in perspective. Whatever may evolve between the individuals later, this overlay will provide a buffer against both exaggerated expectations and a stabilizer when the relationship encounters passing storms.

Composite An argument can be made that the most desirable and beneficial blending of emotional qualities in a partnership is that which produces an unshakable feeling that the individuals can trust and rely on each other. This composite position for Moon seems to offer that potential and, as a result, is a very valuable asset in any sort of partnership. There is great personal loyalty and willingness to meet the obligations of the partnership with this position. We give loyalty to another out of an unconscious but nonetheless strong feeling that they are worthy of our best and, with this composite position, the individuals tend to earn this sort of loyalty from each other. Humans will much more often fail a coworker, lover, or business associate than a friend; perhaps because all of those other relationships were originally entered into to achieve or acquire something of personal significance to the individuals. This self-oriented purposefulness is usually absent in an 11th house Moon position, and the partnership evolves mostly because of the simple fact that the people like each other and find in each other intrinsic good and worth. The result is then a particularly unselfish and supportive kind of interplay based on tolerance, trust and good humor. What form the evolved partnership will take is, of course, going to be dictated by the other links (particularly to Sun and Venus), but it is unlikely that the partners will be dissatisfied with whatever comes. The very nature of this composite is accepting and undemanding. As a result, the partnership should be a durable and pleasant one in any form.

Moon in the 12th House

Synastric This is a troublesome overlay because it creates an element of emotional upset which lies so far beneath the surface that its cause is rarely understood. For the Moon person, there is something about the house person which is unsettling and disturbing. It is not so much an active dislike or feeling of conflict as it is a sense of the unfathomability of the house person: a feeling that the emotional drives and motives of the house person are beyond understanding. By itself, it will tend to discourage a relationship because this feeling of the essence of the other person is concealed. The house person will sense this discomfort in the Moon person and react with some doubt and suspicion, asking "What does that person think I'm up to, anyway?" Even if there are other links which encourage a relationship, there will be a great deal of wary circling and sniffing. There is a kind of incipient paranoia in this overlay which keeps the individuals tense and uncertain in their contacts. Normally this just results in the people going their ways, glancing back over their shoulders and shaking their heads in puzzlement. If, however, this overlay is involved in the environment of an intense romantic/sexual interplay, it can have some very destabilizing effects. The persons may come together for self-gratification, but once that is achieved, an atmosphere of distrust and uncertainty will reappear. The communication is so poor and the blending links so inimical that the relationship can easily deteriorate into angry resentments and irrational, seemingly unprovoked outbursts. It is almost as if the individuals dislike themselves for allowing sexual drives to momentarily overcome their judgement and then project this antipathy onto each other. This interplay won't survive long, of course, but it is probably better to avoid it in the first place.

Composite In this composite, the emotional blending (or rather inability to blend) goes deep into unconscious recesses of the personalities. If the individuals bring to the partnership natal Moons without harsh or destabilizing aspects, this composite can be managed even though there will remain an absence of real emotional bonding. This position activates, through the partnership itself, the natal emotional qualities of the individuals and often in their worst form. Doubts, anxieties, fears, worries, angers and the like which are present but repressed by the individuals will come boiling out in the interaction and be directed at the structure of the relationship. It is as if long-healed-over wounds and punctures have their protective barriers ripped off by the interaction, destroying the hard-won peace the individuals have made with their hurts. This composite digs deep into the unconscious and motivates the individuals to act on long-hidden or deeply repressed urges; personality qualities which, in many cases, would be best left undisturbed. The partnership may cause the individuals to behave in ways which seem irrational and totally out of character. Worst of all, the individuals themselves cannot understand their own behavior or why they respond in such a way in the presence of each other. Clearly this is such an unnerving interaction that usually the individuals will find little basis for a relationship. If the individuals have the bad luck to have this composite within a highly charged sexual interaction and become involved at that level, it can have some strange and even obsessive results. Sex alone closes down the higher, rational mind rather completely, and with this 12th house Moon position, the demons which can escape when reason is turned off are literally invited to come out and raise hell. Except for those whose tastes run to escapism and extremes, this composite position is probably going to have unpleasant results if a partnership is attempted.

THE SECONDARY GROUP

Venus in the Houses

The role of Venus in synastry is best understood as the response humans feel in the presence of another human who embodies qualities which somehow seem to conform to an inner paradigm of value, beauty, joy and some degree of "perfection." This model or paradigm evolves in individuals as they grow and discover what particular qualities most please and excite them. This paradigm or model has complex roots, beginning with those standards which are acquired from the society in which one matures. When we are very young, the standards of our peers influence us greatly, and though we may privately not always share the attitudes of our particular peer group, we feel such pressure to conform to it that we tend to respond to persons who seem to possess the "standard" qualities. Perhaps that is why all Prom Queens, County Fair Princesses and Misses America tend to look like clones. Time and a growing knowledge of ourselves gradually, however, allow us to evolve our own sense of beauty and joy and perfection. In synastric analysis, then, the age and relative maturity of the individuals are vital in evaluating Venus linkages.

In considering Venus and her partner Mars, we must make a distinction between two strongly linked but actually polar opposed human drives: romantic versus sexual responses. Of course, humans have been trying to define both of these powerful drives as long as there have been poets and balladeers and artists, with less than complete success. As potent as they are, they always elude precise definition, probably because, while we all feel these drives, we do not share a common paradigm or model. Beauty is, indeed, largely in the eye of the beholder; at least the kind of personal and special beauty which we individually come to cherish. While we can all see symmetrical beauty with its "correct" proportions and balances, there is a much more meaningful kind of asymmetrical, unique beauty which may only be visible to us. This personal paradigm roots in our own uniqueness and is never completely shared by anyone else, with the result that we never quite totally agree with anyone else's choices or dreams of beauty. Nothing illustrates this better than a blind date (i.e. "Oh, he's very nice; good personality, neat, intelligent. You'll get along just fine." In fact, a first-class nerd.) Or that sense of complete puzzlement over other people's choice of partners which causes us to ask, "what does he see in her?" The root of this personal paradigm of beauty and value, the feeling that we want to simply stand and bask in the perfection and worth of another human, is Venus.

Venus is *not* sexual, in a strict sense, because the underlying response is to give of one's self, to offer whatever is required to be in the presence of the person who stimulates this response. Sexual drives are quite the opposite in that they drive us to take, to possess, to own, rather than offer and give and yield. When these coexist, we call it "romantic love," but the Venus-based response can exist and create strong responses without any sexual overtones. It can operate in relationships between members of the same sex without any suggestion of homosexuality; we simply deeply care for and cherish the individual and believe they are worthy of our admiration, generosity and sacrifice. The overlay of houses on Venus and its composite chart position indicates in what way and form we find beauty and loveworthiness in another human independent of any sexual value they may have for us. It is the "I GIVE" urge or, in the best sense of the word, love.

Venus in the 1st House

Synastric There is a narcissistic quality to this overlay which can be a strong stimulant. The Venus person sees in the house person those qualities which somehow enhance the self-esteem of the Venus person. Being with the house person and a part of their life reinforces the self-appraisal of the Venus person, communicating to the world that the association reflects positively on the capacity of the Venus person to attract and hold such a thing of beauty. There is a tendency to want to "show off" this linkage which is very flattering to the house person. The difficulty with this overlay is that often the house person comes to feel that they are cherished less for their intrinsic qualities than for their trophy value. It seems sometimes as if the Venus person is looking right through the house person to see what effect their coupling is having. Given other links which are less self-oriented, this overlay can provide a strong bond, but it is vulnerable to the erosion of time and of illusion. The house person may come to feel that this valuing by the Venus person is less and less flattering and more and more a burden. This overlay may be the cause of the state of mind which "puts someone on a pedestal"....which is, of course, a bloody awkward place to maintain a real-world relationship of any sort.

Composite The blending of paradigms in this composite comes easily and the individuals will likely satisfy each other in terms of what the partnership seeks in pleasure-giving activity. The partners can spend leisure time together naturally and will rarely disagree over where to go on vacation, how to decorate the house or which restaurant to choose. Their tastes and preferences will be very similar and their appreciation of each other as attractive and interesting people will be durable. This is such a potent composite position that it can, under some circumstances, paper over other less harmonious links. It becomes especially important to see if the relationship functions well in other terms and at other levels, since this Venus composite may blind the individuals to some potential conflicts which could emerge as the glow of the relationship's early excitement wears off. Perhaps the biggest concern is that this linkage is largely a self-gratifying one for both partners and may not, over time, provide a solid base for an enduring and generous friendship which will sustain the partnership through the normal turmoil of life.

Venus in the 2nd House

Synastric In truth, this overlay usually creates very little feeling of admiration or beauty in the Venus person. While the house person may possess all the attributes which society defines as "beautiful," the Venus person is not moved by these qualities. Other linkages may create a response in the Venus person, and it is entirely possible that compatibility or affection or even sexual hunger may be felt, but there will remain an absence of that willingness to make meaningful sacrifices or to communicate a feeling of the house person's intrinsic value and beauty. The house person will sense this absence of true valuing in the Venus person's response and will tend to respond to any effort to establish a relationship in a pragmatic and unemotional way. If there are links which motivate the house person at other levels, some sort of interaction may result, but it will have a rather cold purposefulness about it. Each will take from the other whatever each wants, but only the minimum required to sustain the relationship will be returned. In the end, the lack of generosity with self and the unjudging forgiveness and appreciation will remain as a probable barrier to a truly close interaction. Much depends, of course, on what each person seeks in life and in relationships and, if these are rather practical, unemotional persons who look to other objectives than love and intimacy for life satisfaction, a sort of pragmatic working arrangement can be managed. It will never, however, be a romantic or emotionally interdependent one. Regretfully, it will probably always remain a somewhat self-oriented kind of exchange; one which might well be characterized as a "pay as you go" deal which fills other needs, but not those of romantic love.

Composite While not an especially romantic position for Venus in a composite chart, there is no inherent reason that this cannot function successfully if other more personal blendings exist. The individuals will likely easily combine their energies to acquire what each considers beautiful and life-enhancing in the realm of material things. Their tastes and responses to the physical environment in which they find themselves will blend well, and they may well find their greatest rewards in the partnership through jointly fulfilling the esthetic pleasures of owning and decorating a home, buying art objects or simply sharing their interests and tastes in creative work. Perhaps the most positive aspect of this position is that there will be little disagreement over how to use discretionary resources in creating a personal physical environment within which the partnership can function. The persons will likely respond to the same colors, designs, forms and textures and may even share a "collecting" interest. Given warmer, more personal links elsewhere in the composite chart, this position can be both financially rewarding and stabilizing and, working together, the individuals can achieve much in the way of material and financial security. The danger, of course, is that materiality can become the dominant theme in the relationship and become a substitute for true closeness and regard for each other.

Venus in the 3rd House

Synastric This overlay produces a very relaxed and comfortable response in the Venus person; a sense that the house person will not ask anything in the way of behavior or attitude which will force role-playing or artifice. There is an early perception that the house person can be approached and will usually at least be open to some sort of contact by the Venus person. The persons often slip easily into a companionable and communicative relationship, and even if there are no other significant links to encourage a fully evolved relationship, the interplay will be pleasant and open. The house person tends to appreciate the warm and appreciative tone of the Venus person's initiative and will usually try to respond positively. With this overlay and the excellent opening it provides, whatever potential exists for a more developed and complex relationship will not be blocked by any undue wariness or doubt. There is an underlying trust and harmony in this overlay that allows the individuals to explore the possibilities within each personality and find whatever bonds which may exist. By itself, it is not usually suggestive of romantic or sexual responses, but its ease and openness can make even small links seem worth pursuing. In an environment of strong romantic or sexual linkages, this overlay can produce a delightful quality of understanding and sensitivity to each other; an almost intuitive bond which allows each of the individuals to anticipate and respond to the needs of the other. Any intimacy which may evolve will be light-hearted and full of gentle humor, allowing both persons to express their inner feelings without fear of rejection or ridicule. The timing and priorities of the individuals should work well together, and with any support from other links, this can be a durable and pleasing experience for both, regardless of what form the relationship ultimately assumes. While more commonly an overlay which results in a companionable friendship or easy work relationship, it can be a very happy ingredient of a more intimate interplay if other, more personal, links exist.

Composite This composite position provides a common ground in the individual's perception of the world around them and a capacity to share ideas and values at an intellectual level. While this is a pleasing blending of minds and spirits, it is typically an unlikely combination in more intimate and emotionally based relationships. Because of Venus's constant proximity to Sun, this composite position is most likely to occur in a composite chart which places Sun in the 2nd, 3rd or 4th composite house. With these Sun positions, the likelihood is that this harmonic blending of Venus qualities will focus itself in the arena suggested by the composite Sun position rather than in an intimate romantic sexual interaction. In the less common situation where the composite Sun is in the 1st or 5th house, this then becomes a highly successful place for Venus since it opens communication and establishes a solid intellectual and esthetic basis on which the relationship can pivot. In any situation, however, this position blends the responses of the individuals to the society around them in a harmonious and supportive way and allows the individuals to lean on and trust each other in coping with the struggles of surviving in a demanding and sometimes frightening world.

Venus in the 4th House

Synastric A 4th house overlay will, with other planetary involvement, often create a kind of dynamic and exciting tension which can be a basis for a lively if not always stable response. Venus, however, is a gentle and yielding element in the personality and this stressed and pressing quality of the 4th house is somewhat inimicable to the essence of this planet. The underlying desire with Venus is to make oneself open and available to the other person: to put one's entire ego-identity on the line for the other person either to accept or reject. Obviously, when one makes oneself that vulnerable to another human, it is most easily done in an environment of trust and reasonable shelter from the possible painful rejection by the other person. This overlay is usually too conflict-filled and tense to reassure us adequately and, no matter what other linkages may be operating, there is a self-protective quality to any initiative which may come from the Venus person. The house person will sense this guardedness and hesitancy and will probably interpret it as rooted in either lack of confidence or as an expression of doubt about the motives or integrity of the house person. This overlay is not then one which makes a relationship easy to begin or sustain despite a particular form of magnetism it often contains. By itself it will tend to create too much uncertainty and discomfort to work well. With other more compelling links, its energy and excitement can be reconciled and may, under some circumstances, be rechannelled into an intense kind of interplay. For this to occur, however, links involving other planets (particularly Moon) must provide a reassuring background for the relationship within which the almost inevitable tension of this overlay can operate. There will remain, however, a persisting sense that any bond is based more on the exciting *differences* between the personalities rather than their essential harmony.

Composite This composite position for Venus is, unlike the synastric overlay, a very warm and rewarding placement largely because the individuals can easily blend their aspirations for a life core built around family and home. The partners will find little over which to disagree with regard to what will be the central focus of the relationship. The shared perceptions of the basic source of joy and contentment (primarily the role of the home life and quiet hours away from the outside world) come together with a feeling of naturalness and calm. This does not mean, of course, that every partnership with this Venus composite will result in an old-fashioned, home-centered and familially oriented relationship. It simply means that the individuals will tend not to experience conflict over whatever value and importance the role of kinship and family and home may have in the partnership. Perhaps the most attractive quality of this composite position is that the individuals feel a sense of kinship beyond romantic love or sexual magnetism; a feeling that they are truly "related" in some cosmic way and share a deep-rooted bond which, by forming the partnership, they amplify. Whatever else may evolve in the relationship, this composite position creates a feeling in the partners that they can and will stand by each other in times of stress and present a united and mutually supportive face to the world.

Venus in the 5th House

Synastric This overlay is the most romantic and titillating of the entire circle of houses since, by its nature, the 5th house symbolizes all things joyous, beautiful and magic. With this overlay, the Venus person truly sees the house person as an actualization of what their particular paradigm of human loveliness and perfection dictates. The intriguing part of this response is that the Venus person may well "see" qualities in the house person which not only are not "seen" by others but which, regrettably, may not even exist in fact. There is a mesmerizing quality to this overlay which, while it may not actually blind us to the faults and flaws of another, causes us to be so forgiving and capable of sublimating our judgement that we create a self-serving illusion about the house person. Very few persons object violently to being seen in such a dazzled and misty-eyed way and, rather predictably, the house person is gratified by this response. What the house person elects to do about this adoration depends largely on other linkages, in particular the reverse overlay, but also on the self-image of the house person. In synastric analysis, it is wise to examine the strength of the house person's sense of self-worth and capacity to deal with the world. Persons with a strong natal personality and a firm base of self-confidence will enjoy this response to themselves, but probably only return to the Venus person an honest and straightforward feedback about how they wish to evolve the relationship. A person with low self-esteem engendered by difficult aspects from Saturn and/or Neptune or one whose natal potential is rather self-oriented and lacking in compassion may well seize on this reaction in the Venus person to exploit or manipulate them. At its best, this overlay is immensely gratifying and fulfills what all humans hope to experience: that wonderful glow which is kindled by being with and close to another human who embodies all the lovely and wonderful things in a partner (a reaction which, incidentally, rarely fades with time). At its worst, however, it can trap us in a web of illusion and fantasy woven about the other person which leads the individuals down a path of romantic disillusion and falseness. This is a powerful overlay and when it occurs, one hopes for other more "real-world" links to keep the response within the realm of the possible.

Composite This composite position clearly indicates that the partners can and most likely will fulfill each other's romantic needs. It will seem quite natural and almost "fated" that the partners come together to gaze at each other over dinner, stroll hand-in-hand and bathe themselves in the sensory delight of each other's closeness. No one could possibly object to that, but it does raise the question of what follows this feast of the senses. With this composite position, perhaps more than any other, the analysis must ask whether the partnership has anywhere to go but from one rosy afternoon to the next. The overall composite chart and the underlying needs of the individual natal charts become extremely important in assessing this position for a composite Venus since it alone can trigger a relationship which otherwise may not be unworkable over a span of time. Under any circumstance, the partners will find a great number of ways to enjoy their time together and probably never really tire of each other's company. This is a great contribution to an enduring relationship and can provide one of the most companionable and pleasure-giving interactions regardless of the scope of the ultimate partnership. Its only real weakness is that it is based on the partners fulfilling each other's personal, inner fantasies which typically are not overly realistic. Given the right general environment, this can be a magic interplay, but regretfully more often than not it becomes the underlying cause for those star-crossed romantic tragedies which are the stuff of poets, novelists and soap operas.

Venus in the 6th House

Synastric It is rather unlikely this overlay will produce any depth of favorable response. The Venus person will find little with which to identify in the house person's projected personality as far as sharing a common view of the sources of pleasure or romantic fulfillment. No matter how attractive the house person may be in general societal terms, there will be a doubt in the Venus person that there is much to be shared between the individuals. The house person will likely recognize this reaction and interpret it as a kind of subliminal disapproval or antipathy. Confronted with this, the house person may well feel annoyance or resentment and will not likely seek any contact. Particularly in synastric links involving Venus, we are looking for clearly felt harmony of attitudes about what constitutes a realization of dreams and hopes in partnerships. If this sense of shared dreams is not sensed, we are not very likely to be motivated to invest much of ourselves in pursuing a relationship. Venus symbolizes the endless human quest to find another person who embodies our own paradigm of beauty and worth and to share ourselves with them. The 6th house overlay for Venus typically does not engender this sort of response, and, in fact, may even create a feeling that any depth of contact with the other person would only bring problems and burdens into our lives.

Composite This composite position for Venus can work well enough in partnerships which are not essentially romantic/sexual. Most humans must invest a large measure of themselves in some form of work and, hopefully, from that effort comes the pleasure and satisfaction of doing something well and successfully. In partnerships where the basic bond is work related or involves a shared task, this can be a useful composite position because the individuals enjoy the same sort of activity and seek the same form of satisfaction from their efforts. In more intimate relationships, this "task" quality intrudes into the partnership and the individuals tend to find their interaction either demanding or one in which one individual must fall into a pattern of serving and giving way to the other for it to function. When the partnership involves individuals who come together because one seeks shelter and security behind the strong and dominant personality of the other, this position can probably fill that need. Indeed, this is not an uncommon position for Venus in composite charts which have Sun in the 7th house and often in such situations of basically well blended personalities at other levels, this 6th house position for Venus and its dominance/passivity symbolism is what makes the partnership attractive to the individuals. Much depends on the natal qualities of the individuals involved whether this out-of-balance quality will be contributive or detrimental. In situations where both personalities are relatively self-sufficient and confident, this undertone of imbalance may be initially ignored at the outset of the partnership in the glow of the early good feelings, but in time will become an irritant to the partners. With this position for Venus, ultimately one of the partners will have to yield to the priorities of the other in the search for pleasure and fulfillment. In the end, this subservient role may not be acceptable to either.

Venus In The 7th House
    Synastric This overlay is a classically good one for nearly any sort of relationship

because the Venus person not only finds in the house person a number of pleasing qualities, but in addition to that, these perceived qualities are those which the Venus person has subconsciously defined as specifically desirable in a close partnership. There is a clear sense that the personalities complement each other and compensate for the vulnerabilities and inadequacies in the Venus person's psyche. The house person senses this capacity of the Venus person to mold to their needs and hopes and is both flattered and relieved since such a response tells the house person that a minimum of unwelcome compromise and accommodation would be required to maintain a relationship. Of course, this overlay can work well in nearly any sort of relationship, but it is at its best in romantic/sexual relationships. Given other encouraging links, the individuals can slip easily into intimacy and pleasure-giving activity because their desires are so well blended and the roles each plays for the other is so natural. The other side of this coin, however, occurs in situations where such links from the natal chart of the house person do not exist and do not make the Venus person attractive as a potential partner. This overlay then sets up a powerful push-pull kind of response and exactly the opposite feelings are aroused in the house person. The Venus person seems so pressing and magnetized that the house person's personal "territorial imperative" is violated. The house person may react quite negatively and angrily to any reaching out for contact by the Venus person and not only act to avoid such contact, but sometimes strike back as if the Venus person was enemy or invader. This overlay is very often present in intense but one-sided interactions which generate strong negative emotions and actions. In synastric analysis it is then particularly important to measure the *mutuality* of linkages when this overly occurs.

Composite This is probably the ideal composite placement for Venus since the personality qualities of the partners not only blend in a complementary way, but it is probable that the subconscious paradigm each has for what they seek in a relationship can come together in execution; the thing will just "work." This is true regardless of whether there is a romantic/sexual involvement or not, or whether the partnership involves members of the same or opposite sex. This composite position is just as salutary for fishing buddies, couch potatoes or shopping mall addicts as it is for lovers since the individuals find their pleasure and fulfillment in the sorts of things which are best shared with each other. In fact, the effect the individuals have on each other is largely to accentuate and heighten the pleasure of any activity through the act of sharing that activity. The same pastimes lose much of their value when not done with the partner, but with the partner, new and happy interests and activities emerge. In its way, this composite creates the feeling that just "being together" is the source of pleasure and what else is done when the partners are together is incidental. Perhaps the only real risk in this position is that the partnership can become insular and so satisfying in itself that the individuals may forget to retain their links with the remainder of their worlds. Given personalities which are active and emotionally secure, however, it is hard to find anything about this composite which is negative. Only in a circumstance where the personalities are fearful or reclusive natally and use the relationship to hide from the world can anything really unhealthy come out of this composite position for Venus.

Venus in the 8th House

Synastric This is an intriguing overlay for Venus partially because it creates a smoky and mysterious response in the Venus person as if the house person is somewhat a channel through which the most deep and hidden sources of pleasure can be realized and partially because it makes the Venus person particularly vulnerable to yielding to any pleasure whims of the house person. The house person will probably sense this vulnerability and, if motivated by other links, will have a head full of wild and arcane fantasies involving the Venus person. Because of Venus's association with pleasure-seeking and dreams of fulfillment of fantasies, it is hard to avoid the sexual implications of this overlay. Even if the interaction is between members of the same sex without any homosexual ingredients, this sexual undertone will remain. This may only involve sharing intimate thoughts and attitudes or it may extend to "prowling" together in the sexual chase, but whatever form it takes it will be a strong ingredient in the partnership. Obviously, in romantic involvements it will probably be acted out if the situation makes this possible and both are even moderately motivated. The unconscious response of the Venus person is to at least consider making themselves sexually available and to unconsciously assess the house person as a potential sex partner. Without significant aspects between the charts, this response may never convert itself into action, but a powerful sexual atmosphere will persist in the interaction. The Venus person will enjoy the secret excitement of the sexual presence of the house person and the house person, sensing this, will behave in a way as to heighten this excitement, if for no other reason than most humans are vain enough to enjoy being seen as sexually attractive.

Composite The gods of the cosmos did some devilish scheming here since this composite position for Venus occurs quite frequently in conjunction with a composite Sun in the 7th or 8th house. With the former Sun composite position, it is very likely that the basic bond of partnership will so enhance the effect of an 8th house Venus position that the individual will make every effort to become lovers. Circumstances or other factors may prevent this, but the basic drive to be lovers will remain no matter what outward form the partnership takes. With an 8th house composite Sun, the interaction may well become so sexually charged that the individuals act in the extreme, possibly involving infidelity or sexual obsessions. It is vital to analyze the natal charts in such a situation to determine how strongly sexually motivated the individuals are and how each is likely to seek release of sexual tensions. Given reasonably well matched natal personalities and some motivated synastric links, this can produce a fiery relationship which may not avoid burning itself out, but will be all-consuming while it lasts. The least fortunate situation occurs when the composite Sun falls in the 6th house. This can create a situation in which the persons may simply sexually exploit the partnership, but will likely not be able to create a sound, working partnership. Whatever the circumstances, this position for Venus will not pass unnoticed by the individuals and will probably test their capacity for acting in their own self-interest and with concern for the other person. This is not a position which stimulates good judgment, selflessness or generosity; rather it is one in which self-gratification and deep hungers are triggered by the interaction.

Venus In The 9th House

Synastric This overlay typically produces a pleasant if not exciting response in the Venus person, based largely on a feeling of shared values and responses to those things which are worthy and admirable in an abstract way. Commonly the individuals will have mutual aesthetic or cultural interests, similar preferences in recreational or social activities and be stimulated or emotionally touched by the same books, movies, music or works of art. Given the proper set of natal components, the individuals may also share an interest in outdoor activities, a love of animals or even be interested and active in support of the same social causes and crusades. The house person will welcome the indications of similar standards and responses in the Venus person and enjoy the exchange of appreciations and criticisms. The interaction with this overlay is based largely on a harmony of response to what is beautiful and culturally significant at an intellectual level. To the degree that religious or political interests are based on ideals and actions which bring a sense of personal fulfillment to the participant and somehow make the world "a better place," the individuals will find much in common in their attitudes and values. While this overlay in itself does not stimulate the more intimate and personal responses, with other more personal links or a warmly emotional composite chart, it can contribute a large measure of harmony to an interaction. Persons whose world view and personal values, ethics and priorities are harmonious certainly have a head start on a pleasant relationship, and since this harmony involves Venus and the coming together to share what is beautiful, good and valuable in life, this overlay can produce a very satisfying and stimulating interaction.

Composite This composite position for Venus, while essentially a harmonious one, in some ways tends to be restrictive in its effect on the scope of the relationship. In composite charts, the blending of the Venus components of the natal charts usually indicates the capacities of the individuals to find in each other the realization of romantic (in the broadest sense) hopes and dreams. The individuals will find little conflict in their interaction and may well find a considerable range of ideas and abstracts on which they agree, but the partnership will tend to remain at that somewhat arms-length distance. This presents no problem, in fact it is rather desirable, when neither of the partners has romantic or sexual aspirations for the relationship, but if one or both are stimulated by synastric links to try to move the relationship to that more intimate level, the individuals may not find it easy to accomplish this. This composite position is an excellent example of how mutual attraction and even real compatibility triggered by synastric interplay may not always translate well into a working partnership. The absence of a common ground for romantic intimacy or sexual freedom which grows out of this composite position can leave the individuals wondering why they can't seem to feel emotionally and romantically close despite their attraction and seeming compatibility. This composite position lacks the fantasy-fulfilling, romantic electricity to truly bond an intimate relationship and, because of this, the individuals will most likely remain warm friends, but never quite translate that into a love-based partnership. Sometimes this interaction becomes so puzzling or frustrating to the individuals that they abandon the relationship despite its many good qualities, sensing that it will never fully meet their most romantic and intimate needs. The memory will linger and the question, "We had so much in common. Why didn't it work?" remain unanswered.

Venus in The 10th House

Synastric This overlay usually establishes a somewhat impersonal response, at least in terms of what the Venus person perceives to be the personal qualities and value of the house person. Not only is the interaction somewhat stressed, it also contains the feeling that there is little warmth or humanity to be shared. The 10th house symbolizes the general public identity, the "place" an individual establishes in a society and the Venus qualities in a personality have only minimum interest and concern for this arena. The exception might be an individual with very strongly activated natal need to achieve a position of status and influence and who, therefore, might respond to the house person as a resource to achieve this. The individuals probably will not have difficulty working together in an impersonal setting and may even come to respect each others abilities and skills. The house person may come to rely on the Venus person where some joint effort requires creative or inventive insight or a talent lacking in the house person. The Venus person usually will accept this role since it offers an opportunity to use talents in a productive and possibly status-enhancing way. This is not an unfavorable overlay within the limited context of work or career related activity or simply a joint undertaking for mutual benefit, but it is unlikely either person will feel much in the way of personal warmth or closeness no matter how the interaction evolves.

Composite How successfully the Venus qualities in the personalities blend in this composite position depends very largely on the composite positions of Sun and Moon. The individuals, can probably share (or at least reconcile) their priorities in the areas of career, position, public recognition and "honors" and, given positive links elsewhere, they may form a very effective partnership. Nearly all humans derive some sort of pleasure and fulfillment from a self-defined form of success and recognition. With this composite position, the individuals will likely find much in common with regard to the type of "success" which creates that special sort of pride and exhilaration that recognition can bring. They may well be able to combine their talents in creative or imaginative enterprises since the creative side of Venus in the composite chart flows easily and productively. It is, however, rather uncommon for this position to signal a close personal or romantic relationship. More often, it characterizes successful business partners, cooperative forms of inventiveness and successful work relationships. It appears to function best when the composite Sun is in the 10th or 11th house, but despite its rather impersonal blending, it can find a useful role in nearly any otherwise positively blended composite chart.

Venus in the 11th House
Synastric In many ways this may be the most rewarding and promising overlay for the Venus person. The response is very warm and appreciative without being unrealistic or clouded by impossible aspirations. The qualities which the Venus person perceives in the house person are the sort that encourage an almost immediate offer of acceptance and unhurried willingness to search out the wishes and interests of the house person, trying to find areas of common ground. The house person will usually find this undemanding and open initiative a welcome respite from the jockeying and fencing which accompanies the typical contact with a new person. The individuals will find a number of common attitudes and interests in recreational activities and in their preferences for using the free hours of their life. There will be shared appreciation of particular relaxing and restorative situations and the individuals will find it easy and pleasant to spend their leisure time together. The scope of the relationship will depend on the links to Sun and Moon between the chart, but whatever potential this creates for the relationship will be given its fair chance to emerge. While this overlay most typically suggests a relaxed and agreeable friendship, it can provide a solid core of acceptance and tolerance for each other's idiosyncratic quirks which is a great asset for any sort of relationship. The Venus person will find it possible to laugh off and treat as unimportant qualities in the house person which in others might not be accepted so easily. The house person will, of course, feel much more free to lay down the masks all of us wear in our

daily lives and express their inner selves without fear of being rejected. Certainly this overlay holds at least the promise of warm, good natured and durable interaction regardless of the eventual resolution of the relationship.

Composite At its center, this composite position for Venus indicates the individuals will seek the same sort of outlets for pleasure and recreation. Given other links which might bring the persons together, it is probable that they will seek each other out as leisure time companions. If the Sun's composite position is in the 10th house, this is the sort of blending which prompts persons to extend work or professional contacts into areas of common recreational interests to become bowling partners, concert companions or sailing pals. With Sun in the 11th house, this may well establish one of those rare lifelong friendships which time and distance cannot erode. While less common, a 1st house Sun position in the composite chart establishes one of the very best sorts of combinations for marriages: the natural blending of basic personality form with the calm and open undertone of a shared love of the same entertainments, hobbies and activities which roots in the 11th house Venus placement. The greatest value of this Venus placement is the durability of the admiration and respect the persons develop for each other. This combining of personality qualities is in itself, neither romantically or sexually rooted and, in the young, may not be as highly valued as it is in more mature relationships. The blending of capacities for pleasure and response to the beauty is so relaxed and amiable that it may seem to lack the electricity and excitement of other placements. Because of this, it may not immediately suggest a romantic interaction. Nonetheless, this placement is often the basis for one of those slow growing, sturdy relationships which comes to be appreciated only after time and other disappointments reveal its true value. It is not uncommon to find this placement in composite charts of second marriages between more mature persons.

Venus in the 12th House

Synastric This overlay has a special significance with Venus. This gentle planet is the source of our consciously constructed and deliberately evolved dreams and fantasies of joy, happiness and the realization of including something beautiful in our lives. Over time we evolve a fairly well defined paradigm for this scenario which we can call up and experience in our imagination. Beneath this conscious paradigm, however, lie other elements which, for a variety of reasons, we do not easily confront in ourselves. These elements may be aspects of our own personality with which we are not entirely comfortable or they may be outside the range of "proper" modes of behavior which we have been conditioned to believe is appropriate for a love response. Occasionally we let them rise to consciousness, but usually they are tucked away out of sight of even our inner mind. This overlay, however, may tap these deep needs and elements and cause the

Venus person to respond in ways which even they find puzzling. The projected qualities of the house person trigger the release of these unconscious drives without necessarily revealing them, with the result that the Venus person may find themselves offering themselves in unusual and out-of-character ways. The house person will, of course, confront this hard to understand behavior with a response based on their own interpretation of the Venus person's qualities, but there will likely be some unsettling doubts about the motivations involved. We like to persuade ourselves that we have some working understanding of what the other person is about, but with this overlay that reassuring sense of understanding each other's hopes and objectives will be elusive. Other linkages may cause the relationship to be pursued, but these uncertainties and occasionally off-the-wall interplays will remain, and it is unlikely that the persons will be entirely comfortable with each other as a result.

   Composite This combining of personality elements seems to cause the relationship to be driven by forces which neither person fully understands or ultimately with which either is comfortable. It is as if the relationship has a hidden underside which is only revealed in moments of intimacy and emotional intensity. This is a common position for a composite Venus when the composite Sun falls either in the 11th or 1st house terms. It then may come as something of an unsettling surprise to both persons that, at times, the relationship seems to stray from these comfortable confines to take on an entirely different identity when the situation permits the exploration of love fantasies and hopes. Persons who usually perceive themselves to be "good pals" or "very compatible and, as a result, believe they have a rather straightforward and easily managed relationship, can suddenly find themselves behaving towards each other oddly. A relationship which, on the surface, may not have a strong sexual overtone may, with this Venus position, trigger sexual behavior rooted in the repressed needs of the individuals which is subsequently hard to reconcile with the main thrust of the relationship. The result of this interplay often is a situation in which the effect the individuals have on each other seems disturbing and not entirely appropriate to the basic relationship structure. More typically, however, humans are rather frightened by the unaccountable and difficult to understand rumblings within themselves and, troubled and confused by these, will back away from the partnership out of some unfocused fear or anxiety.

Mars in the Houses

   Mars symbolizes the marshalling of the energies of the personality to aggressively reach out and capture those things for which we feel "want": the desire to possess and control and to enhance our self-image. It may require the creative sensitivity of Venus to produce a master painting or a beautiful piece of jewelry, but it requires the ego-need of Mars and the initiative which pours forth from this lively planet to produce a buyer. In relationships and in synastric analysis then Mars symbolizes the opposite side of the interactive coin from Venus; the "want" or drive to capture and hold another person as a means of fulfilling the Martian need.

Mars, of course, can be a very sexual planet because the sexual drive, standing by itself, is an intensely self-gratifying and demanding urge. Much of what is celebrated as "romantic love" is, in truth, not romantic at all, but rather that explosive need to grab what one wants and drag it back to the cave, to own and use as one will. Somehow this entirely natural and healthy urge makes humans a bit uncomfortable with themselves, perhaps because it reminds us that we are not that far evolved up the evolutionary scale from our animal cousins. We romanticize this urge, rhapsodize it and coat it with all sorts of more attractive patinas to persuade ourselves that what we want is, after all, not just simple lust or desire, but something more tolerably "sensitive and caring." Of course, it *can* be that tool, provided Venus is an active participant in the response. To understand the function of Mars, it is probably best to lay aside any apologies for this wholly normal and not entirely attractive quality in humans and accept it for what it is: the potent and energizing "I WANT" drive.

The role of Mars in synastry then is to identify and give form to the "wanting" urge, and to suggest the particular character that this urge adds to the scenario of synastric interplay. Links with Mars and house overlays typically place other persons in various categories relative to how we would "use" them if we had the opportunity. Do not, however, respond too harshly to this concept of "using" another human. Relationships are, if balanced and durable, a working combination of giving and taking, of fulfilling and being fulfilled. There is nothing inherently dishonest or selfish about wanting to get as much in return as one invests in a relationship, regardless of the form which the relationship takes. The question then is not whether "want" plays a role in synastric interactions; it does. The question really is whether the give/want balance is reasonable and whether there is a workable exchange between the persons involved. With Venus we see what the partners are willing to offer. With Mars we see what they want in return. This is not a bad basis for arriving at an agreement but, if the bargain is not an equitable or harmonious one, it also can be fair warning that someone may come out on the short end or that such a bargain is not even within the realm of the possible. To state the obvious, "want" must be present on both sides or there is no deal.

Mars in the 1st House

Synastric With this overlay, the Mars person perceives the house person to be an ego-enhancing partner in that there is considerable physical attraction and a sense that, by any standards, the house person would be seen by the world as a reflection of the Mars person's capacity to attract a desirable consort. This is just as true in non-romantic relationships or relationships between members of the same sex as is it is in conventional romantic relationships. We enjoy the reflected recognition which comes from being with a person we believe (and assume others would agree) is a "fine specimen." The house person may, if there are motivating links in the reverse overlay, bask in the awareness that the Mars person finds them so presentable and clearly enjoys the association with them. The basic response then is rather more one of "display value" than a deeper, more profound need and may not have much staying power. The house person may tire of being put on display or being prodded to always be at their physical best for the benefit of the Mars person and, of course, the Mars person may ultimately want something more substantial in a partnership than physical attraction.

Composite The energies of the individuals will tend to focus on the same objectives and goals; a blending which has both good and bad possibilities. It can be very useful in achieving some common end, but there is always the possibility that the individuals will struggle to occupy the same air space and become very competitive. This composite position is highly energizing for the individuals in that they seem to stimulate each other to reach out for shared objectives, but there will often be a contest over who is steering. In highly competitive and demanding situations, this composite position can produce some remarkable joint achievements, but it really is too fraught with a boiling sort of confrontational aggression to work well in multilevel relationships. It is probably at its best where the individuals can come together for some specific, highly demanding task, then separate for periods of more tranquil interactions.

Mars in the 2nd House
Synastric This overlay brings together the traditional house of possessions and property and the powerful acquisitive energy of Mars; a combination which suggests a rather material form of response at least and, in the most extreme situation, a desire in the Mars person to "own" the house person outright. To what end this ownership might be directed depends on other links, but the Mars person will tend to see the house person as one who can play a role in acquiring whatever that may be. This may be as innocent as an agent/client relationship or the hiring of someone to replace the roof on your house. It can, because of the subliminal sexual character of the 2nd house, stimulate a quality of possessiveness and dominance in the Mars person. How the house person responds to this depends not only on what they seek in the interaction, but even more on the natal qualities of the house person. Self-sufficient and confident individuals will resent this tendency of the Mars person to attempt to dominate the relationship. More passive and unsure individuals may well find exactly what they seek in strong hand of Mars. No relationship is ever entirely balanced and almost inevitably one of the partners accepts

a more "following" role. When there is a clear polarity of strength and independence in the natal charts of the individuals, this overlay is not an uncommon one because it leaves little doubt over who is in charge.

Composite In a here-and-now, material sense, the combining of Mars energies is quite successful with this composite position. To the degree the partnership comes into being for some real-world, tangible purpose, this is an excellent placement since the partners will work well together in this sort of environment. Clearly this is a sound position for work tasks which are non-abstract and hands-on in character, but there is no reason this position cannot function well in more complex or emotionally involved situations. In any partnership, situations arise frequently in the daily routines of living in which people must cooperate in the ordinary tasks of getting through the day. This combining may not produce an inspired collaboration on a symphony or novel, but if getting the fence repaired or the car washed and polished is required, the energies of the individuals function in harmony. It is a sensible and stable position for a composite Mars, but without other more sensitive or caring links, the partnership will probably remain just that: "sensible and stable."

Mars in the 3rd House

Synastric This overlay has great potential for fun and activity and shared dabbling in a myriad of things. The Mars person casts the house person as one with whom pairing up for "doing and going" seems quite natural. Nearly everything available to humans is more fun to do with another person than alone and the Mars person usually will identify the house person as the sort who probably would enjoy the same excursions and explorations. The house person will typically find communication with the Mars person delightfully easy and effortless and there may even be a pattern of regular phone calling or correspondence for the sheer fun of chatting with each other and sharing experiences. This overlay can obviously add a great deal to any interaction and usually does not require a major emotional or romantic commitment to sustain the relationship. The individuals can seek whatever level of involvement is open to them and consistent with what each of them wants from the other without the unfortunate background noise of wanting more than can be achieved. If circumstances and other links indicate a close romantic exchange, this overlay adds light-heartedness and good humor, but if that level of involvement isn't possible or just isn't present in the remainder of the linkages, the individuals can still enjoy the interaction at the more superficial (but entertaining) level.

Composite The combining of Mars energies in the 3rd house establishes a basis for shared ideas and exchange of responses which will be an active and continuing part of the relationship. The individuals not only respond to the world in the same general way, but act in response to their perceptions similarly. The same personal environments, the same concepts of how one's personal world ought to function and where things fit into the routines of the day will provide a useful common ground for the individuals. Often they will enjoy similar reading tastes, decorating styles and even work interests. Maturity and experience will tend to have the same evolutionary effect on the individuals and their ideas about how life should be lived and the priorities for one's personal application of energy and resources flow along parallel lines. The individuals enjoy their time together and commonly use it to let off steam about the pressures and frustration of their lives, assured that the other person will be empathetic and in general agreement. While not a romantic or sexual placement for Mars, it is a good blending of the most actively expressed mental energies of the individuals and allows them to function together in pursuing whatever courses these mental energies move them. Perhaps its most attractive content is that such a blending provides each of the partners with an interesting and companionable ear into which everyday anxieties, fears, angers and frustrations can be vented without risking being told to take their troubles elsewhere. With this placement, one will never hear the complaint "we never talk" or that difficulties in the partnership grew out of a breakdown in communication.

Mars in the 4th House

Synastric With this overlay, the Mars person will tend to respond to the house person in a parental or avuncular way, feeling a need to extend a protective and perhaps even a "guru" sort of initiative. While this may be, in some circumstances, a pleasant way in which to be dealt with, the house person may not be looking for a big brother, a Dutch Uncle or a guide to the universe and may resent the paternalistic tone of the Mars person's actions. At the risk of sounding like a chauvinist, it does seem this overlay functions best when the house person is female and the Mars person is male since the interplay is more harmonious with the society's established concept of male/female roles. It also can work well when there are major age differences between the individuals since there is an element of parent/child interaction in this overlay. Obviously, just as there is built-in tension in a parent/child, teacher/student or sibling relationship, there will be in this overlay. Much depends on what other ingredients there are in the relationship and what each seeks generally from the other. There is a strong magnetism in this overlay, but over time it will tend to develop a pattern of dependency in one of the persons which may not be harmonious with the circumstances or the motivations of the remainder of the interaction. It certainly can make sharing a home or living together a more stressful and tension-filled experience than most people enjoy.

Composite Despite the association of the 4th house with home and family, this is often a too conflict-filled and aggressive place for a composite Mars. Instead of the atmosphere of sanctuary and kinship which returning to a home and hearth ought to provide, this combining of energies can easily produce a stressed and demanding environment. The tendency to try to control and dominate which goes with Mars and to demand satisfaction of ones desires is not harmonious with the focus of the Martian energies in the 4th house. This position often is the source of anger and arguments over family ties or dependencies or simply of the role of home and family in the partnership. The partners may contest who is setting the priorities in this general area of their life and may even not be able to easily come to terms over what portion of the partnership's resources and time ought to be invested in domestic versus outside activity. Even in non-romantic relationships in which traditional "home" or "kinship" is not present, there is likely to be a struggle over turf and primacy. Not uncommonly, the individuals have such divergent views on what the proper interaction should be within an extended "family" or group that conflict or competition may arise in such diverse settings as offices or the factory floor. Office feuds and angry factional divisions can have their roots in this composite position. It seems as if all the negative sides of inter-tribal brawling and animosity are triggered, and finding common ground for an enduring peace is hard to manage.

Mars in the 5th House

Synastric This is the overlay which causes moonstruck lovers to write impassioned letters, dreamy poetry and stand under balconies and practice on their guitars... at least in the fantasies which fill the imagination. Whether these or similar actions really are undertaken depends on motivating aspects, but the moments when one lays one's head on the pillow at night and conjures up romantic dreams are vividly colored by this overlay. The Mars person feels all the rushes of emotion and ecstasies which are triggered by "Ms./Mr. Wonderful" and is, with any sort of other activating links, eager to act out this intensely romantic fantasy. The house person, realizing they are inspiring this sort of behavior, will respond as both personality and response to the Mars person dictate, but at the very least they will be flattered and buoyed. This is a fun overlay, with a great potential for batting of eyelashes and intricate, ritualized "courting" activity... except that it really isn't "courting" in the true sense, with an eye toward a full partnership. The underlying motivation, particularly in the Mars person, is questing for romantic gratification and realization of fantasy triumphs. As delightful as this overlay can be, it is essentially a limited one unless more stable and enduring links occur elsewhere. The senses are overwhelmed, the heart is pounding, but most of the energy will go to self-gratification and bathing in the pure excitement of the interaction. There may not be anything else on which to anchor the interaction beyond rosy images. If there is an overlay which makes "all lovers fools and all fools lovers," this is probably it.

Composite The Mars energy and initiative from the individual charts combine in this composite position to focus on the search for excitement and realization of romantic/ sexual dreams and hopes, at least in the potential. This is such a lively and responsive composite for Mars that it is almost inevitable that the individuals will at least try out the idea of romantic relationship. Whether this comes to fruit depends on the remainder of the linkages and, of course, circumstances, but almost from the outset the interaction will have this tone. Given the right set of conditions and basic attraction, the exploration will probably be realized to some degree. The problem with this position is that it so strongly activates this prospect of a romantic relationship that the individuals may overreact to it. Most humans carry around a pocketful of unfulfilled fantasies about love relationships and these are not hard to catalyze. With even a modicum of encouragement, they will rush out and dance about, spinning fairy dreams of bright, exciting futures. The great burst of expectations which occurs when individuals with this composite come together is, more often than not, illusory since it is not based on any substantial harmony of personalities beyond the quest for sensory fulfillment and pleasure. In many ways, this composite is more valuable in non-romantic relationships because it focuses on shared forms of recreation and amusements or even on mutual creative interests, but contains much less potential for ultimate disappointment. With this composite, individuals can easily come together in any activity designed to give pleasure and release from routines and responsibilities with considerable success. If you are considering building a boat or planning a trip to the Bahamas, a cohort whose chart produces this composite Mars with yours would be ideal. If your plans are more intensely personal and complex, then be sure to take a good hard look at the rest of the linkages to see if the bond between you extends beyond fulfillment of romantic fantasies.

Mars in the 6th House

Synastric In the context of other, more attention getting linkages, this rather drab and unexciting overlay will not even be an active element in the initial response. By itself, it hardly causes a ripple and the house person will pass largely unnoticed if this overlay is echoed by those involving Sun and Moon. If, however, there are more sparkling overlays to the rest of the planets, then this Mars position may subsequently make a useful contribution to the interaction. The Mars person will develop a feeling of obligation and loyalty to the house person, particularly in terms of any task-related contacts. The house person, in turn, will come to trust and rely on the Mars person and, from this base, a solid and functionally successful relationship can evolve. Probably the best quality of this overlay is that it seems to bring out the best efforts in the individuals and the most honorable and self-sacrificing qualities. While not the most electric or energizing overlay, it can provide a basis for a durable and unflappable interaction which, in a world of many ups and downs, can be a valued anchor. This overlay works well enough in romantic relationships and while not contributing much in the way of excitement, makes sharing space and the daily unavoidable chores of life less of a strain. It is nice to be around someone who does their share and will remember to stop and get the pizza when it's their turn.

Composite The aggressive qualities of Mars and the focus of self-gratifying and assertive energies with this composite position may make it a less than ideal position for close personal relationships. While the efforts of the partners may blend well enough in some more mundane tasks, in partnerships which extend beyond these work-oriented environments the essential imbalance of this composite position may become burdensome. Intimate relationships may become more a matter of "doing one's duty" than a mutually enjoyed process and there often is a recurring problem of bad timing and unsynchronized responses. Over time, the only resolution may be for one of the partners to accept a serving role, meeting the needs of the other and deriving gratification from filling the role successfully. In situations where there is a striking imbalance of assertiveness and confidence in the natal charts, this master/servant quality can go beyond reasonable scope and the interaction can become so fraught with abuse and dictatorial pushing and shoving that the relationship fails. More commonly, however, this placement simply results in one partner being forced to constantly yield to the demands and wishes of the other and falling into a passive and unfulfilled role. Even in nonintimate interactions, this imbalance is likely. This composite position is often the foundation for a partnership in which one of the individuals plays the role of toady or sycophant to the over-sized ego of the other. The results of this composite position are not always so severe or intolerable and, with more compassionate and empathetic links, it may fill a need in some persons for either a clear cut leader role or a sheltered position for a nonassertive personality. It is unlikely, however, that the behavior of the partners will not reflect this fundamental imbalance to some degree.

Mars in the 7th House
Synastric There is an interesting ambivalence with this overlay of the 7th house on Mars. At one level, the Mars person is very strongly drawn to the house person as a natural partner or companion and will usually find the house person both physically attractive and a person with whom the Mars person would enjoy being openly associated as a reflection of the Mars person's self-image. Yet, within this positive response is an inconsistency. The house person projects an aura of leadership or at least that of a peer capable of successfully meeting the Mars person on their own turf. Since Mars is a very assertive planet, symbolizing the need for everyone to find their "place in the sun," the

The Secondary Group 117

house person may also present something of a threat to the Mars person. Normally the Mars reaction is confident and secure, but with this overlay there may be an undertone of doubt about the ability of the Mars person to hold their own with the house person. The house person will usually respond positively to the Mars person, sensing the naturalness of the interplay, but also may feel, at some level, this potential for competitiveness of confrontation. Perhaps more than in any other overlay of Mars, the basic compatibility of the natal charts and the aspects formed between Sun, Moon and Mars is critical in anticipating how this polar response will work itself out. By its nature, this overlay pits the temperament and basic statement of "I AM" of the house person against the most aggressive elements of the Mars person's chart. There is no fundamental reason why these strong, assertive qualities can't work together, but with this overlay, synastric linkages which might otherwise be only minor sources of occasional disagreement or competitiveness will tend to be exaggerated and make a successful partnership more difficult.

Composite This is really a very healthy and positive composite position for Mars unless the composite chart contains exceptionally difficult aspects between the composite positions of Sun and Mars (i.e., a square or opposition). The energies of the two personalities flow outward in a harmonious and complementary way, making both the individual and mutual expression of the partner's pursuit of any goal easier and more likely to be successful. For non-intimate relationships it is a highly productive position for any joint enterprise in which the individuals must invest a great amount of personal energy and effort. At a more personal and intimate level, the partners function together smoothly and with great mutual supportiveness when they team up to reach some joint objective. This is, then, an excellent position for romantic/sexual relationships and this very personal element of the partnership will likely not be an area of difficulty. Perhaps the only caution is that the interaction of the individuals is so reciprocal in vitalizing the release of life energies that the very presence of the relationship may cause the individuals to overextend themselves, perhaps physically, emotionally, financially or even in challenging the world in ways which may threaten their own security and well-being. This is not a common result, but if the natal charts of the partners show a tendency to over-expansiveness or risk-taking, the coming together will tend to encourage these qualities rather than moderate them.

Mars in the 8th House
Synastric This overlay is responsible for most "double-takes:" that neck-wrenching response when another person reaches across a room or a crosswalk and hits us right in our procreative urges. This is perhaps the most apparent and energetically pure sexual response which is likely to be kindled by the physical presence of another human. There

is nothing particularly elegant or generous in the reaction since it triggers a powerful "I WANT THAT ONE!" feeling comprised mostly of a desire to possess and overwhelm. The Mars person will mostly likely be the one who is bug-eyed, but the house person knows this is happening and will be very tempted to at least allow the Mars person to enjoy the feast of responses. Of course, nothing much will come of this beyond a rise in the room temperature and some enlarged pupils unless the house person is experiencing some similar twinges, but if they are present, there is a powerful magnetism being generated. Given some more gentle and compassionate links elsewhere, this overlay gets its share of relationships off and running with great energy and enthusiasm. In other situations (i.e. members of the same sex of heterosexual persuasion, someone else's spouse or a person boarding a transcontinental flight just as you are deplaning) the same tension and base-of-the-spine response will likely occur, but its expression will take the form appropriate to the moment. Members of the same sex may share intimate thoughts and aspirations, spend time in the mall secretly comparing notes on passers-by or rely on each other as allies and co-conspirator in social situations with sexual potential such as bars and parties and singles cruises. The interaction of the individuals is based on a link-up of this very basic need and, in one form or other, it will likely be the continuing theme. While the 8th house is associated with many other elements in life, if you look closely at those traditional associations, they are all devices to wield power and control (i.e., money, magic, secrecy) In the end, humans are motivated to master these devices primarily for their own self-gratification and this overlay triggers the strongest urge to fill that need.

Composite More than most composite positions, this placement of the composite Mars depends almost entirely on the elements of attraction and, to a lesser extent, compatibility to manifest itself. Many composite positions provide such an obvious flowing together of planetary energies that even with a minimum of initial support from the initial linking of overlay charts, the individuals will come together at some level to realize the potential of the composite position. With the composite Mars in the 8th house, however, the interaction tends to be so narrowly sexual that without initial sexual attraction, the inherent unblendability of this position becomes dominant. Arguably, sexual interaction is a form of incompatibility in which individuals compete, even "war," to achieve their own ends without a great deal of regard for the other. If the individuals are sexually attracted to each other, this conflict is resolved through each gratifying themselves and produces only an exciting tension and energy. If, however, one or both are not attracted physically, the tone of contesting and demand (accentuated by the aggressive qualities of Mars) becomes a basis for irritation and confrontation. While the position may offer some potential for nonsexual interaction, particularly if the individuals are brought together for some activity involving investments or investigation and research, the inherent unblendable nature of this position will probably not permit a very broad range of cooperative interaction. It is also important to note that a strong sexual link can function between individuals without their becoming sexual partners in the normal sense. Two members of the same sex linked by this position can just as easily become "partners" in the sexual hunt as they can in the joint search for fulfillment of any other shared interest. Humans are social, companionable creatures and very few do not welcome an ally in any cause.

Mars in the 9th House

Synastric This is a rather inconsequential overlay for Mars since there is little in common between the assertive, "hands-on" energy of Mars and the abstract and esoteric qualities of the 9th house. To the degree that the Mars person shares intellectual interests or perhaps is brought by circumstance to appraise the potential companion in either actual physical or intellectual explorations (i.e., a travelling companion, co-researcher, etc.) there may be a positive response. Certainly there is nothing in this overlay to create any conflict or divergency, but there is also little to arouse a clear sense that the house person will play a meaningful role in the Mars person's life. The house person will, no doubt, sense both this low level of response and the absence of any potential competition or threat and, if the circumstances dictate, be comfortable and at ease with the Mars person. This can be a helpful overlay when the individuals encounter each other in a work environment since it suggests just enough capacity to cooperate and understand the objectives of the partnership to make joint efforts go smoothly without any undertone of incompatibility or "hidden agendas." Again, the other links between the charts will play a much larger role than this Mars overlay in determining how the individuals respond to each other. If there are strong indications with Sun and Moon that a more complex interaction may exist in potential or actuality, then this Mars overlay will not interfere with that realization. Nonetheless, even with such strong links elsewhere, the interaction will probably never be a highly intense or energized one. It will be marked more by its tranquil, noncompetitive qualities and essential harmony of method of reaching out for what each wants from the world than for any high level of aggressiveness, energy or electric interplay.

Composite This is an excellent composite position for Mars when the individuals come together for any sort of learning or personal development. The blending of Mars energies as they are directed toward understanding, intellectual growth or even the search for self-development and realization work well together. It is a natural position for a teacher-student relationship or even coworkers in some complex and demanding problem-solving task. The innate potentials in the individual personalities of the partners are stimulated and energized by the coming together and the persons seem to be able to aid each other up the steps of any difficult intellectual challenge. There is such a harmonious expression of the talents and insights of the individuals that the problem of competition or jealousies rarely seem to arise. Perhaps the best word to describe the product of this composite position for Mars is "collaborative" and it can create one of those highly successful interaction of contributions where the product of the collaboration is greater than the sum of the contributions. It is certainly no barrier to a more intimate or complex interaction, but in itself adds only a harmonious blending of efforts (particularly at the mental level) rather than any emotional or physical impetus. This is the composite position of the successful team which blends its talents to write the words and music, do the field and clinical research or divide the planning and execution of less abstract chores with happy results.

Mars in the 10th House

Synastric This is a powerful, if somewhat impersonal, overlay position for Mars since it brings together the natural aggressive energy of Mars in striving to achieve the desired goals of the personality and the critical issue of status and position in the society. It is likely the Mars person will perceive the house person to be an individual somehow important or useful in achieving recognition and fulfilling of any goals the Mars person has in this arena. The house person will inspire a degree of admiration and respect in the Mars person and will at least be seen as reflective of what the society which surrounds the individuals counts as noteworthy and successful. The house person will respond to this admiration and deference and be reinforced in their own self-image by the way in which the Mars person deals with them. Because of the quality of initiative and assertiveness of Mars, it is likely the Mars person will make a deliberate effort to associate themselves in some way with the house person and enjoy the aura of accomplishment which is derived from being linked with the house person. Whether this effort is one of honest admiration and respect, or is self-serving and exploitive depends, of course, on the basic natal qualities of the personalities. If the house person's natal chart shows strong, expansive aspects between Sun and either Jupiter or Saturn, the response of the Mars person will tend to exaggerate the already substantial self-esteem of the house person. If the Mars person shows excessive natal self-orientation (perhaps shown by strong presence of planets in angular houses or hard aspects from Saturn or Uranus to Sun) this may be expressed in a manipulative way, trying to utilize the house person as an instrument of status achievement. More commonly, however, this overlay simply creates a "high acceptability" sort of interaction; not particularly warm and generous or affectionate, but one which can bring the individuals together to accomplish a wide range of worldly objectives. Certainly in more intimate relationships, this position suggests that, whatever other motivations may be involved, the social "rightness" of the interaction plays a strong role.

Composite While the individuals may function reasonably well together in casual relationships and even evolve an effective work-related interaction, there is a basic stress in this composite Mars position that has the effect of blocking more personal and generous urges. Without really understanding why, the individuals will feel a strong sense of competitiveness and perhaps even threat from each other which is difficult to overcome even in the absence of any real evidence for such a response. When the individuals come together in some common environment or task, it seems as if they are born adversaries and, even if this takes a good-humored and amicable tone, there remains that atmosphere of competition and jockeying for position. Of course, in professional fields or high-intensity work environments, this is the sort of competition which can stimulate the individuals to extraordinary levels of achievement, but it rarely produces friendship or warmth or cooperation. It is a rather unlikely composite placement for Mars in romantic/sexual partnerships because of this confrontational quality. Most humans are quickly put off in the early stages of intimate relationships if there is a constant tone of "one-upmanship." Close personal relationships ought to give us respite from head-butting and struggling for space, but this composite position for Mars can rarely promise that. In certain situations where both individuals have strong career drives and rely on that area of their life for personal fulfillment as much as they do on personal relationships, it may be reconcilable, but it takes a special sort of partnership to tolerate the level of competition and scorekeeping this position seems to stimulate.

Mars in the 11th House

Synastric Arguably this is the most agreeable and natural overlay for Mars since the energetic qualities of this outgoing planet will be focused by the 11th house's amicable and companionable tone on activities which bring a welcome release of the underlying tensions of Mars. The Mars person will respond to the house person as one with whom they can let down their hair and act without concern for disapproval or disharmony. Typically the Mars person will take the initiative in offering friendship and a willingness to share whatever pleasure resources are available. With a modicum of links to the Mars person, the house person will enjoy the openhanded and warm initiative of the Mars person and slip easily into a relaxed and unstressed interaction. Usually the Mars person will be the catalyst for shared activities and adventures, discovering the opportunities and pulling the house person into flow of enthusiasms and interests. The underlying calmness and naturalness of the interaction will open up avenues of shared interests and projects. The individuals will typically enjoy joining forces for some undertaking which, without the invigorating interplay between them, might not be initiated. When impulses strike either to launch off on some unplanned but attractive recreational effort, there will be a natural inclination to turn to each other to participate with an assurance that the impulse will be welcomed. In many situations, Mar's aggressiveness and self-oriented demands create an atmosphere of competition or contentiousness, but with this overlay most of that drive will be harmonized into an unchallenging, sharing kind of bond.

Composite This is the classic composite position for "teamwork," for the blending of energies to produce a more effective and formidable effort than either could achieve alone. Probably no other composite position for Mars allows for the combining of the prickly and assertive qualities in the natal charts so effectively and with so little abrasion. In nonintimate partnerships, the individuals will seem to flow together without any conscious effort in joint efforts as complex as running a business or as mundane as where to go to lunch. There is a particularly good feeling of timing and the individuals will usually find that they are marching to the same drummer as they pursue their objectives. Even if there are major differences in educational or cultural backgrounds or even significant age differences, these normal restraints on the degree of harmony will seem not to interfere with the partnership. A very high level of tolerance and good will usually results from this composite position with the result that shared tasks or extended periods of time do not result in impatience or conflict. In more intimate partnerships involving romantic/sexual closeness, the same excellent timing and amiable acceptance of each other's foibles occurs. Probably no other composite position for Mars produces as good bed partners as this one, largely because the individuals come together not only as lovers and for sexual gratification but also as friends.

Mars in the 12th House

Synastric This overlay is not likely to evoke much of a conscious response of any sort, at least in terms of any perception by the Mars person that the house person has a particular role to play. The house person will likely seem a person from whom the Mars person would not seek any sort of connection, one who offers the Mars person nothing of interest. It is not so much a feeling of dislike or enmity, but rather a lack of connectedness and common ground. The house person will likely perceive their "invisibility" in the view of the Mars person and, unless there are motivating links in the house person's chart, the individuals will likely just pass in the night. In an unconscious way, Mars is always appraising other individuals in terms of what those individuals offer of value. This is not as hard-hearted and selfish as it may sound because it is only one component in the individual's response and usually not the most meaningful one. Nonetheless, this overlay exemplifies the fact that we do, in fact, become consciously aware of a relatively small percentage of individuals who brush by us in life and, unless they appear to fit some paradigm or need or project something akin to our own essence, we just erase them from the tape. The aggressive acquisitive nature of Mars has so little in common with the inward-looking, self-abnegating qualities of the 12th house, there is no synapse made which causes Mars to respond. The house person will likely sense this fundamental disharmony and shrink from any contact unless there are very strong links elsewhere. Even if thrown together by work or circumstance, there will remain a distance and inability to link with this overlay that is unlikely to be bridged.

Composite Composite charts are prepared usually only when a relationship evolves to a point where the individuals believe it has potential and are motivated to explore that potential. While this Mars composite position can, of course, occur as often as any other in purely arithmetic terms, it is an unlikely one to find in composite charts of evolved partnerships because the Mars energies blend (or fail to blend) in such a troublesome way that a relationship is unlikely to be pursued. The individual expression of the Mars qualities in each of the natal charts not only do not harmonize well, they seem to trigger irrational and unpredictable responses between the individuals. The people are likely to annoy or irritate each other although both would be at a loss to explain why this happens. They normally will try to avoid being in close proximity, but if circumstances force them to be in prolonged contact, there will be a hard to repress strain and bottled-up irritability which most likely will come out as sarcasm or only partially concealed disapproval. Neither will really be able to give a sensible reason for their reactions and others observing this will be puzzled, but there isn't much either can do to sublimate these responses. Everyone has experienced "love at first sight" occasionally in their lives and remembers this experience with great fondness. We also experience "dislike at first sight" just as often, but obviously act to disassociate ourselves as quickly as possible from the person. Since we did not pursue this latter reaction with the fervor we did the former, it was not the sort of thing we tend to want to store in our memories. We forget that such a reaction is no more rare than immediate positive ones. The root of this sort of negative response is often this composite Mars position, particularly in contacts between the sexes. One does wonder why friends inevitably choose someone whose Mars produces this composite with ours for blind dates.

Uranus in the Houses

With the inner planets, the synastric responses are usually clearly felt and, to some degree, consciously understood as they are experienced. The scenario which they stimulate is more or less explicit, like watching images in a movie. With Uranus we begin to see the unconscious impulses function in synastry; those urges which bubble up from deep inside us and trigger behavior which we don't fully understand nor entirely control.

Uranus-based behavior is particularly apparent under any sort of stress or anxiety. We see the function of the natal Uranus most clearly in individual behavior in times of high demand, depression or fear. The same general characteristics appear in synastric interaction, largely because dealing with any other human involves some stress and response to demand, particularly if the person is important to us. It is no coincidence that the so-called Age of Aquarius which is allegedly upon us is characterized by, among other things, an increasing percentage of our population who chose to live alone, free from the demands and inconveniences of sharing their lives with another. Human interaction, even at its best, is filled with compromise, stress and elements of competition. Uranus, the traditional ruler of Aquarius, plays no small part in this unconscious need of a large share of the populace to maintain distance between other humans. As stress-filled urban societies and the seemingly insoluble problems of the world surround individuals, the Uranian impulse to push away intimacy unconsciously affects many humans. There is no other time in human history when a premise like "happiness is being single," would have gained such currency; a stressed and unhappy retreat from the age-old procreative need to pair up and the obligations which accompany that.

In the synastric analysis of Uranus we are then examining the form of stress/anxiety response which is triggered by contact with another person. The house position of Uranus, both in synastric overlays and in composite charts, gives us an insight into what arena, what form of interaction, is being unconsciously built into the script and how the individual, without really quite understanding why, will be impelled to play out that part of the interaction. Most humans have experienced relationships which, despite conscious hopes and plans to have it evolve in one direction, seems determined to follow a contrary course. Uranus is often the culprit in such situations, causing us to behave in ways which, on the surface, seem irrational or outside our conscious script, but in fact, in ways which our deep impulses propel us. Uranus is often the key in initiating relationships and that original impetus continues to reappear in one form of specific behavior as long as the relationship continues whether we really welcome it or not.

Uranus in the 1st House
   Synastric This overlay likely will create a feeling of immediate identification and empathy in the Uranus person. There will be a sense that the house person somehow shares a place in the cosmos with the Uranus person. The house person may not feel this response, but will likely at least open the door to finding out what common ground exists between the personalities because of the strong initiative shown by the Uranus person.
   Composite The relationship will probably be marked by out-of-character behavior or at least an extraordinarily high level of impulsive opening up with each other. Often,

with this composite Uranus position, the relationship starts quite suddenly and in an unusual way. Whenever the individuals are together, they find themselves feeling a stronger than normal need to break out of routines and find new adventures. Sometimes this interaction forces one or both persons to confront any stagnation or worn-out elements of their life and the individuals stimulate each other to discard these and consider new avenues.

Uranus in the 2nd House

Synastric This overlay often stimulates a desire to include the house person within the circle of associates of the Uranus person as a sort of decoration or enhancement of self-image. Because there is no strong sense of harmony of personality between the individuals, the response is somewhat impersonal and possibly largely self-interested. This overlay is not usually the cause of any immediate interaction; however, if the situation is such that either party needs the help or service of the other as a way to achieve some tangible objective, there may be an unconscious perception of the person as "useful" or worth some effort as a possible resource in the future.

Composite The self-indulgent impulsiveness and need for freedom from restraints of the Uranian drives do not blend well with the stable, security-oriented qualities of the 2nd house. It is rather unlikely that this position will come up in functioning partnerships largely because the individuals tend to destabilize each other. Most likely the individuals, once having experienced an underlying feeling of a shaky foundation for the possible partnership, will not feel secure enough with each other to pursue a full partnership. If this position does occur in an evolved partnership, it is probable that difficulties in maintaining a stable, secure and practical framework for the relationship will be a recurring difficulty.

Uranus in the 3rd House

Synastric Many relationships are initiated by an impulse to simply strike up a conversation with a relative stranger, to reach out in a communicative way. This overlay creates in the Uranus person a feeling that if they do attempt such communicative link with the house person, it will not fall on the proverbial "deaf ears." The house person will usually share at least this willingness to open up the lines of communication but will tend to interpret the motives of the Uranus person primarily in terms of whatever links exist between their own chart and the Uranus person. This overlay can just as easily result in a gross misreading of each other's motives and interests as it can be a basis for continuing communication, largely because the communication is based on somewhat irrational impulse rather than a conscious assessment of the situation.

Composite This composite position for Uranus can contribute a very valuable ingredient to a partnership: the breaking down of any barriers to letting each other know what is going on in each other's heads at any given time. The effect the individuals have on each other is much like a sudden release of fears or doubts about "letting it all hang out," a willingness to open up and reveal anything which is troubling the partners or causing worry. While this can, on occasion, produce a certain amount of "dumping" on each other, given a good general link-up between the partners, it will be accepted as part of the obligations the individuals feel toward each other. Certainly with this composite position for Uranus, the partnership should not be troubled with repressed annoyances or inability to share worries and doubts.

Uranus in the 4th House

Synastric This overlay usually creates an uncomfortable and stressed response in the Uranus person, rooted primarily in the feeling that the house person somehow presses too closely or that the house person's personality would somehow be limiting or repressive. It is probable that there is an unconscious association of the house person with parental authority and any residual resentments toward that authority which the Uranus person retains. If, however, the individuals are seeking a relationship in which a protective or parent/child link-up is involved, it is possible that the response may be positive. Certainly the house person will tend to behave in a rather hovering or parental way and will take on some responsibility for the Uranus person without really understanding why.

Composite While this is not an easy composite position for Uranus because of the essential conflict between the sheltering and protective, family-oriented qualities of the 4th house and the Uranian demand for freedom of action, it occurs in functioning partnerships more often than one might suppose. The reasons appear to be twofold: first there is an impulse which comes out of the blending of Uranian energies to take the partnership into a space-sharing mode, often rather hastily and without much forethought; and secondly, there is a certain wacko charm to the partnership; an "odd couple" quality that can bring together some rather unlikely candidates. Actually, it may be the very eccentric and unusual qualities of the partnership which create the impulse to come together, whether the partnership is a limited, non-intimate one or a full romantic/sexual involvement. Whatever the result of this impulse, it will likely not follow conventional lines nor be a tranquil, stable interplay.

Uranus in the 5th House

Synastric This overlay can create some rather unsettling impulses in the Uranus person who may become unaccountably attracted to a person who would not consciously be found interesting. Often this results in a kind of impulsive flirtatiousness or little outbursts of behavior which puzzle the Uranus person as much as the house person. This is a rather potent impulse coming up from the unconscious and may motivate the individuals to experiment with some kind of contact, only to find themselves wondering "what am I doing here with *this* person?" Much depends here on the placement of Uranus in the natal chart. If it makes easy and harmonious natal aspects to the inner planets, this impulse will simply bring about a quick starting, impulsive interaction. If there are natal Uranus squares or oppositions to the inner planets, however, it is likely to cause a number of frustrating false starts in relationships.

Composite This blending of Uranian impulses can trigger a rather impetuous jump into a relationship. There is no reason inherently that this is a harmful phenomenon provided other, more fundamental positive links exist. It is not strong enough, in itself, to support a relationship, but if it occurs in a composite chart in which the inner planets blend well, it can cause a very rapid and very intensely romantic evolution of the partnership. Actually, it is a rather nice component in an ongoing partnership since it helps to keep alive and vital the initial magic of the interaction. Even in non-intimate partnerships it adds a lively undertone which gives a liberating zest to the interaction. More than any other position for composite Uranus, this will prevent the relationship from becoming boring because of the unconscious "recharging" effect the individuals have on each other.

Uranus in the 6th House

Synastric This overlay may actually create an unconscious negative response since the Uranus person may feel that the house person represents a potential burden or troublesome obligation. Now and then we do encounter people who, without any evident cause, make us back away because we see in them personality qualities which might intrude on us or get us entangled with problems we don't really care about. The Uranian impulses are always looking for a way to break out and follow new paths and any hint that another person might add to our load rather than lighten it is typically unattractive. More likely, however, is simply a neutral or "invisible" response to the house person who will typically return it in kind with the result the two individuals won't interact in any significant way. If there are strong attraction links elsewhere in the synastric interplay, then this Uranian response will not prevent the relationship from functioning, but there will probably be some lingering sense that even if good things generally come from the relationship, there will still be some penalties to pay in taking one another's problems.

Composite This composite position for Uranus will probably not play a large role in the partnership and creates no significant problems in an otherwise promising one. The partners may possibly feel an unusual depth of obligation to each other, particularly in responding to each other's needs or problems, which can be an agreeable addition to the relationship. Perhaps the most important consideration with this position is the natal qualities of the individuals, particularly any substantial imbalance in aggressiveness and personality strength. In a relationship which involves one very dominant partner, this composite Uranus will add to the difficulty of the passive member in resisting the demands of the stronger personality. In extreme situations, this position can create an unconscious undertone of constant demands for attention and support from one partner and an inability of the other partner to free themselves from this endless burden. This, however, would be the exception and typically this composite position for Uranus only tends to enhance the sense of interdependency and mutual support within the partnership.

Uranus in the 7th House

Synastric We have all heard someone say, "I knew I was going to marry him/her the first time we met," and then, in fact, subsequently do just that, not uncommonly after a very short acquaintance. This overlay of Uranus is the probable source of both that impulse to cast another person as a partner, and any rush to accomplish that goal. One hopes that, in such situations, the natal Uranus is well aspected to the inner natal planets since things obviously work out better if that powerful impulse to join with another is harmonious with the basic personality qualities. The house person, in this situation, will also have their own agenda and write their own script for the relationship, but the awareness that the Uranus person sees them in this most meaningful of all possible roles is a powerful aphrodisiac and the house person will likely open the door to exploring the possible relationship. The greatest risk is that this strong impulse roots in the unconscious and often is not really understood by the Uranus person. They feel a potent drive to latch on to the house person, almost without regard to the rationality of the goal, and may well allow it to drive them when good sense would argue against such a project. Fortunately, despite the strength of this impulse, it will not prevail against fundamental incompatibility and, while the impulse may linger, most persons will eventually repress it when all the other links indicate the impulse is ill-advised. In harmonious interaction, of course, this overlay acts like an accelerator and moves a relationship along at an amazing pace with no unfortunate results. Whether we are looking at quick forming friendships or really serious romantic/sexual relationships, this overlay gets things up and moving with alacrity.

Composite This is a happy composite position for the free-wheeling composite Uranus because it seems to eliminate some of the feeling of compromise and restriction which goes with any partnership. With this composite position, the individuals usually feel that they are getting from the relationship a great deal more than they are forced to give up by forming a partnership. Uranus in the 7th house will often give the individuals a liberating boost when they come together and, functioning in tandem, the two persons can have a livelier, more varied and interesting lifestyle than either can manage alone. Perhaps the only caution with this position is that any attempt to fence in the partnership with imposed restrictions or conventions may cause resentment. The partnership got some of its original impetus from its liberating qualities and trying, after the fact, to box it in and make it follow more conservative and traditional patterns will probably diminish its value. It is well to look back at the natal charts of the individuals to see if there is any evidence of insecurity or rigidity in one of the partners which might cause them to try to force the relationship to conform to "acceptable" or traditional rules. A composite Uranus in the 7th house simply won't allow this behavior within the partnership without eventually causing irritation and annoyance.

Uranus in the 8th House

Synastric While not as potent in its effect as overlays to Venus or Mars, this 8th house overlay of Uranus can cause a strong and unsettling sexual response. Where overlays to the inner planets tend to trigger the spinning of conscious scenarios in which the planet person is quite aware of the roles in which the house person is cast, responses of Uranus are much less intellectually grounded and are felt in the pit of the stomach (or wherever one keeps one's deep drives). Instead of a deliberate and conscious effort to bring about a particular sort of interaction, this overlay seems to create a magnetism that draws the Uranus person to the house person in an unthinking but strongly impelled urge to possess. By itself, it may only cause a continuing sexual fascination with the house person, but if it is supported by other links, it can be the stimulus to a very impulsive and almost driven kind of sexual quest. The house person's response to all this will be dependent on what sort of scenario they may be writing, but feeling such a powerful response in another can be hypnotic and it is likely the house person will at least try to find reasons to agree with the Uranus person's objectives. Such a relationship may be characterized by a pattern of contacts which, despite any plan to the contrary, inevitably slip into a sexual encounter; sometimes to the upset or despair of one or both of the individuals who may not truly want this to be the fulcrum of the interaction. Uranian unconscious impulses can be strong and hard to resist.

Composite When the Uranian energies combine to produce an 8th house composite, the wider implications of this house tend to become an element in the partnership. There often is a shared interest in occult or New Age subjects or some other manifestation of an unconscious reaching out for a link with the cosmos which the coming together of the individuals reinforces. In some ways the individuals find within each other half-hidden suggestions of the great mysteries of life and are stimulated to come together because of the fascination with these subliminal clues. While the individuals may trigger sexual responses in each other, it is just as likely that the combining of energies will stimulate the intense and probing curiosity associated with Uranus: the search for cosmic order amid earthly chaos. The partnership may have a quality of almost compulsive magnetism for the partners who will find themselves drawn together despite barriers which might otherwise prevent or at least discourage a relationship. There is sometimes an ambivalence in relationships with this composite Uranus position created by a conflict between the unconscious magnetism of this house position and the resistance of Uranus to binding or confining situations. In extreme situations, this position can cause sexual obsessions and rather odd behavior (i.e., impulsive telephone calls, exhibitionism, etc.), but this is rare. Most commonly it is the fascination with the cracking of the gateway to the mysterious and unknown which the partners seem to offer each other which adds intriguing elements to the relationship.

Uranus in the 9th House

Synastric This overlay is very subtle and its effects tend not to reveal themselves unless the individuals are drawn together by stronger and more urgent links elsewhere in the charts. If that occurs, this overlay will cause the Uranus person to believe that many unconscious and unarticulated feelings and attitudes can be revealed to the house person safely and without fear of rejection or ridicule. The house person may play an uncritical listener role or even perhaps a teacher or counselor part for the Uranus person as concerns or anxieties are released from the unconscious. There is a quiet but fundamental harmony between the individuals with this overlay which can have a liberating effect, especially on the Uranus person. Such an interaction is valuable for release of tensions and stresses which have been accumulated by the individuals in their efforts to conform to whatever social or cultural rules within which each is required to function. The nonconforming and freedom loving qualities of Uranus work in this overlay to allow the individuals to cast each other as confidants and trusted repositories for ideas and hopes which otherwise remain private and unshared.

Composite This is an essentially harmonious blending of Uranus energies in the composite chart, allowing the individuals to combine in a partnership in which the alliance is a device to break out of social or cultural constraints otherwise difficult to breach individually. In some cases, the partnership itself represents this rebellious discarding of social standards or subcultural mores. It can bridge barriers such as interracial partnerships, major differences in education, ethnic or economic backgrounds or even vastly different religious orientations. More often, however, the effect is to send the individuals on life expanding, mind enlarging explorations together which cause each to grow and mature more rapidly than either would have managed without the interplay. Sometimes this overlay triggers efforts on the part of one or both of the partners to try to achieve some professional, intellectual or social goal which previously had been deferred or repressed because of fears of failure. The effect of this composite position is nearly always supportive and reassuring in the partnership even if it lies quietly below the surface and seldom reveals itself in the conscious interaction between the individuals.

Uranus in the 10th House

Synastric The initial unconscious response to this overlay will probably be somewhat negative because the Uranus person will sense that the house person seeks a different life mode and content. Even if there are other links which cause the house person to seem attractive or compatible, the feeling that it would be difficult to reconcile the priorities and life goals of the two individuals will persist. Without other links, the two people will likely not seek any contact because of this underlying disagreement on what counts in one's life content. There is a basic discordance between Uranus and this house as the nonconforming, somewhat eccentric, qualities of Uranus and the rather staid and conventional qualities of the 10th house confront each other. This initial unconscious response will not prevent people who have many other harmonious qualities from coming together and even forming a rewarding interaction, but the harmonies will also not entirely override this residual element of differing world views. In relationships which do form and continue with this overlay, it is probable the Uranus person will be unable to restrain an urge from time to time to be critical of the choices the house person makes with regard to anything which reflects the public image of the house person. Whether this is only a minor squeak in an otherwise smoothly functioning relationship or becomes a serious area of disagreement depends largely on the strength of the feelings the house person has for the Uranus person and how much of this periodic criticism they are willing to accept to keep the relationship.

Composite This composite position for Uranus has a two-edged impact on the individuals, the eventual significance of which depends entirely on the other ingredients in the relationship. At one level, it allows the needs for individuality and exploration which may reside in the personalities to be realized within the partnership and be reinforced by it. The relationship itself may be a vehicle for the partners to jointly explore new aspects of their talents or interests in a tandem and mutually supportive way. At another level, however, this composite position for Uranus can have a destabilizating effect on the efforts of the partners to establish a firm financial or social base for the relationship. The interaction between the individuals can trigger discontent with the inevitable routine of living and the grind-it-out necessities of pursuing a career or stable home life. In a way, the almost unavoidable periodic boredom and discontent most persons have to deal with feed on the interplay between the partners and they uncon-sciously reinforce each other's dissatisfaction. If the natal qualities of the individuals point to an ability to find satisfaction in a life mode with many changes of direction and ups and downs, this can be an invigorating contribution to the partnership. If, however, one or both are really needful of stability and security in any partnership, this composite position may create too much turmoil and destabilization for a durable relationship.

Uranus in the 11th House

Synastric This overlay typically results in a non-threatening, even warmly amiable unconscious reaction in the Uranus person. The house person seems somehow a likely candidate for some easy, low-pressure interplay and the Uranus person will probably deal with the house person from the outset in a friendly and accepting way. This kind of a pleasant and amiable response is rare enough in a generally hostile and indifferent world and the house person will likely return at least a gracious and nondefensive response. Typically the Uranus person will find themselves motivated to do little, off-the-cuff things to express feelings of friendship and concern for the house person: sending humorous greeting cards for no particular reason, showing interest in the events in the house person's life and generally offering what is, in many ways, the most welcome human gift: non-intrusive interest and concern. What other elements enter into the relationship depends, of course, on the links between the inner planets and the natal needs of the individuals, but this overlay of Uranus will provide an agreeable, unjudging ambience within which the best possibilities for the relationship can bloom and realize themselves.

Composite This composite position is perhaps the most natural and comfortable for Uranus, allowing the most positive of the Uranian qualities to be realized while moderating the less attractive qualities of this eccentric planet. The energies of the two personalities flow together in basic harmony in any exploratory initiatives or inventive openness which the partners feel. With this composite Uranus position, the partnership remains fresh and interesting, always open to new inspirations and experiences. The responses of the partners to opportunities or simply to the unplanned and impulsive enjoyment of little happenings in life seem to always be in tune and the individuals see each other as the best preventative to boredom and discontent. Perhaps the most attractive quality of this position is its great value in allowing the partners to spend a great deal of time together without annoying each other or feeling a stagnation in the relationship. If a partnership can be said to have "entertainment value," it is likely this composite position for Uranus is the root cause. Certainly one of the most charming aspects of this position is that the relationship will often begin in a very atypical and impulsive way, but not fall victim over time to a winding down of expectations as so many other impulse-motivated events do. This is a real contribution to the durability and tolerance in a partnership and will do much, in itself, to sustain the partnership through difficult times.

Uranus in the 12th House

Synastric This is a rather neutral overlay of Uranus, neither motivating nor preventing the individuals from coming together. If anything, the house person may feel some trepidation about any efforts of the Uranus person to reach out for contact, but have considerable difficulty in rationalizing this response. The inward orientation and otherworldly qualities of the 12th house have little in common with Uranian energies and any bond which develops between the individuals will gain little from this overlay. The relationship may even have to cope with a persistent undertone of uncertainty and doubt. We all prefer to have some clear sense that we understand what motivates the people with whom we establish any bond. This overlay may engender an unconscious feeling that those motivations are somehow hidden and, therefore, possibly worrisome. This response is not sufficient to prevent individuals who find much else in common from coming together, but if either person has natal qualities which make them particularly vulnerable to self-doubts or anxieties over the unknown, this overlay may enlarge those uncertainties. At best this overlay has minimal effect and remains only a muted, unimportant undertone. At its worst, however, it undermines the individual's feelings of security and trust and exaggerates any paranoic tendencies either may have.

Composite This composite position for Uranus is probably more likely to have its affect by what is absent in the partnership than what it may cause to be present. The unconscious impulses in any personality will inevitably find a way to express themselves and, within a successful partnership, there must be some sense that these can be released and perhaps even shared in an environment free from criticism or condemnation. With this composite Uranus position, this ability to be relatively free from anxiety about being judged or measured when releasing these unconscious tensions may be absent. The result may be a feeling that one or both of the partners must repress significant elements of their personalities, particularly those most likely to be visible under stress or pressure. None of us behave calmly and rationally under all circumstances, and at times we inevitably act like bubble-headed idiots or lose control momentarily. Within a good partnership, we would like to believe we'll be forgiven for these lapses, but with this composite position, that unconscious reassurance may not evolve. To the degree that communication at an intuitive and unconscious level contributes to the functional success of a partnership, this Uranus position may create a small problem; not enough to prevent a good partnership, but one which will require a measure of conscious effort and patience from both individuals.

THE TERTIARY GROUP

Saturn, Mercury, Jupiter, Neptune and Pluto play lesser roles in synastry, but over time make significant contributions to a relationship. The principal distinction between these five planets and the five already discussed is that the influences of this tertiary group is not as evident in the early stages of the formation of a relationship. They contribute only subtly to attraction and early probing for compatibility and then principally at the unconscious level. As a relationship evolves, however, their influence becomes stronger and, in the end, they fill out and give dimension to a partnership which probably began as a less complex and more highly focused enterprise. *Saturn* is perhaps the most powerful of this group, providing both the skeletal strength and stability on which the relationship can develop, yet indicating the area of the interaction where goals will be most difficult to achieve and frustrations most likely to occur. *Mercury* makes its contribution in the daily interplay between the individuals, indicating how successfully they can blend their efforts and remain on a harmonious wavelength in dealing with the everyday demands and needs of a partnership. *Jupiter* suggests the avenues for continuing evolution of the relationship which prevents it from becoming stale and repetitive, but also the areas in which the individuals may exaggerate each other's weaknesses and flaws in judgment. *Neptune's* subtle influence can tell us what fantasies and dreams play a role in the relationship, yet also where persistent areas of disappointment and uncertainty may crop up. *Pluto's* deep and remote influence appears to emerge largely in times of crisis for the relationship, suggesting both how the partners might utilize the relationship to meet any crisis and, in a less positive sense, what carefully buried or repressed urges the relationship might allow out in the light.

In appraising the influence of these five planets, emphasis should be on the long-term effect both house positions and aspects will have as any relationship unfolds. The previously discussed five more powerful planets tell us what the individuals consciously want from each other and are prepared to offer in return, while these five less powerful, but still important, planets tell us how the individuals will "get along" over the long term. They suggest what areas of mutual interaction will provide both the support for the primary focus of the partnership and possibly the slow-growing but corrosive problems. Their role is to fill in the spaces between the primary building blocks of compatibility, affection, romantic love or sexual desire with the mortar of everyday interaction; the less obvious elements of a relationship which attract little original attention, but which, in the end, bind the relationship into a durable structure capable of surviving both routine and crisis.

Tertiaries in the 1st House

Synastric *Saturn* captured in the 1st house tends to inhibit the confidence of the Saturn person that a relationship can be initiated, creating a rather heavy atmosphere within which any sense of fun and pleasure seems unlikely. The house person will tend to see the Saturn person as overly serious and somehow likely to be a "wet blanket" in any interaction. *Mercury* in this overlay will open channels of communication and allow the Mercury person to articulate their responses and feelings about the house person. The house person will not likely misinterpret the hopes of the Mercury person and will have a feeling of confidence and understanding about the unspoken motives and objectives of the relationship. *Jupiter* in the 1st house stimulates a large measure of open affection and generosity in the Jupiter person and a willingness to go more than half way in creating and sustaining the relationship. The house person responds warmly to this openness and comes to rely on and be reassured by the Jupiter person's forgiving and open-hearted actions. *Neptune* introduces an element of unrealistic assessment of the house person, often causing the Neptune person to attribute qualities and even responses to the house person which may not exist. The house person may become uncomfortable with the seemingly unfounded assumptions made by the Neptune person about what might be expected from the relationship. This overlay will probably create persisting misunderstandings of motives and aspirations in both persons.

Pluto in the 1st house may create mildly obsessional tendencies in the Pluto person about the house person and a commitment to the interaction which may or may not be justified. The house person may find the presence of the Pluto person unsettling or disturbing in some hard-to-decipher way and may never find it possible to be fully at ease in any interaction. There seems to be some faint but persisting tone of threat in this overlay which makes it hard for either person to relax and develop trust in the relationship.

Composite With a composite *Saturn* in the 1st house, the relationship will tend to have a stable if somewhat unexciting foundation on which to build. There will be a rather insular and inward-looking quality to the relationship, perhaps causing the partners to withdraw into the partnership as response to the demands of the world. The biggest problem with this position is that the relationship does little to reinforce the self-esteem or confidence of the individuals and may be troubled with a persisting feeling that the relationship represents some sort of a compromise or "make-do" arrangement. *Mercury* in this house establishes a strong intuitive bond between the individuals, making it possible for them to anticipate the reactions of each other accurately and avoid behavior which might cause irritation or disagreement within the partnership. A strong sense of truly understanding each other and the type of responses each hopes for within the relationship contributes much to ongoing tranquility and satisfaction of daily contacts. *Jupiter* in this composite house opens the door to a great deal of shared fun and exploratory adventures with the partners finding many areas of common ground in the mutual use of resources directed to pleasure and fulfillment. There will be a deferential quality in the interaction with either partner usually willing to bend to the desires of the other graciously and with obvious affection. This position may trigger some extravagance with shared resources, but whatever the individuals do together will be greatly enjoyed and rarely regretted. *Neptune* in the composite 1st often makes bringing the partnership to any clear focus difficult. The individuals will feel such uncertainty and confusion over what role the relationship is supposed to play in their lives that a number of false starts and abortive attempts at creating a durable relationship may follow. The interaction lacks a sound basis of clear-headed judgment and the individuals trigger unrealistic and probably unachievable daydreams in each other which can send the partnership down unhappy and even disastrous paths. This is not an uncommon position for extra-marital affairs which individuals, discontent with their personal lives, see "escape" in the other person and fall into rosy but unrealistic fantasies. *Pluto* in the composite 1st may have little effect until one or both individuals are threatened or tested. In such a circumstance, the individuals can fall back on the partnership itself as a bulwark to meet such a crisis. The position may, however, create an undertone of contesting for dominance within the partnership. This is not normally serious unless the individuals involved are both highly competitive and dominant personalities. In rare and unusual situations where the natal charts of one or both individuals contain strong indications of violent behavior or deep emotional turmoil, this position may trigger this sort of behavior either directed toward each other or as a mutual "Bonnie and Clyde" assault on the world.

Tertiaries in the 2nd House

Synastric *Saturn* in this house overlay gives a rather serious and practical quality to the response: an unconscious classification of the house person as one with whom the Saturn person will probably deal in a real world and no-nonsense way with little emotion.

The house person will find the Saturn person a useful contact, but is unlikely to offer much in the way of personal warmth or generosity. *Mercury* captured in this house is somewhat inhibited by the unimaginative qualities of this overlay and the Mercury person will probably have some difficulty in establishing any effective mental linkage with the house person. The house person will not likely find it easy to communicate with the Mercury person because of the absence of any clear sense of common attitudes or life view. *Jupiter's* linkage with this house is typically helpful in any common enterprise aimed at mutual gain. The Jupiter person will find it comfortable to focus on any material goal which requires the house person's participation. The house person will usually find the Jupiter person as a natural partner and will have an unconscious sense that the Jupiter person can be relied upon when some joint project is involved. While not a compelling position for either individual, it can be helpful in material terms. *Neptune* overlaid in this house usually produces a feeling that the house person does not share with the Neptune person any common value systems or priorities with regard to the role that possessions or wealth play in an individual's life. One or both of the individuals will likely come to feel that the other person has an unacceptable or unattractive attitude toward material things and somehow places them improperly on the scale of life content; either "greedy" or "impractical." *Pluto* in the 2nd house will probably reveal its effect only if the interaction has a material focus. The Pluto person may come to feel that the house person sees them only as a source of material support or advantage and the house person may develop a resentment over the Pluto person's need to control any joint resources. Over time, this overlay can produce slow building irritation over money issues.

Composite *Saturn* in the composite 2nd house is a rather unhappy placement since it suggests that the planetary energies do not blend effectively in achieving material security or agreeing on priorities in use of joint resources. At the least, there will be a very conservative and even gloomy attitude about the partnership's capacity to provide a secure base for the individuals and, in some cases, it almost appears the partners work against or inhibit each other in achieving any material goal. *Mercury* in this composite house makes it easier for the partners to deal with the daily rigors of budgets and allocation of resources.It prevents serious misunderstandings or conflicts over practical, everyday management of the partnership's assets and should allow the individuals to make the most of whatever resources they have. *Jupiter* is well placed in the composite 2nd house and the natural affinity between the Jupiter's capacity to attract and expand personal wealth with this house indicates the blending of planetary energies should produce inventive and profitable partnership efforts. Perhaps its only drawback here is that the partners may reinforce each other's yearnings for showy or ostentatious expenditures which might, if not otherwise managed, cause some overextension of the partnership's capacity to sustain itself. *Neptune* here contributes an unfortunate impracticality and over-optimistic quality to the partnership; the all-too-common kind of problem which results from poor management of credit and unrealistic expectations for the partnership's material future. The individual's influence on each other tends to make them brush aside reality and blithely use joint resources for a Caribbean cruise while forgetting to pay the monthly utility bill. With this composite position for Neptune, an especially strong effort is needed to not take financial risks out of some illusory sense that "everything will work out." *Pluto* in this composite house adds to the partnership a capacity to recoup from financial difficulties and survive hard times. The planetary energies muster themselves in times of trouble and find ways to regenerate the partnership's ability to restore its material security and financial future. With natal charts which have a strong material orientation to begin with, this position for Pluto can produce rather ruthless partners who tell each other that it's okay to foreclose on widow's mortgages, make loans at double the normal interest rate and sue for whiplash damages annually.

Tertiaries in the 3rd House

Synastric Despite *Saturn's* reputation for restrictiveness, this overlay appears only to give a degree of depth and seriousness to the intellectual exchange between the individuals. The Saturn person will appraise the house person as one with whom something other than "small talk" can be exchanged and, as a result, will tend to treat the house person's abilities and insights with respect. The house person often adopts a role of counselor or sounding board and will normally respond well to the earnestness and regard shown by the Saturn person. This is not a light-hearted linkage, but it can contribute depth and stability to an interaction. *Mercury* is in its natural home with this overlay, stimulated and enlivened by the projected qualities of the house person. The Mercury person will find it easy to "open up" to the house person and typically will initiate frequent contacts between the individuals, using the house person as a resource to articulate ideas and plans to clarify their own thinking. The house person will enjoy this undemanding and open exchange (unless they are particularly reclusive by nature) and join in comfortably with trading of responses and insights. If you're looking for someone to have coffee with often, this is the place to find such a companion. *Jupiter* responds well to this overlay, principally because the house person seems to have an encouraging and uplifting impact on the Jupiter person. The Jupiter person will usually find contacts with the house person a fine antidote for depression or discouragement and the house person is motivated to be more generous and supportive in the relationship than perhaps might be the normal pattern of behavior. Over time, this is a very warm and pleasant foundation for a relationship since continuing contacts between the individuals is restorative and pleasant; a rather uncommon experience in a world which seems largely populated by people who are either indifferent or determined to be "downers." *Neptune* is in a rather harmless position in the 3rd house overlay, opening avenues for the individuals to share their fantasies and dreams at a more communicative level than usual, but probably not, in itself, befuddling things as severely as this planet can in other positions. The Neptune person may be a little too trusting in revealing themselves to the house person or the house person may, if the natal charts suggest an ego-centered personality, use this interaction to play "head games" with the Neptune person, but normally this overlay adds only a certain dreamy and mildly escapist quality to the interaction. *Pluto's* affect in this position will likely reveal itself in a significant way only if the individuals decide to live together. In this situation, the Pluto person may be prompted to exercise excessive control over the shared environment and, in extreme situations, actually unconsciously cast the house person as part of the "decor" of their life. If other, more powerful links bring the individuals together into a relationship, this position can add the rather unattractive unconscious drive to use the presence of each other as a kind of display and ego-reinforcer; the urge to have a companion who is as much a decoration as a friend.

Composite A composite *Saturn* in the 3rd house may be the most common cause of the complaint "we never talk" from one or both partners. Each individual in such a partnership is exceptionally protective and insular in trying to create and preserve a particular personal environment which suits them, but often finds it difficult to accommodate to the personal needs of the partner. The result is often an ongoing unconscious contest over the shared environment and use of resources. It seems especially difficult for any sort of partnership with this position to find those many little areas of consensus on the daily living process which must exist if two individuals are to be together. The root cause probably is, as the "we never talk" complaint indicates, a real barrier within the partnership to easy communication. This is the sort of thing which only reveals itself over a long period of time, yet can lay down stratum after stratum of minor resentments. If this potential can be recognized and the partners make a major effort to listen to each other, the consequences can likely be avoided, but it does take a special effort with this composite position. *Mercury* in this composite house is like popping the cork on a champagne bottle; the partners literally bubble (and babble) in each other's presence with great energy and enthusiasm. The energies of the two charts spark and crackle with the need to get inside each other's heads and compare notes. Considering how vital good communication is in a partnership, this usually is a very healthy interaction. Certainly this composite position for Mercury makes staying in touch, spending long hours in amiable, idle chatter and doing things like traveling together or just sitting on the deck in the sun pleasant and relaxed. *Jupiter* in this composite house usually reveals itself in the happy discovery that the partners enjoy the same kind of living environment and priorities in allocating the hours of the day. This position for Jupiter gives the partnership a bustling energy that gets the individuals out and going together, finding the same opportunities for pleasure and stimulation of the mind and emotions interesting to both. Oddly, one of the hardest things to find in a partnership is the ability to fill the hours not occupied by work or other mandatory requirements in a mutually satisfactory way. With this position for Jupiter, these hours should be happy and mutually pleasing ones rather than sources of disagreement or discontent. *Neptune*, while not especially powerful in this house, can create a problem of understanding the needs and motives of the individuals. At least in some instances, the complaint that "my husband/wife doesn't understand me" roots in this position for Neptune. The source of this fogginess is probably that the individuals project their own hopes and motives onto each other rather than try to understand each other. When we see others in our image (as occurs with this position for Neptune) and find they don't behave or respond as we anticipate, the result is at least confusion and often discouragement. The only cure is to remember that each individual is the center of their own universe and, with this Neptune position, the centers are in different places. *Pluto* here can bring together planetary energies which stimulate a deep, unconscious need to jointly probe some of the most private and profound ideas held by the partners. Even if the individuals initially come together for other purposes, they will find themselves slipping into explorations of things usually withheld from the world at large and rarely shared. This position has a "confessional" tone and, as a result, may function as a catharsis for the persons. If, however, there are indications of emotional instability or severe repressions in the natal chart, this may reveal itself in more negative ways. It's nice to feel that one can be open and reveal the most private things to another, but given the wrong combination of factors, this may result in partners stimulating the worst rather than the best in each other.

Tertiaries in the 4th House

Synastric *Saturn* overlaid in this house arouses a strong unconscious sense of kinship and even sometimes a feeling of déja vu or that odd sensation of having been "fated" to have some sort of interaction with the house person. The house person will sense this bond and may well respond to the Saturn person as one who is, because of an unfathomable heritage, entitled to some special status. This response, while likely to influence the interaction to some degree and lend a quality of bondedness, is not an especially upbeat or exciting response. The undertone is more like the feeling of responsibility or obligation we have toward a seldom-visited relative or old classmate: unavoidable and permanent, but not entirely welcome. *Mercury* in this overlay establishes a clear sense of shared attitudes toward social mores and customs and a basis for the Mercury person to assume that their established way of going about the daily business of living will not trouble the house person. The house person will likely accept the Mercury person's attitudes and approach to social values without difficulty and include that person within the daily circle of activity without any concern that that normal pattern will be disrupted by the Mercury person's presence. *Jupiter* in the 4th house stimulates a parental or protective response in the Jupiter person which will reveal itself over time in small but usually pleasant ways. The house person may well welcome the continuing level of concern about their well-being shown by the Jupiter person in the same way that we count on the unshakable loyalty of a parent or sibling. In continuing relationships this overlay adds a quality of relatedness which makes any sort of ongoing contact unusually warm and trustful. *Neptune* here can cause the Neptune person to doubt that the house person will accept them as worthwhile persons or kindred souls or that there is a common ground of priorities in personal relationships. The Neptune person will, if motivated by other stronger links, seem to be constantly seeking the approval of the house person and, because of this, the house person may respond in a way which seems to be pushing away the possibility of a relationship. Over time, this position for Neptune may erode away some of the self-confidence of one or both individuals because of a lingering feeling that there is not a fundamental mutual respect or feeling of intrinsic worth between the individuals. *Pluto* here reinforces the quality of kinship and almost cosmic bonding, but can bring a dictatorial quality to the interaction. Under stress, the Pluto person may adopt an authoritarian attitude toward the house person as a device to make the relationship proceed as the Pluto person wishes. Depending on the natal qualities of the house person, this may trigger either ill-advised yielding to this demand or angry rebellion. While not a major element in a relationship, this position can add an often unwelcome quality of bullying or overreaction to minor problems.

Composite *Saturn* in the composite 4th house presents some difficult problems in a partnership. Ultimately, a partnership works well if there is a feeling of belonging to the same genus, the same "sub-tribe" within a culture. With this position for a composite Saturn, there seems to be a lingering sense that the individuals just don't have that sort of linkage; that whatever may have brought them together will eventually be undermined by a vague but pervasive lack of kinship. This may be something as evident as a major difference in cultural or educational background or even age which works against the partnership, but is just as likely can be a much more subtle and unconscious feeling that the partnership somehow violates an unspoken rule, an ill-defined more, or runs against the grain of the universe. With this composite position, the Saturnian energies directed toward establishing a joint social identity within the subculture do not blend well and can, over time, create a corrosive kind of discontent within the partnership over the question of "who we are and where do we fit into the world?" *Mercury* in this composite house makes the sometimes abrasive process of sharing space much easier and more natural, whether the sharing occurs in a home, work place or just a casual social interaction. Over time, it is harder to share a refrigerator than a bed. The daily exposure to another's little habits and quirks make much greater demands on human patience and tolerance than the intense but short-term demands of the lover's bed. With Mercury in this composite position, the simple and basic processes of getting through the day function well together and it is unlikely that there will be any anger and upset over who forget to get milk or put gas in the car. *Jupiter* in the composite 4th house is a happy position for a partnership, particularly a romantic/sexual one. The warm and benign energies of Jupiter come together in a supportive agreement on such basics as what makes the whole living process rewarding, what part of the society is most comfortable and natural for the individuals to inhabit and what sort of sheltering retreat from the rigors of the world provides peace and a sense of well-being. Even in the work place, such a composite allows the individuals to create a relaxed and pleasant atmosphere in which to carry out daily chores. No matter what the basic aim or function of the partnership is, it will retain the nuclear warmth of persons who are at peace with each other and have a caring and generous concern for the happiness and fulfillment of the individuals involved. *Neptune* in this composite can add a sweetness and gentle quiet to the interaction based largely on a strong, unspoken intuitive link-up of the psyches of the partners. There is a risk, however, of the partners over-romanticizing the basic strength of the relationship. Each is drifting in the glow of their own inner vision of the relationship and perhaps not being entirely realistic about what actually bonds the relationship. If this Neptune position occurs in a composite chart, it is probably wise to look particularly closely at the fundamental compatibility of the individuals. It can gloss over some troublesome conflicts in the personalities for a time, but they will ultimately emerge and even Neptune's magic won't prevent them from forcing the individuals to deal with them. *Pluto* here seems only to give added strength to the partnership when it is under stress, providing an almost "clan bond" when the partnership is under assault. In unusual situations, it can add an obsessive quality to the partnership, making the individuals cling to the relationship even when their own self-interest might argue for abandoning it. If either partner is prone to violent emotions or behavior, it occasionally exaggerates this in the form of physical abuse or raging diatribes, a rare result, but still one to consider.

Tertiaries in the 5th House

Synastric *Saturn* overlaid in the 5th house will, with other more potent linkages, awaken one of the most curious of human reactions: the conviction that the Saturn person will be inexorably drawn into a relationship by the house person which, while seemingly almost impossible to resist, will nonetheless bring sadness and disappointment to the

Saturn person. By itself, this overlay only gives a rather somber quality to the interaction, but when it occurs with strong links to the inner planets, the unconscious fear and anxiety which can haunt most humans about close relationships seems to be triggered. The house person will probably succumb also to this pull even in the face of this deep doubt, but share with the Saturn person the unshakable feeling that things will ultimately "go wrong." Perhaps because the need for relationships is so strong in nearly all humans and we want to find that "fated" bond with another, we unconsciously fear the disappointment of failure in this part of our lives very profoundly. With Saturn in this house, those fears are seemingly most aroused. *Mercury* in this synastric house awakens the qualities of humor and cheerfulness in the individuals, making continuing contact easy and light-hearted. The Mercury person will likely be prompted to be their most amusing and entertaining self, offering encouragement and sunny reinforcement to the house person in the usually less-than-exciting routines of life. The house person will, no doubt, find the amiable good nature and upbeat pleasantries of the Mercury person a welcome bright spot in a world seemingly largely populated by indifferent or complaining humans. In almost any sort of interaction, this Mercury position keeps the relationship from bogging down in discouragement and boredom. *Jupiter* here will add to any other links which motivate the Jupiter person to cast the house person as a companion. The Jupiter person will feel a deep quality of generous concern and interest in the house person's happiness and fulfillment and will typically do what can be done to contribute to that. The house person will be quite secure and open in such an overlay and, depending on the natal chart needs and proclivities, come to rely on the Jupiter person for reassurance and "recharging" when these natal needs seem to be in jeopardy. To the degree that we can turn to any other human as a trusted source of support when we are depressed or anxious, this overlay casts the individuals as such resources for each other; the Jupiter person is the energy source and the house person is the warmed and radiated reflector. *Neptune* in this adds a subtle and unconscious romanticism to the interaction, awakening in the Neptune person a sense of the beauty and inherent "perfection" of the house person: the classic "rose colored glasses" effect. The house person will feel a bond with the Neptune person of an almost ethereal or other-worldly quality, as if they share some special tie in the world of myth and spirits. This is a harmless and mild reaction, but in situations where powerful romantic/sexual magnetics are operating on the inner planets, the circumstances would dictate caution. The capacity for objective judgment of each other and the situation in which the individuals find themselves is blurred by this overlay and can contribute to a lack of realism and sensibleness in the interaction. *Pluto* here can contribute an undertone of romantic/sexual obsession and aggravate any urge to abandon one's present situation in favor of some rejuvenating escapade. With this overlay of Pluto, any sexual links between the individuals is given a darker, more intense tone, stirring some very primal urges. Certainly the Pluto person, if motivated by other links to inner planets, will sense an unconscious drive to "possess" or somehow dominate the house person beyond a typical reaction to another human, a response which will be sensed by the house person and responded to largely in terms of natal chart potentials. Pluto in this overlay makes itself felt more clearly than in most; and no matter what form the interaction takes, it will add intensity and depth... for better or worse.

Composite When *Saturn* energies flow together to produce a 5th house composite position, the rather depressive effect the individuals have on each other is severe enough that it often prevents a partnership. Because of this, this composite house position is not often found in relationships which have matured enough to prompt the constructing of a composite chart. When the weight of other linkages does bring the individuals together into a partnership, this position for Saturn is not fatal, but also offers little in the way of light-hearted or warm interaction. In such situations, there is a high probability that the partnership exists to fulfill some pragmatic or self-oriented need of one or both of the individuals independent of emotional or romantic/sexual goals. In any event, it is unlikely the individuals come together because they enjoy or admire each other, but rather because they provide each other a means of achieving some external, worldly need, the nature of which will probably be suggested by the natal charts. *Mercury's* normal effervescence and liveliness is heightened with this composite house position and the partners find it very natural to simply have fun together. With this position, the hours spent together are probably the best of the day and a shared response to all sorts of leisure outlets and ways of relaxing and enjoying life makes this an ideal placement for persons who, either by choice or necessity, must spend much time in each other's company. Playing off each other, the partners are livelier and more outgoing when together than either is by themselves. *Jupiter* in this composite house so enlivens the capacity for pleasure-seeking and daring that, however, pleasant this may be, it always risks the possibility of the individuals going to excess. Normally prudent or level-headed sorts who combine to produce this composite house seem to abandon their fears and anxieties. The optimism and boundless energy is so amplified that risky or extreme actions seem much less so. Jupiter's ebullience and golden glow is tapped by this blending of energies and, with some occasional prudent reassessment, much can be achieved. The partners will, however, have to guard against over-confidence and excess. *Neptune* in the composite 5th regrettably so muddles the capacities of the individuals to view each other realistically that all sorts of foolishness can result. This may be only a harmless blindness to each other's faults and foibles, but it can extend to blindness to the facts such as marital obligations, age differences or financial barriers. Alone, this composite position for Neptune can be managed and may even contribute a sweet and gentle forgiveness to the partnership, but in the context of a highly charged interaction with powerful romantic/sexual contents, it is likely to make getting a second opinion on just about any partnership decision prudent. *Pluto* here seems to strengthen any bond between the partners, particularly those which have their roots in a conviction that the partnership is a means for the individuals to make significant changes in their life direction, purpose or content. If the partnership is formed largely because the individuals see in each other the ingredients for achieving some long-sought objective, of "starting over" or breaking out some confining circumstance, this Pluto position reinforces that feeling and adds a binding quality to the partnership when the individuals join forces to this end. The partnership may have a somewhat obsessive undertone, but the contribution of Pluto in the 5th is usually helpful and supportive.

Tertiaries in the 6th House

Synastric *Saturn* in the 6th house is not an altogether unfavorable overlay. Despite the rather dreary reputation of both the planet and the house, the response of the Saturn person is often a measured and durable sense of obligation to and responsibility for the house person which can be the foundation of a long-term and deeply trusted relationship. The house person will gradually come to feel that the Saturn person is a bulwark against the trials of living and that the bond will survive time and separation. Over time, as the relationship is tested, this foundation will be a valuable stabilizer, perhaps keeping the interaction from losing its axis and flying off on divergent courses which would be later regretted. *Mercury* in the 6th is somewhat muted in its effect, the sturdy practicality and concern for sensibleness of this house being antithetical to Mercury's buzzing curiosity and surface-skimming energy. The Mercury person may feel compelled to restrain normal tendencies to spread their mental energy over a broad spectrum and, because of the influence of the house person, at least try to be more practical and focused on specific tasks. The house person may react to the Mercury person's approach to daily living with a growing lack of confidence that the Mercury person will stay the route. Depending on the natal chart qualities of the individuals, the effect of this may range from a helpful stabilizing otherwise a rather unsteady life course to creating a feeling of boredom and restraint which, over time, might be a corrosive problem. *Jupiter* in this house is a bit squashed by the essential pragmatism of the placement. The Jupiter person will likely respond to the house person as one who does not share any inner urge for adventure and exploration, at least, not parallel kinds of ways to enliven one's life. The house person will probably doubt the stability and reliability of the Jupiter person and come to doubt that the individuals really seek the same rewards in life. Given other harmonious links, this placement will not prevent a successful relationship, but there will likely remain a lingering feeling that the individuals will have to seek some of their life satisfactions outside the relationship. *Neptune* overlaid by the 6th house has a rather insubstantial impact, perhaps creating an element of uncertainty in the Neptune person that the general influence of the house person will be helpful or supportive. The house person may find that the Neptune person will have, despite other attractive qualities, a distracting impact on their life course at times, side-tracking them from the primary business at hand or unconsciously planting seeds of doubt about the achievability of goals. The influence of this placement is not, however, very strong and may only reveal itself if the individual natal charts are significantly lacking in self-confidence and assertiveness. *Pluto's* influence with this overlay is also rather minor. The Pluto person may, under high demand situations, find that the influence of the house person is to add a level of commitment to any joint effort, perhaps even triggering any latent obsessive qualities about life goals in the Pluto person. The house person may unconsciously try to manipulate the Pluto person as a device to achieve personal goals or to use the Pluto person as a buffer in high stress situations. This overlay will not likely play a noticeable role in a relationship unless the individuals are highly ambitious or self-oriented. In that context, the interplay may reinforce any tendency towards materiality and greed.

Composite The composite *Saturn* placement usually indicates the life arena in which the individuals will share a need to overcome difficulties and satisfy a lingering inner sense of deprivation. In the 6th house, this Saturn person suggests that the common ground will likely be demonstrating a real utility and value to the world and garnering some recognition for competency and ability. This composite house then is probably at its best in a work-related partnership. It can, however, be a bonding element in a more complex and intimate relationship when the individuals choose to come together at least in part to take on a difficult personal task. Couples who go on missions to remote countries or combine a personal relationship with long, difficult research or studies typify this sort of partnership. Regrettably, this composite can also play a role in partnerships burdened with difficult and painful tasks such as caring for an invalid family member or the like, particularly when the task was a factor in initially bringing the individuals together. *Mercury* here lends a steadying quality to the partnership's approach to life, making sensible long-term planning easier and establishing of a solid financial foundation for the partnership a cooperative effort. The 6th house placement for Mercury, however, does little to stimulate the intellectual growth or willingness to expand the horizons of the partnership. This placement suggests that the partners will have to guard against becoming too routinized and narrow in their relationship; there is a rather high probability of getting in a rut and staying there. *Jupiter* in this composite house makes taking the "long view" natural and comfortable for the partnership and is useful when the individuals come together for some purpose which requires a steady, unwavering commitment to some joint goal. This house position constrains Jupiter's tendency to be over-optimistic and grab for the main chance, an effect which has to be appraised within the general context of the partnership. If the individuals are aggressive, high risk people with large scope hopes and objectives, this position provides a stable underpinning for these efforts. If, however, the individuals are natally prone to fearfulness and lack of initiative, this exaggerates this anxiety over the risks of any undertaking and will tend to make the partnership overly cautious and self-protective. *Neptune* in the 6th sometimes has the curious effect of aggravating any tendencies toward self-pity, hypochondria, paranoia or similar personality qualities in the partners. The coming together of Neptune's yielding and dissolving energies with the 6th house's focus on "duty" and health may cause the partners to become so absorbed in their own personal well-being and so obsessive in their pursuit of that end that they become extremists. This Neptune position will not, in itself, cause the partnership to take such a turn, but if the potentials for such personality disorders are present in the natal charts, the partners will heighten these tendencies in each other. *Pluto* in the composite 6th will likely reveal its influence only in the uncommon partnership situation which brings together individuals at the extreme ends of the aggressive/passive scale. This Pluto position can cause the individuals to behave in ways which exaggerate these innate qualities and, particularly under stress-filled situations, heighten any proclivity toward either sadistic behavior or martyring passivity. The influence of Pluto in the 6th house is not profound or compelling except in that unusual situation, however, and will likely only be a contribution to the capacity of the partnership to cope with occasional unstable behavior or actions by either individual with patience and dedication.

Tertiaries in the 7th House

Synastric *Saturn* captured by the 7th house creates an unconscious response in the Saturn person which is, in some ways, the negative reflection of the Uranian reaction: a sense that the house person represents a kind of partner who is highly desirable, but somehow forever denied the Saturn person. If this is the only significant linkage, the response is fleeting and accepted with the resignation experience brings, but if there are other links to inner planets which establish a strong conscious impetus to reach out for contact, this can create an ambivalent hope/doubt atmosphere. The tone is a bitter sadness over the realization that some paradigmic dreams will forever be beyond our reach... and we really don't understand why. The house person will feel this karmic linkage, but will also unconsciously feel the barriers which exist and probably also turn away. This overlay is sometimes the source of that depressive doubt that ones hopes will ever be realized in a partnership and, if it is encountered in a synastric analysis, will present a difficult chore to explain in a way which the Saturn person can accept without frustration and resentment. It is not an absolute barrier to a relationship, but it is perhaps the most difficult of all Saturn overlays to overcome in creating and sustaining one.

Mercury establishes a very positive ambience, with the house person not only being seen as one with whom an easy communication could be maintained, but also a sense that the Mercury person's fundamental attitudes and approaches to life would probably be acceptable to the house person. The house person feels comfortable in the presence of the Mercury person, relaxing into surprisingly open and intimate conversation almost from the initial contact. Over time, this linkage assures continuing openness in exchanging responses and appraisals of the events which mutually affect the individuals and a strong intellectual bond. *Jupiter* in this overlay will almost certainly contribute to the warmth and selflessness of the Jupiter person's feelings about the house person. This creates the kind of responses which make it seem quite natural to send flowers, remember birthdays and find a myriad of opportunities to do little things which compliment and reassure the house person. Considering how rare such kindness and concern is in human interaction, the house person's response will tend to be charitable and tolerant in accepting the Jupiter person even if there are not other, more potent links between the charts. Perhaps the only difficulty that arises here is when all this good feeling between the individuals cannot, because of circumstance or the absence of other more personal motivations, be expanded to a full relationship. In such a situation, the Jupiter person in particular is vulnerable to that feeling that they have made a major unselfish effort in the relationship and have not gotten a fair return. This overlay is sometimes the source of a sad but useful lesson: you can't make someone feel about you as you would want, no matter how hard you try and how kind and considerate your behavior. *Neptune* can be a real muddler in this overlay, creating a false sense of kinship and bond with the house person. The Neptune person may proceed on the assumption that the house person is a natural and willing participant in the relationship, only to find that the motives which had been assumed in the house person were not at all those which actually existed. With this overlay, the Neptune person in particular must guard against wishing onto the house person either personal qualities or aspirations which don't exist. If you have ever been shocked and disappointed about the behavior of a person who you believed to be worthy of your trust and candor, it is probably because of this overlay and the illusions it can create. *Pluto* here, if it is accompanied by other more personal and intimate links between the inner planets, can have strong romantic/sexual undertones. The Pluto person can be motivated by a potent unconscious drive to possess the house person because the house person seems to epitomize a perfect love partner. Even without other links, the Pluto person will be motivated to explore the possibility of an intimate relationship, often to their own conscious surprise. The house person will feel this tug and may well be unsettled by the deep rumblings it can create. Most often this just creates a temporary atmosphere of rather steamy flirtatiousness, but given other romantic/ sexual links, it can add a darker, more intense hue to any relationship; a quality of compelling passion which may, in some situations, lock the individuals into an obsessive romantic sexual bond.

Composite *Saturn* in the composite 7th house appears so disproportionately often in the composite charts of functioning partnerships, it has to be assumed that this is more than just happenstance. The probable reason for this is that the long-term cyclic energies of the individuals flow together in such a way that the need and opportunity to form a partnership converge. Successful partnerships, like much else in life, are a product of fortuitous timing and circumstance. With Saturn in the composite 7th, the persons find their individual life objectives and aspirations are not only attuned, but that by coming together in a partnership, they become more attainable. Seen in a more metaphysical way, this composite introduces an element of "fatedness" into the partnership and should, over the long term, contribute to the harmonious and parallel evolution of the individuals. The partners are less likely to mature away from each other and find themselves no longer in tune and compatible after a time within the relationship. *Mercury* in this composite house creates a very pleasant "meeting of the minds" of the partners. There will likely be little misunderstanding or uncertainty about attitudes and priorities and perhaps even a strong element of seemingly "intuitive" linkage. This is really not a mysterious phenomenon when the Mercury mental energies of the partners are so essentially similar and, therefore, tend to respond to stimuli in the same way. With this composite position, it is not so much that the partners think alike as it is that their combined reaction to the processes of living are, in combination, more complex and three dimensional than either could manage alone. The result is then a better, more useful combining of abilities and actions which usually bring happy results for the partners. *Jupiter* in this house arguably may be the most desirable single placement in a partnership, especially a romantic/sexual one. Jupiter makes such a winning contribution in this house because the individuals come to realize that it is the partnership itself, not just specific qualities in the individual personalities, which is the true source of their pleasure and happiness. With such a placement, in the context of a generally harmonious composite chart, the partners will come to feel that life without each other would be a difficult and sorry prospect. There probably is no better mortar to bind a partnership than a shared feeling of gratitude to the gods for bringing the individuals together. Even in partnerships with less complex and intimate goals, this Jupiter placement serves well and, over time, sustains warm friendships and close bonds. *Neptune* in this composite house contributes an element of rosy romanticism to the partnership, but often makes it difficult for the individuals to settle on a workable form for the relationship. It probably is that the individuals are so entangled by the romantic fantasies triggered by the relationship that it is hard for them to deal with the reality of the situation. Though not an unmanageable element in a partnership, it does make bringing the partnership to some satisfactory level of functioning more difficult. People who have a long relationship, but never can seem to get it organized enough to commit to it, will often had the placement; a source of both lovely dreams and fuzzy execution. *Pluto* in the composite 7th has a subtle effect which will go largely unnoticed unless the relationship actually evolves into a full partnership for other reasons. If this occurs, this position for Pluto will contribute to the capacity of the partnership to survive significant changes and to hold together during such traumas and demands. Pluto's role here is much like the reinforcing steel in a concrete structure: invisible until the structure is tested, but of greater inner value when the hurricane hits.

Tertiaries in the 8th House

Synastric *Saturn* overlaid by the 8th house stimulates one of the less benign responses in the Saturn person. The cold and unyielding qualities of this stony planet combine with the manipulative and dominating elements of the 8th house to produce a rather cold, calculating unconscious impulse. The house person is seen as an object to obtain, to utilize and exploit without particular regard for any pain or damage done. The house person, like a wary animal sensing danger, will normally retreat and maintain a safe distance. This overlay typically only results in a disturbing discomfort and a quality of hunter/prey in the interaction which keeps the individuals in tense and distrustful stances. If there are other, stronger sexual links between the individuals, however, the overlay will amplify any tendency toward falling into self-punishing and unbalanced relationships. If a person has a history of repeating a pattern of relationships which cause them to be exploited and abused, this overlay can trigger that kind of self-destructive behavior mode. *Mercury* overlaid in this house tends to swing this planet's normally light-hearted and mundane focus toward a more calculating and self-oriented direction. It may only give a more tightly focused purposefulness to the intellectual interplay between the individuals with the Mercury person directing the dialogue and the house person responding with deliberateness and precision; a useful interaction when the two individuals are involved in an activity which requires clarity of thought. The interaction, nonetheless, seems always to have a "hidden agenda," with each of the individuals using the communicative linkage to achieve their own somewhat veiled goals. *Jupiter* captured by an 8th house overlay is in an unnatural and awkward place, with the probable effect of losing this planet's normally positive influence in a relationship. The inherently free-wheeling openness and unselfish qualities of Jupiter do not harmonize with the indirection and self-orientation of the 8th house and the most unattractive qualities in the Jupiter person's personality may be amplified: greed, falseness or role-playing, self-importance or the like tending to come to the surface. The house person may not be able to rid themselves of the feeling that they are being "conned" and, as a result, may remain insecure and distrustful in the interaction no matter how strongly motivated by other links. *Neptune* in this overlay can stimulate some rather bizarre sexual fantasies in the Neptune person but blind them to both the consequences of these and the essential character of the house person. The Neptune person may pursue the relationship in an attempt to fulfill these sexual fantasies without consideration for the feedback from the house person, creating some very awkward and uncomfortable interplay if the house person does not share these goals. The house person will have a sense, at an unconscious level, of being sought after, but there will be so much uncertainty and absence of reality in the atmosphere that the response will be defensive or fearful. Sometimes there will even be a degree of frightened hysteria over the unspoken motives of the Neptune person. *Pluto* is at home in this overlay... which is a little like saying the fox is at home in the chicken coop. Pluto is our link with the most primal and unreasoning drives and, in this house, a channel is opened to those ancient needs. As with all influences of Pluto, this typically provides only a lower octave harmonic to the main theme of a relationship, but if the interaction has a major sexual content, this Pluto placement adds a quality of animal vitality and deeply rooted motivation, in a word, "lustiness." Typically, however, this only causes the Pluto person to feel an undefined, but still detectable, cosmic link with the house person, a feeling responded to by the house person almost instinctively. In a casual and uncomplex interaction, this has only minimal effect, but in a fully evolved relationship, it contributes a bond deep in the unconscious. The individuals seem somehow "brothers to the boulders and cousins to the clouds," linked at the most fundamental cosmic level.

Composite *Saturn* in the composite 8th house is a rather unlikely placement in close, personal relationships, because it tends to keep the individuals at a distance from each other and inhibit their ability for intimacy. Still, it is not an entirely discordant placement since it probably allows individuals to retain a degree of objectivity and pragmatism in dealing with each other. It would seem to be best placed in a business or professional relationship or as an element in the partnership which forces the individuals together for long periods, but also requires them to remain detached and uninvolved at a personal level. Certainly, a tone of formality and conservatism will remain in any partnership with this composite placement of Saturn, no matter what other contents the relationship may have. *Mercury* in the composite 8th house brings a high level of intuitive bonding between the individuals; a quality of attunement and simultaneity in responses to the events surrounding the partnership which is helpful in any situation where such unspoken coordination is important. With this placement, the partners may experience such an intimate mental link that it seems almost like ESP at times. The urge to contact each other, to speculate about a particular question, make a change in life direction and even similar life experiences all seem to occur in close synchronicity. To the degree that being in such mental lockstep contributes to the effectiveness of the partnership, this placement is useful and supportive. *Jupiter* in the composite 8th house has both useful and potentially detrimental potentials. It contributes to the partners's ability to function well as a team, particularly in high-demand or competitive situations and, whether they are sharing a tennis court, mutual fund or a bed, they work well together in getting what they want out of the situation. This placement, however, can amplify any elements of materiality, selfishness or vulnerabilities to excess which exist in the natal charts of the individuals. At best, it brings energy to any joint venture aimed at enhancing the shared life content and pleasures of the partnership. At worst, it sends the partnership off on ill-advised and risky tangents which undermine both the stability and durability of the relationship. Which manifestation will prevail is largely a matter of the natal and composite chart context in which this Jupiter placement occurs. *Neptune* in this composite house is a relatively harmless placement, usually adding only an element of romantic daydreaming and tendency to chase a few rainbows: a quality not without its charm and certainly a sometimes welcome antidote to the harsh reality of making one's way through life. The partners can share their fantasies and fairy tale dreams and perhaps even realize a few. Neptune's effect here is only potentially dangerous if either or both of the partners are vulnerable to escapist behavior. In this situation, the interaction can exaggerate this tendency. *Pluto* probably has a more evident impact in this composite house than any other, amplifying any shared interest in metaphysics, religion or other mode of finding ones place in the universe. It can add a bit of an obsessive quality to any materially-oriented efforts of the partnership, but contributes to the ability of the partnership to evolve and carry out long-range plans for the partnership's material well-being. In intimate relationships, it gives a gutsy eroticism to any sexual interplay and helps blow away any latent inhibitions in the relationship. In any situation where the partners are working together to fill some deeply felt personal need, this Pluto place adds muscle and staying power... and more than a little ruthless determination.

Tertiaries in the 9th House

Synastric *Saturn* overlaid by the 9th house often stimulates the Saturn person to play the role of mentor or guide to the house person, a response which might be likened to a teacher's response to a worthy pupil. With such an overlay, it is not uncommon for substantial age differences to be bridged in the interaction and for two persons who, on the surface, might not have much in common to find a strong intellectual bond. The house person will sense the interest and the absence of any manipulative or possessive drive in the Saturn person and normally respond with appreciation and without unwarranted self-protectiveness. The relationship will gain depth and profoundness with this overlay, although in itself it does not suggest emotional closeness or warmth. *Mercury* with this overlay brings a depth of thought and seriousness to any exchange between the individuals. The house person may bring their most acute problems and concerns to the Saturn person as a means to focus and articulate them. The Saturn person will usually accept this role since it tends to be flattering and offers an opportunity to play a role which contains personal interest without any substantial personal commitment. This interplay is an exercise in the old axiom, "If you want to make a friend, ask a small favor. If you want to lose a friend, ask a big one." If the interaction remains impersonal, it typically is a pleasant and supportive one. *Jupiter* captured in the 9th house encourages the Jupiter person to open a long and rewarding dialogue with the house person; one which allows the Jupiter person to find both reassurance in their own evolving thought and attitudes and stimuli for further philosophic growth. The house person will normally play a patient and interested listener, offering encouragement and agreement to the Jupiter person in areas of uncertainty and discouragement. Often this can be the basis for an enduring friendship; an example of the maxim, "If you talk like me, think like me and agree with me, you can't be all bad!" *Neptune* in a 9th house overlay will cause the Neptune person to wonder about the world view of the house person and shake their head over how such a perception of the world could come to be. There will be a vague feeling that the individuals originated on different planets and, try as they may, will not find an area of philosophic agreement no matter what other links bring them together. The atmosphere of "foreign-ness" will tend to make the house person defensive and sensitive in dealings with the Neptune person; a feeling that there is a real absence of a shared perception of the world and its workings. While not an overwhelming barrier, this position can be abrasive over time for the Neptune person who just can't fathom the attitudes of the house person. *Pluto* seems to have little effect in this position, perhaps contributing in small measure to a feeling of cosmic linkage between the persons and some deep, underlying common link with the universe. If the individuals are brought together by a common political or philosophic agenda, this position can give a more urgent and messianic tinge to such a shared interest.

Composite If *Saturn* falls in the composite 9th house, the partnership will have a strong flavor of social conventionality and adherence to whatever the norms are for the subculture in which the individuals find themselves. It sometimes has the curious effect of causing the individuals to behave more conservatively and cautiously within the partnership than they might otherwise normally act. Whether this is an inhibitive influence or one which helps the individuals to avoid non-beneficial behavior is entirely a matter of context in which it occurs. Under any circumstance, it gives a degree of formality and reserve to the partnership and contributes a keen social sense and courtesy to the interaction. *Mercury* in this composite house strengthens the intellectual and philosophic bond between the partners, largely eliminating any significant areas of conflict or disagreement over cultural, political or religious issues. It can often provide a helpful bridge in partnerships involving persons of very different life experience, cultural heritage or educational background since it contributes not only tolerance, but also a fundamental concord on the really basic matters of everyday life which occupy any relationship. *Jupiter* in the composite 9th is a great invigorator of the growth and development potentials of the individuals in a partnership. Coming together with another human can often be the catalyst for venturing onto new paths and searches and this should be the impact on the partners with this composite placement of Jupiter. Many intriguing avenues attract us, but are not explored because we are reluctant to do so alone. With this placement, the partners can come together to experiment and explore with that marvelous reassurance of having a "buddy" to share the discoveries and the risk. *Neptune* in this composite house is relatively harmless, perhaps only giving an ethereal tone to any shared philosophic or intellectual interests. It can amplify any tendency to want to "get away from it all" or to break away from social norms, but more often it only gives a certain romanticism to opportunities for travel and exploration. Given relatively stable individuals and a modicum of good sense, this composite position will only soften any areas of disagreement over social or philosophic issues, making them seem irrelevant to the partnership. In rare situations, however, it can exaggerate any tendencies toward political or religious extremism in the individuals, causing them to behave in almost fanatical ways. *Pluto* here can add to the excitement and fascination of exploring unconventional or eccentric interests. If the partnership shares an interest in the occult or metaphysical, this Pluto position will spice that interest with a feeling that the partners can jointly reach levels of understanding which alone they could not. Obviously, if the individuals are, by natal inclination, very strongly oriented toward such areas of interest, this Pluto placement may be a factor in bringing them together, particularly if there is a strong sexual undertone to either their interests or in their response to each other. In rare situations, this placement may contribute to drawing the partners into investigation of really arcane matters which might be best left alone.

Tertiaries in the 10th House

Synastric *Saturn* falling in the 10th house overlay establishes the house person as "acceptable," at least in terms of the Saturn person's self-image and aspirations. Despite the fascination of the foreign and exotic, most humans ultimately are most comfortable and form relationships with other humans who appear to fall within the parameters of the particular subculture to which each belongs. The house person is perceived as being somehow the "right sort" and there is a natural inclination on the part of the Saturn person to associate themselves with the house person. The house person, if typical of most humans, will respond positively to this appraisal if the Saturn person appears to offer any other desirable qualities. We may make fun of the need for "acceptance" in humans, but it is nonetheless a strong element in the sustaining of a strong self-image and only true eccentrics and rebels (some might say "social misfits") are unaffected by this need. There is nothing particularly warm or winning in this response, but when it is absent, there is a lingering doubt about the "appropriateness" of the relationship which can be a source of long-term difficulties. *Mercury* in this overlay appears to play a relatively minor role in the response of the individuals; in part, because there is not much of a bond between the curious and inquisitive Mercury and the rather staid 10th house and, in part, because the areas of life which are influenced are rather drab and routine. The Mercury person will probably not find any serious areas of disagreement with the house person over career aspirations or goals and may, in fact, be perceived as useful in the quest. The house person seems largely unaffected by this overlay and will respond to the Mercury person only if other links exist. This position for Mercury creates no special problems, but is minor in its influence. *Jupiter* in this overlay can play a major role, particularly if the individuals are career-oriented persons with well-formed and ambitious aspirations. The Jupiter person will appraise the house person as one with whom an effective partnership can be formed to achieve some important life goals, or at least a person with whom the Jupiter person can work constructively. The house person, sensing that the Jupiter person finds value and substance in them, often will put forth their best effort to try to live up to this response. The interaction may remain only a simple, utilitarian one or, with other links, become more complex and intimate, but in any circumstance, this overlay will contribute to deriving the maximum rewards from the interaction for the persons involved. *Neptune* overlaid in the 10th can stimulate some of the less charitable and self-centered responses; in the extreme, what might be characterized as the "gold digger" syndrome. The Neptune person may see the house person as an instrument through which some status-based aspiration can be achieved, or at least as an individual who enhances the Neptune person's social image. This is a relatively harmless response if the Neptune person is natally self-sufficient and confident, but if the natal chart indicates a combination of weakened self-image and an excessive need for wealth, position or recognition, this overlay may trigger an assessment that, "It's just as easy to fall in love with a rich man/physically beautiful woman as it is a poor/plain one." This response is the exception, of course, but it can't be discounted in synastric analysis when the right combination of factors exist. *Pluto* here is not especially important, contributing largely to the perception that the house person may be a source of strength or support in achieving some worldly end. On occasion, with a pattern of intense romantic/sexual linkages, this may cause the Pluto person to perceive the house person as one who enhances the Pluto person's public image as a lover and sexual performer with the result that the "acquisition" of the house person is undertaken in part as a demonstration of sexual prowess. More commonly, this overlay only enhances the general acceptability of the house person in the unconscious mind of the Pluto person: a response most humans appreciate even though they may not be disposed to satisfy the responder.

Composite *Saturn* in the composite 10th can have two quite different results, depending on the overall content of the partnership. Perhaps most commonly it indicates that the individuals do not share common worldly aspirations or life goals and, when the Saturn energies combine, there is a neutralizing or counterproductive result. The individuals tend to hinder each other in achieving their individual objectives. Less commonly, in situations which have very strong links elsewhere in the synastric and composite charts, the individuals can negotiate an "arrangement" which allows each to pursue their own careers or aspirations, but still come together on rather pragmatic terms to fulfill personal needs. This composite placement occurs not uncommonly in relationships which match two strong independent and assertive people who do not want to give up much of their freedom, but as with all humans, need some companionship and central personal reference point in their life. The partnership may be very durable, but likely will remain limited and without major commitment. *Mercury* in the composite 10th house is a useful and practical placement, allowing the individuals to cooperate successfully on a continuing basis in any activity aimed primarily at enhancing the career or professional status of the partners. This Mercury position occurs frequently in business partnerships in which the composite Sun is in either the 10th or 11th house and seems to be a good prognosticator of a successful and harmonious blending of abilities. *Jupiter* in the composite 10th indicates a very complementary blending of abilities which often result in material success; a good teaming of talents and skills which allow the individuals to be more successful as a partnership than either could on their own. It may cause the partners to focus too acutely on simply acquiring wealth and material success, leaving other aspects of the partnership undeveloped, but given a reasonable balance within the other links, this position for Jupiter will make a prosperous contribution to the partnership without creating any great difficulties. *Neptune* here seems to bring out the least practical and sensible elements of the individuals, causing them either to give inadequate concern to the simple daily requirements of a relationship (e.g., paying the bills) or a false sense of their own role in the world. Perhaps the most common result of this composite placement is that individuals misjudge their ability to function together successfully in any situation which they cannot easily later escape. Second marriages where children are involved, live-in mother-in-laws, conflicting work schedules or the like can be blithely ignored as potential difficulties for a partnership. Reality will, however, inevitably intrude and this failure to see the partnership in terms of the real world in which it must function can cause some troublesome problems. In synastric analysis, this composite position for Neptune obligates us to gently remind the partners of these realities. *Pluto* here does, as is often the case with this remote planet, not reveal itself unless the partnership comes under stress or encounters some real practical troubles. In these times of difficulty when falling back on the strength and shelter of the partnership to recover and go on with life is necessary, the blending of Pluto energies come forth and the partners will usually find surprising durability and recuperative resources within the relationship.

Tertiaries in the 11th House

Synastric With *Saturn* in this overlay, the probable reaction of the Saturn person is to confront major disagreements with the house person; in a sense there is a "generation gap" or inability to agree on social priorities. The unconscious perception is that what one person holds dear and wants to preserve is seen as having little value or even as undesirable by the other. The house person will tend to evaluate the Saturn person as stodgy and over-cautious, out of sync with the times. The Saturn person will similarly unconsciously appraise the house person as immature and trendy. In a casual interaction, this overlay creates no great barrier and, if there are other more positive links, the individuals will show a good natured tolerance of each other. In more personal and intimate relationships, however, this is probably too discordant of a response to not cause some irritation and discomfort. *Mercury* overlaid by the 11th house is in a very benign place, with the Mercury person almost immediately responding to the house person in an open and communicative mode. The house person will be seen as a natural companion with whom ideas and responses can be shared. Such a friendly and undemanding reaction is normally welcome and the house person, given any other positive links with the Mercury person, will find the cheery, upbeat tone of the interaction pleasant. The warm but easy pace of the relationship gives it an opportunity to evolve into whatever general form other elements of interaction indicate and establishes an atmosphere of tolerance and patience valuable in any relationship. *Jupiter* here stimulates the Jupiter person to unconsciously reach out to the house person with little acts of kindness and generosity ranging from just a simple but genuine interest in the well-being of the house person to small gifts, cards and other demonstrations of caring and concern. Unless the house person is wholly disinterested in the Jupiter person, this show of human warmth and interest is a welcome exception to the normal self-interested behavior of humans. No one has too many friends and, with this overlay, the door is open to a long and genuine relationship based on undemanding interest and unjudging concern. *Neptune* captured by the 11th house overlay creates some difficulty for the Neptune person in getting the house person "in focus;" a feeling that one can't really get a good hold on the personality of the other person and, as a result, is vulnerable to making a poor judgment about them.

No one enjoys this sense of being unable to "read" another person and even if strongly attracted by other links, will remain somewhat ill-at-ease. The house person will usually sense this uncertainty, but likely will give it a more negative connotation than it deserves, assuming the hesitancy in the Neptune person roots in disapproval or distrust. Obviously such an uneasy atmosphere is not the best for a useful interaction and may cause the individuals to remain at arms length despite any other links. *Pluto* in the 11th house normally only adds an undertone of "fatedness" to any response which is reassuring to the Pluto person and usually accepted by the house person with an unconscious sense that some sort of linkage is natural. In situations where either natal chart has powerful aspects to Pluto from the inner planets, this can go beyond just a background factor and become a central theme of the response. The Pluto person may pursue the relationship almost obsessively, refusing to accept any limits or restraints set by the house person. Whether this only gives a particular intensity and depth to that response or creates a damn nuisance depends, of course, on the context in which it occurs.

Composite *Saturn* in the composite 11th house occurs with the same disproportionate high frequency as the 7th, probably because the Saturn energies flow together in a way which makes bridging some extraordinary differences in personalities and situations much easier. Saturn often suggests the unconscious aspirations of the individuals which life and circumstance seem to frustrate and, with this composite house, the individuals seem to find in one another a kindred soul form of bond. Sharing and understanding disappointments and anxieties can often create a stronger bond than links based on common skills or successes; in a sense, it is an exercise in the old saw that "misery loves company." In any event, this composite placement of Saturn is a fair indicator of a bond based on a shared interpretation of life experience and is a strong unpinning for any sort of partnership. *Mercury* in this composite house amplifies the element of friendship and companionability, making it much easier for the partners to articulate their feelings and hopes and providing a very positive opportunity for the individuals to lay out their personal goals and arrive at some sort of a joint plan to achieve them. With this house, communication is not blurred by romanticism, made manipulative by sexual aspirations or too uncritical by an overly rosy image of each other. The partners will likely find their common ground realistically and without the probability of later disillusionment. *Jupiter* here is nicely placed, enhancing the ability of the individuals to play and dawdle together without the relationship becoming stale or repetitive. Free time and discretionary resources can be used with a happy accord about how they should be expended and the partners will probably feel that no better pals exist with which they would choose to spend their recreational time. While the individuals may encourage each other to play a bit more than sometimes might be good for either's career or bank account, this is such a relaxed and agreeable flowing together of Jupiter's expansive energies that it is hard to find much bad to say about it. *Neptune* in the 11th seems not to cause much harm, given reasonably sensible and stable partners. There may be an over-idealizing of both the partners and of the soundness of the relationship, a kind of "I can forgive you anything!" But unless the individuals are complete airheads, this just smooths the hours together and gives a creamy tone to the way in which the individuals deal with each other. It may make those nearby a bit nauseous, but if you like relationships punctuated with baby-talk and pet names, this is the ideal composite position for Neptune. *Pluto* in this composite house gives a "through thick and thin" quality to a partnership, gluing the commitment with an unconscious adhesion which provides great resistance to time and turmoil. Normally this is a valuable asset in a partnership and keeps it whole under some real strains. It can, however, become negative if the relationship has fundamental troubles since it makes it harder for the individuals to admit these problems and confront the possibility of separating. Partnerships in which one member accepts excessive abuse or unfaithfulness or refuses to face such problems as alcoholism or drug abuse in the other person may well reveal this Pluto placement. This is, of course, the exceptional outcome of this placement, but it does contain the potential for such blind clinging to a relationship when good sense would dictate another course.

Tertiaries in the 12th house

Synastric The 12th house, by its nature, is always a slippery concept to cope with and any planet which is overlaid by this house tends, in its response, to reflect this amorphous quality. *Saturn* will tend to feel an unconscious tug in this house which is not entirely pleasant. The house person will be perceived as someone to whom the Saturn person has a kind of karmic debt, an unavoidable obligation, which must be paid even if the price is unwelcome. Even a normally assertive and confident personality may feel disarmed by the house person if their Saturn is overlaid by the 12th, almost as if some of the structural firmness of the Saturn person's self-image is weakened by the presence of the other person. Still, there is a deep pull in this response which leaves the Saturn person often unable to avoid the demands of the house person. How the house person responds to this depends largely on how much compassion and integrity they possess, a synastric analysis problem for us to solve. Clearly, if the Saturn person is in a position to be badly used or exploited, we should try to point this out and create an awareness of this vulnerability. *Mercury* in the 12th house can establish an intuitive link between the individuals; sometimes it is so strong that the Mercury person is unduly influenced by the house person. The Mercury person will probably feel that they can sense clearly the feelings and responses of the house person and "understand" them at a subliminal level. Not everyone enjoys this sort of anticipatory insight, real or imagined, and the house person may not feel comfortable with the Mercury person's interpretations of their motives and thoughts. If there are strong links from other planets, this Mercury overlay probably only adds a level of communication below the verbal plane, but it can exaggerate any fearfulness and self-protectiveness if the links are sexual and self-oriented. *Jupiter's* normally benign qualities seem neutralized by this overlay, not necessarily made negative or harmful, but rather simply nonoperative. The Jupiter person may feel a protectiveness or desire to try to solve the house person's problems, but often is paralyzed by a feeling that nothing they might do would help. The end result is likely to be a recurring sense of frustration over some perceived quality in the house person. In the same way, the house person will feel an ambivalent response, appreciating the concern but not really wanting to be "saved." For obvious reasons, this overlay can be the unconscious stimulus for relationships which have a strong element of martyrism and self-imposed suffering in the name of helping another. While not always a bad thing (most of us do need "saving" at times), it does introduce the sort of imbalance in a relationship which can become a source of annoyance and resentment. *Neptune* here opens the Neptune person to unconscious manipulation by the house person and, if there are any self-punishing qualities in the personality or a weak self-image, the Neptune person can be pulled into a very passive and undefended posture. Usually the house person will only respond to this weakness and malleability in the Neptune person with an effort not to injure or offend, but if there are powerful romantic/sexual links, this vulnerability may be felt as a channel for exploitation. Other factors may draw the individuals into some sort of relationship, but this element of imbalance and the potential for exploitation and manipulation will usually remain as part of the content of the interactive response. *Pluto* here is more or less unfathomable, reaching so deep into the primal foundations of the personalities that it is very difficult to anticipate the result. There is no essential disharmony between the qualities of Pluto and the 12th house and it is probable that the only effect is a contribution to the number of levels at which the relationship can operate, perhaps giving a vague but persisting quality of metaphysical linkage. If, however, this overlay occurs with a number of other links which produce a seriously out-of-balance and abusive interaction, the Pluto person may find themselves caught up in an inexplicable tangle of violent responses to the house person which have their roots so deep in the psyche that they are completely irrational and senseless... but potentially dangerous to both individuals.

Composite *Saturn* in the 12th house is not a happy placement in a composite chart. It occurs rather infrequently in the charts of functioning partnerships largely because, when such a blending produces this house position, the unconscious reaction of the individuals is permeated with suspicion and misinterpretation of motives. The individuals seem to be out of rhythm, so uncoordinated in their hopes and aspirations, that any hope of successful blending of personalities is remote. The instinct, with this composite placement, is to move away from each other rather than together and no matter how attractive the partners may be to each other at other levels, this is a troubling and divisive factor in the relationship. Since all this dark uncertainty percolates below the conscious level and is, therefore, very hard to understand or explain, the individuals may never grasp why they dealt so badly with each other and wander off wondering what prompted them to try in the first place. *Mercury* here can produce a higher level of effective nonverbal communication between the partners, but it is just as likely to muddle the ability of the individuals to communicate at a real-world pragmatic level. The effect of this blending of Mercury energies is not necessarily detrimental to a partnership, but the individuals will have to rely strongly on their ability to "sense" what the other person thinks and feels rather than trying to articulate these motives. This composite placement for Mercury probably works better in partnerships which have strong emotional foundation (i.e., lovers, friends, family) than in an intellectually based, problem-solving environment. If precision of communication and complete, detailed understanding is required, this composite position can be the source of confusion and misunderstanding. *Neptune* in the 12th is probably more at home than in any other composite placement, making the blending of energies from this often puzzling planet flow into positive channels. The individuals will have an uncanny intuitive capacity to anticipate and act to fulfill each other's fantasies and dreams, rarely making an awkward or ill-advised move in any environment from the bed to the bank account. Perhaps the hardest thing to share with another, no matter how close the relationship, are one's very private and secret dreams and visions. With this placement of Neptune, that revealing of the most protected and vulnerable self is much easier within the partnership. While this blending can, with highly self-indulgent and undisciplined natal personalities, lead to extremes of escapism stimulated by the interaction, much more commonly this placement contributes the delicious mystery suggested by the phrase "behind closed doors." *Pluto's* contribution, if in the composite 12th house, is so speculative and remote that it is almost an arrogation to specify what it might be. Probably the most accurate thing which can be said is that it acts like a subtle spice, not directly detectable, but giving any main component of the partnership added flavor and complexity. Pluto energies have a base-of-the-spine sexual quality and, when they flow together in the 12th house, they may give a mind-boggling (or whatever boggles in a sexual relationship) depth to any sexual content of the partnership. In all honesty, the proper observation here is probably "come back in several centuries and check on what we've learned about this strange, new planet."

ASPECTS IN SYNASTRY

In the simplest terms, the overlays and composites of houses establish the roles in which we cast people: the particular function we perceive them to be "equipped" to play in our lives. Standing by themselves, these casting responses are only a form of categorizing of people with regard to ourselves and our needs. Aspects formed between the planets of two charts or in the composite chart provide the necessary motivating energy to translate this passive casting into an active effort to cause the casting to come to life. Without the aspects to motivate us, we will normally not reach out to the other person to actualize our scenario for a relationship, typically contenting ourselves with abstract conclusions about another person. With the forming of aspects, however, we will try to find a way to make the script generated by our reaction to the other person become a reality.

Since the other person's projected solar chart usually is the basis for our initial casting of that person, the aspects formed between the natal chart of one person and the solar chart of another indicate the catalytic impetus for the natal person to act, to communicate the hoped for scenario to the solar chart person. Conversely, the aspects formed between the natal chart of that person and our projected solar personality determine the other's initial willingness to respond to any such opening. Clearly then the early reactions of a relationship are based, in large measure, on a potentially faulty reading of the inner personality qualities of the individuals, on the often illusory projection of the solar chart. This phenomenon is probably the source of the conventional wisdom that initial attraction between people is only "chemistry" or "physical attraction" and is, therefore, somehow invalid and not to be trusted. This is really a misconception. The projected solar personality is a real and functioning element of everyone's personality because it is the "public" self which is created by the interplay of the ascendant and planetary positions in the natal chart. There is nothing unreal or untrue about the solar chart in the sense that it is a fake or deliberately deceptive projection. We cannot control what we project to others anymore than we can control the color of our eyes or timbre of our voices. The caution then about the solar chart and the initial attraction which it creates is not that it is "false," but only that it often is a *different* self than that which lies concealed in the natal chart, the inner personality which dictates the way a person responds and reacts to life. The solar chart tells us much about how the world reacts to us. The natal chart tells us how we will react to the world.

As the links formed between solar and natal charts suggest the quality and content of *attraction*, the aspects formed between the *two* natal charts indicate the probable harmony or discord which will arise as the individuals come to know each other and their actions and attitudes play off against one another: in short, the *compatibility* of the individuals. If the individuals find themselves sufficiently attracted and compatible and elect to really try to combine their two separate personas into a blended third entity, a *partnership*, the aspects formed in the composite chart tell us how successful this blending is likely to be and what the ingredients of this partnership will produce. It is always well to remind ourselves that these three important qualities in a relationship, *attraction, compatibility,* and *partnership*, have no consistent astrologic relationship to each other. Any one can exist without the other and in any combination. Obviously we can be strongly attracted without being compatible or able to form a partnership (and who hasn't had *that* experience), but we can just as likely be quite compatible without the presence of meaningful attraction ("can't we just be friends?"). Oddly, we can be strongly attracted and be able to establish a functioning partnership, yet there may be deep incompatibilities (the ultimate cause of divorce, perhaps, in lengthy marriages). Perhaps the most frustrating of all, we can both be strongly attracted and very compatible, yet still not seem to be able to bring a working partnership into being. To make the matter even more complicated, the element of attraction may be strongly present in one person, but absent in the other; yet there may be a powerful mutually felt compatibility. (Remember, attraction can be one-sided because of the interplay of solar and natal links, but compatibility is mutually felt because of links between the two natal charts.) This sets up a mismatch of objectives and hopes (i.e., "I like you, but not *that* way.") which is guaranteed to drive everyone up the wall. As pointed out earlier, it is remarkable that we ever get all this untangled and reach any sort of agreement about relationships. We often do, however, because while the two persons may not have the same ends in mind, both manage to get what they want from the relationship and do not mind giving what the other person needs. The objective then in synastric analysis is not to look for exact matches of personality qualities or needs, but rather to weigh whether some sort of a satisfactory "give/get" arrangement is possible without too severe compromises or unwelcome demands. It is this energetic giving and getting which is activated by synastric aspects.

As discussed earlier, aspects are measures of closeness and the resulting synaptic linkage between planets which permits the crackling leap of energy to flow between them. In traditional overlays of two charts, the planetary positions of the two persons are analyzed to see if, when overlaid, they fall within the normal orbs of aspect. To measure attraction, we overlay the solar chart of one person and the natal chart of the second person, telling us *only* what attraction the *natal* person is likely to feel. To measure compatibility, we overlay the two natal charts to test the interplay of natal planets. To measure the probable results of attempting a partnership, we calculate the midpoint positions of the planets in the natal charts and, from those, set up a composite chart. In all of these techniques, the house information stresses role-casting and aspects the flow of energy between the individuals to bring those roles to life. Having done all this, we are in a position to forecast not what *will happen*, but rather what *potentials* exist at each level. There are too many other factors which influence and constrain relationships to believe that any synastric analysis is enough in itself to accurately forecast an "inevitable outcome." Done well and with genuine commitment to thoroughness and compassion, however, a synastric analysis can help the individuals understand what brought them together, what common ground they share, where there may be compromises to be made and how well, over time, they are likely to function in a close and blended bond. After that, the good will, sensitivity and generosity of the individuals will tell the tale... and no set of astrological factors can overcome greedy self-interest, insensitivity and lack of human compassion in making a relationship work.

Synastric Versus Composite Aspects

In a synastric overlay of aspects, we are examining how two different natal elements blend; how the style of one person blends with the needs and qualities of another person. The aspects formed between overlaid charts then tell us much about the "give/get" exchange between people. If one person has a high level of emotional need and is seeking someone who can fulfill that, but encounters another person who is very reserved and unwilling to express their emotions, it indicates a rather poor exchange. Other factors may still bring the two persons together, but this particular element of the relationship of emotional interplay will remain something of an unfulfilled segment. Synastric aspects then give us an indication of what sort of an active bartering of needs and capacities will take place.

Aspects formed by the mid-point composite "planets," however, reveal something rather different. As noted earlier, the composite chart is a graphic method of examining the structural similarity or dissimilarity of the two charts; in a sense, a way to see if the individuals share common qualities in the holistic assemblage of their personalities or if they are put together differently. A composite planet position signifies the *blended* qualities of the individuals within a partnership (e.g., the composite Sun is a statement of what form the combined qualities of integrated self-expression of the two personalities will take if the individuals form a partnership). Aspects formed between composite planets tell us not how one person will or will not fill the needs of another, but rather how the two persons functioning as partners find that their planetary energies work together. For example, we may find that when the two persons unite, the resulting composite style of expression is very stable and conservative, but the emotional blending may be highly charged and volatile (perhaps characterized by a square between the composite Sun and composite Moon). This can set up an element of stress and conflict within the partnership which cause the individuals to behave much more erratically or aggressively *within* the partnership and toward each other than either typically might behave outside the partnership.

Perhaps the best way to keep the distinction clear between synastric aspects and composite aspects is a general rule that (1) synastric aspects indicate how well the individuals can satisfy each other's needs and (2) composite aspects indicate how contact with each other will influence the behavior of the individuals within the partnership. This distinction is, of course, why persons who are highly compatible can, in a united partnership, still make a bloody mess of each other's lives... and never really understand why.

Planetary Aspects To The Ascendant

In synastry, it really is not necessary to distinguish between the impact of planetary aspects made to the ascendant and the general qualities of planets in houses. If the overlay produces close enough contact between any of the house cusps of one chart with the planets of the other, the assumption could be that the planet/house role-casting will be energized and transformed into a drive to actualize the casting decision. In interpreting aspects made by planets to the ascendant one need only look back at the relevant discussion of the effect of planets in houses... and turn up the volume. For ease or reference, the following guidelines can be used to analyze aspects made by planets to the ascendant:

Conjunction	- see "planet in the 1st house"
Sextile	- see "planet in the 3rd or 11th house"
Square	- see "planet in the 4th or 10th house"
Trine	- see "planet in the 5th or 9th house"
Quincunx	- see "planet in the 6th or 8th house"
Opposition	- see "planet in the 7th house"

ASPECTS TO SUN

The Sun is the integrative force in the personality, gathering up one's life experience, filtering it through the particular qualities of the sign and house in which the Sun falls and distributing that experience throughout the chart for interpretation and response. After all this churning around is complete, the Sun again gathers up the product of the other elements in the natal chart, shapes it up into a presentable form and expresses it to the world as a statement of what and who we are. The mechanics of the Sun's function is, of course, strongly dictated by the sign and house in which it falls. The Sun itself is, without these influences, only a giant double convex lens without any particular qualities, colors or area of focus. In combination with these factors, however, the Sun takes on very definable colors and qualities and becomes sharply focused. In synastry then, aspects formed to Sun show how the various natal elements of one chart respond to this great uniting force of the other, how the way in which the Sun person takes in and interprets life experience and re-channels the results of that life experience outward, functions with the natal elements of the particular planet in another person's natal chart which it aspects.

Traditionally, the Sun has been seen as vital to the essential compatibility of individuals and, along with Moon, the most critical determinant in measuring whether we "like" another person. Actually, it probably is more accurate to say that Sun aspects tell us whether we approve of the way in which the Sun person goes about life in a general way; the style, mode of expression and central point of reference in dealing with the world. If the general and overall qualities of the Sun person are harmonious with our own, we are comfortable with them, are not disturbed or disoriented by their reactions to the world and can usually find a wide range of common ground. If that harmony is not present, no matter how much affection, romantic love or sexual yearning we feel, the Sun person will eventually bug us too much to allow a peaceful and pleasing continuing close contact. In the same sense that it is clinically demonstrable that most people choose as mates persons who physically resemble themselves, we ultimately choose to be in relationships with persons who are as much like us in basic personality traits as possible. Because the Sun plays the greatest role in forming the overall personality, aspects to Sun then tell us the quality of basic personality harmony. As fatuous as the query, "What cher sign?" may be, it is not entirely without sense.

Sun Aspects To Moon

Synastric These aspects indicate how the fundamental style and overall personality of the Sun person works with the underlying hopes and needs and emotional qualities of the Moon person. The *conjunction* establishes a bond of shared and identical qualities, with the Moon person finding the basic approach to life of the Sun person highly agreeable and pleasing. The Sun person will come to trust the instincts and unconscious responses of the Moon person, knowing that their normal and comfortable way of dealing with life will be accepted by the Moon person and usually approved of as the "right" way to respond. The *sextile* brings together different but related qualities of self-expression and emotional fulfillment with the result that the persons find within each other nothing especially upsetting or difficult to deal with. The individuals will not always respond the same way to the circumstances which surround them or to each other, but these differences will not be hard to reconcile and will usually add a dimension to the relationship because of what each stimulates in the other. There is a solid and valuable invigorating quality to this aspect which promises the interaction will cause the growth and evolution of the potentials in each of the persons which might not otherwise occur. The *square* between Sun and Moon is perhaps the most stressful and demanding of the aspects. The entire life mode of the Sun person and their interaction with the world seems inappropriate and unfulfilling to the Moon person. The individuals will likely find that even if they are able to satisfy each other at a personal romantic and sexual level, they want such different things from life in general that there is a constant tone of discord and contention. While there may be some excitement which comes from this discordance, over time it is wearing and discouraging to the degree that the individuals will find there are narrow limits to the relationship.

The *trine* creates a tranquil, easygoing harmony between the individuals suggesting an almost unconscious capacity to blend lifestyles and objectives. While the individuals may seek different forms of life satisfaction and superficially may have somewhat different objectives, over time it will become apparent that these needs are only different manifestations of the same basic needs. It is unlikely the individuals will stimulate each other to explore new avenues or develop any latent potentials as a result of the contact between the persons, largely because the personalities do not challenge each other. This has its good and bad sides, offering great stability and peace, but perhaps lacking in vitality and energy. The *quincunx* between these luminaries has a subtle influence which will probably require the individuals to leave a part of their personality outside the relationship to be fulfilled in other ways. As long as the individuals are not troubled by the need to allow a major amount of independence and separate activity, this aspect is no barrier to a good relationship. To make it work, however, requires both a large measure of tolerance toward each other's personal activities and, even more important perhaps, a coming together of two persons who have strong self-images and are not threatened by such an only partial commitment to the relationship. The *opposition* is typically a successful linkage in male/female relationships since it complements the bipolarity of such pairing, especially if the individuals are comfortable and happy with traditional gender roles. It is less successful and can create deep resentments in relationships between the same sex or in nontraditional male/female relationships because it is essentially inimical to androgenous interaction. If the individuals are seeking a completely "peer" relationship in which there is no clear-cut, traditional male/female role assumption and the partners prefer essentially asexual division of responsibilities and attitudes within the partnership, the opposition may make this difficult to achieve. By its nature, the opposition brings into contact counterpoint qualities, the balancing yin yang, "mirror and its reflection," elements of personalities which usually result in a sense of completeness and equilibrium. If, however, the two individuals are so much the same sorts of personalities in terms of basic qualities, the opposition results in competition for dominance and territory and can generate deep enmity.

Composite The composite *conjunction* between Sun and Moon is such a strong bonding element in a partnership that it can allow the relationship to withstand a wide range of assaults and turmoil without collapsing. Even if there are other discords and discontent, the individuals find that their energies blend so well and the frameworks in which they choose to live their lives flow together so easily and naturally that neither is likely to look outside the partnership for satisfaction. The individuals will treat each other with tolerant friendship and patience and usually shrug off the less than satisfactory qualities in each other as "the price one must pay" for a close relationship. Perhaps the only negative of this composite aspect is that it is so comfortable and stable that the individuals may resign themselves to some major dissatisfactions and frustrations in the partnership beyond what might be wise in the long term for the happiness and fulfillment of the individuals. The composite *sextile* allows a very high level of communicative availability between the partners, the result usually being an unusually quality of closeness and understanding of each other. The largest contribution this aspect makes is to prevent misunderstandings and enhance the capacities of the individuals to share their concerns and fears with each other. Given other bonding links, the partnership should result in the individuals becoming more evolved and developed as humans as a result of the interaction. The composite *square* infuses the interaction with both a highly charged energy and the potential for confrontational conflicts. Partnerships characterized by intense, fiery interaction and constant challenging of each other typically have this composite aspect. Whether this is a good or bad thing depends on the natal characteristics of the individuals. Some people thrive on such an intense and vitalized personal environment. Others, of course, find it exhausting and not at all what one seeks a partnership to achieve. In any situation, the electric interplay between the personalities will keep the partnership churning at a very high level of energy and the two individuals will not suffer from indifference or unresponsiveness to each other.

The *trine* between Sun and Moon in a composite chart so softens the interaction between the contact points of the personalities that the two individuals feel no sense of invasion of privacy or restriction of action in each others presence. The partners just go on their way, doing what comes naturally in concert without pulling against each other or stumbling over each other's feet. While this may sometimes result in a partnership much like a team of oxen placidly toiling with their load, it provides a deeply harmonious general environment for the individuals. Hopefully, within this tranquil and pastoral peace, there are other links between the partners which bring some excitement and enlivening tension. With only the trine as a bond, the partners will celebrate their 60th wedding anniversary by going to the same restaurant where they first met... trying to remember what happened in between visits. A composite *quincunx* between the Sun and Moon pits the natural evolving mode of the partnership in expressing itself against a largely discordant way of deriving emotional satisfaction from the pairing. the problem here is that the form in which the partnership perceives and responds to the world is at odds with emotional needs of the partners. For example, the partners may stimulate each other to be very socially and communally active and busily involved in many joint ventures outside the personal confines of the personal relationship, yet the natural form for the partners to feel emotional contentment and security requires a more insular and self-contained life mode. The result is often discontentment and irritation, with the partners easily blaming each other for this failure to adequately fulfill both needs: active participation in the world and personal contentment. Often each complains that the other is not responsive to the personal emotional needs of the partner (i.e. "all you ever think about is your work" or "you never want to do anything!"). This is simply a difficult pairing of personality qualities and requires an extraordinary amount of love and commitment to manage.

The composite *opposition* typically polarizes the behavior of the individuals within the partnership, reinforcing the strongest personality traits in each. This, of course, may or may not have a happy result. At its best, this aspect allows the partners to fully realize themselves, developing their own particular strengths and relying on each other to guard their individual weaknesses. It can, however, just as easily exaggerate weaknesses and vulnerabilities. Tendencies toward dominance or passivity, dictatorial behavior, or abject dependence, self-indulgence, or self-sacrifice all may play off against each other with this aspect. The partners are likely to feel that they are sheltered and protected by the partnership and made less vulnerable to the slings and arrows of the world by it, but whether this generates a powerful and effective tandem or simply causes an ingrown, fearful and restrictive symbiosis depends entirely on the natal qualities of the individuals and other links between them. Whatever the result, this aspect creates a potent link between the individuals which will have the effect of altering their behavior and approach to life if the partnership is pursued.

Sun Aspects to Venus

Synastric Overlay aspects between Sun and Venus commonly occur in romantic relationships, but these aspects can just as easily be a major factor in any close relationship in which a forgiving and accepting kind of response is felt. These aspects bring together the summation of one personality (Sun) and the capacity for giving of oneself in the other (Venus). The flow of energy between the persons when this linkage occurs seems to bring out the most kind, most warm and tolerant qualities in the individuals and allows each to see the beauty which resides in each other which may not be apparent to others. The *conjunction* creates a tendency to idealize each other and to find what most others might consider rather ordinary and mundane qualities filled with extraordinary beauty and worth. The axiom that "beauty is in the eye of the beholder" is exemplified by this overlay aspect and, with the conjunction, the Sun person sees the Venus person as a personification of their paradigmic companion. The Venus person is stimulated to give the best and most gentle of themselves, often finding in themselves warmth and openness not ordinarily drawn out by others. The *sextile* aspect between Sun and Venus seems to be the most effective in opening the doors and overcoming the barriers between individuals in a way which causes each to make themselves freely available to each other. The responses are so uncluttered and without artifice that the individuals find being together entirely natural, requiring no role-playing or careful early maneuvering. With the sextile, there is less of the romantic idealization of each other, but more of the good-natured, pragmatic recognition of mutual worth. The quality of response has a wholesome and unselfish tone, leaving each person with a feeling of pride and comfort with their own motivations and behavior. The overlay *square* is likely to trigger the less attractive qualities of the planets involved. The Sun person will tend to respond in an exaggerated form of whatever the Sun sign suggests (i.e., Aries' self-gratifying impulsiveness, Taurean possessiveness, etc., etc.) in dealing with the Venus person and in expressing themselves. Venus's vulnerability to excessive self-gratification and hedonism may emerge in the responses of the Venus person. The result is an interplay which, while lively and vital, will contain a high quotient of ego gratification. The square reduces the gentling effect of contact between these planets and heightens the tendency to exaggerate the real value of the relationship. Ultimately, the responses of the individuals tend to be too selfish and indulgent to sustain a relationship.

The *trine* draws out what is perhaps the most perfect form of non-sexual, selfless love in the individuals, the best elements of denying self as a way to please and sustain a companion. Of all the aspects, it seems to make it possible for the relationship to endure long periods in which the individuals are content with whatever is possible and not motivated to press for some content or form which may not be possible. In fact, no word better captures the nature of the responses growing from the trine than "contentment"... with each other's appearance, ideas, attitudes and choices and just about anything else. Seen from the outside, this can get a little slurpy, but the individuals are happy and that is what counts. The overlay *quincunx*, while not a strong linkage and one with a very small (1 degree to 2 degree) orb, can give what is typically not primarily a sexual aspect a peculiar spin. Inherent in any response which is based on a perceived beauty and value of another human is the imbedded concept of "price"... to be paid or demanded. The quincunx sometimes makes the individuals unconsciously vulnerable to the idea that part of their interaction implies obligation, the requirement to either extract a tangible result from the contact or to yield to the wants of the other. In male/female relationships, this commonly takes the form of a sexual exchange, not so much based on a strong physical desire, but rather a response to this unconscious obligation. In nonintimate relationships, this quality of obligation may be only a tendency to impose on and make demands or feel unable to say "no" to such demands. The overlay *opposition* is classically the "mating" link, especially in the responses of the Sun person. This aspect is, by its nature, an expression of the male/female polarity and will have a much more profound impact in contacts with the potential for romantic/sexual involvement than in less personal interactions. In less personal and polarized contacts between persons of the same sex or in casual contacts, the result may be more a wariness and that peculiar sensation of disliking a person because they display some of the same flaws present in our own make-up. In romantic/sexual contacts, however, the tendency is to deal with each other as potential partners with all the implications of that word. Certainly, this weighing and measuring begins almost immediately at either a conscious or unconscious level and the future of the relationship will tend to hinge on the availability of the individuals for such a role. Anyone who says, "I knew I was going to marry him/her the first time we met," will likely be experiencing this overlay opposition.

Composite A *conjunction* between the composite Sun and Venus is, because of the limited distance Venus can travel from the Sun in natal charts, a rather commonly occuring aspect (remember, an aspect which is impossible in a natal chart is equally impossible in a composite chart. Venus can only range up to about 48 degrees from Sun). Since all composite aspects indicate a structural similarity within the natal charts, this conjunction simply tells us that the partners share a common Sun/Venus linkage in their natal charts and will, therefore, tend to respond to beauty and joys of life in a similar way. The result then of this composite aspect is that the partners find it easy to combine in their seeking of pleasure and fulfillment through the partnership and find in each other's company an enhancement of this part of their lives. This conjunction is an indication of what may be best described as "companionability;" a quality which will probably be lacking if this conjunction is not present in the composite chart.

No other meaningful aspect can be formed in the composite chart between Sun and Venus. Sometimes, however, in the calculation of planetary midpoints required for a composite chart the raw results produce the astrologically impossible Sun/Venus opposition. Robert Hand, in his definitive book on composites, recommends that when this happens, the *opposite midpoint* be used to eliminate this oddity in the composite process. I find no reason to disagree with this recommendation, however, I would add that when this phenomenon occurs and the raw calculations initially produce a Sun/Venus opposition, the adjusted Sun/Venus "conjunction" then appears to take on a stronger romantic tone in keeping with the traditional interpretation of the Sun/Venus conjunction in synastry.

Sun Aspects To Mars

Synastric Conjunction This can be a highly sexual aspect, or at least one which amplifies the physical attraction between the individuals. In casual contacts or contacts between members of the same sex, the response may simply take the form of recognizing the physical attractiveness and perhaps being motivated to be in the company of such a person for whatever enhancement of one's public image may accrue. In the male/female interaction, however, this generates a strong urge to introduce a "touchy-feely" element into the relationship. The natural inclination is to seek physical contact with each other and, given other links, to quite possibly carry this inclination to a full sexual involvement. The Sun person perceives the Mars person as "definitely my type" and the Mars person senses that their natural communication link with the Sun person is a physical one. The ultimate form of this linkage will be, of course, determined by a number of other factors, but in nearly all instances, strong physicality and a bond of energetic activity will play a role in the relationship. Great for doubles partners, hiking companions and lovers. The *sextile* has some of the same elements as the conjunction, but with a lower quality of urgency and compulsion. The individuals will sense a harmony of motivations and styles in expressing their physical energies and be motivated to seek each other out as partners when the urge strikes to "be physical." The tempo and style of personal energies will blend well and have a high recreational value. The Sun person will enjoy the willingness of the Mars person to adjust themselves to the pace and form of activity which attracts the Sun person. The Mars person will find the Sun person stimulating and capable of arousing them from depressions or lethargy or just simply getting them out of ruts. The *square* brings into contact two quite different and largely inimical forms of energy expression, sometimes with highly abrasive results. This aspect tends to polarize the leader/follower aspect of the interaction, requiring the individuals to take much more exaggerated roles in being the aggressor or the passive recipient than either might normally assume. Under some circumstances, this can be exciting in that it introduces a quality of going to extremes in physical and energy interplay, but in the end it probably is too exhausting and fraught with potential conflict to allow an enduring relationship.

The most attractive quality of the Sun/Mars *trine* is that neither individual is required to alter or repress their normal life pace or tempo within the relationship. The personal inner clocks of the individuals tick along in harmony (if not unison) with the result that the life rhythms and cycles of activity blend very well. The Sun person's basic approach to meeting the demands of the day synchronize with the Mars person's biorhythmic flow and the individuals function just as easily and successfully in tandem as they do separately. While this aspect is unlikely to force either into learning how to function in different and more testing environments, it promises the ability to spend large amounts of time together without using up undue energies in constant and annoying adjustments and repressions of natural life tempos. The *quincunx* between Sun and Mars seems to bring out the most frustrating responses in the individuals. The problem is less a matter of negative reactions to each other than it is a feeling of being out of step and getting in each other's way. The Sun person will have difficulty anticipating and understanding the Mars person's actions and reactions. The whole style of managing situations and events used by the Sun person will seem ill-advised and contrary to the Mars person's natural responses. Ultimately, this inability to get into sync and work well together, to harmonize actions and responses, will cause the individuals to look elsewhere for partners. The exception to this is one of those unusual situations where the individuals so segment and separate the elements of a shared task that their different modes do not interfere with each other. This can work in non-intimate relationships, but hardly seems promising in intimate personal relationships. The *opposition* between Sun and Mars, while potentially confrontational, is more likely to introduce a reciprocal quality to interaction not unlike tossing a frisbee back and forth. The "ping-pong" sort of energy interplay can, at times, make the individuals somewhat competitive and testing, but given other elements of harmonious interaction, it can have the same reciprocal balancing effect in a relationship as the pendulum swing in a clock; a rhythmic shuttle of initiative and rest between the individuals which can give the relationship durability and stability. This effect is most pronounced in male/female relationships and offers the potential for a true peer relationship with neither partner dominating the relationship. The Sun person will see the Mars person as a natural instrument to express their assertive qualities, but the Mars person will typically have no difficulty in responding in kind, with the result that the two persons achieve a highly rewarding ongoing exchange which keeps both alive and invigorated.

Composite The composite *conjunction* of Sun and Mars steps up the voltage of the partnership, making the mutuality of overt expression of the primary themes of relationship easier and more natural. This does not necessarily dictate what those themes may be, but rather gives the central content of the partnership greater potential for full expression. If synastric links suggest a romantic/sexual content, then this conjunction will give vitality and urgency to the fulfillment of that drive. If a less intense and personal interplay is suggested by synastric links such as simple friendship or the coming together for some common task, this aspect invigorates that basic motivation and the partners find contact with each other energizing and productive. This can be a very helpful aspect when the individuals are not natally self-starting personalities. With individuals who are already highly motivated, the coming together is like plugging into an extra power source: potentially explosive and inflammatory. The *sextile* gives the partnership great potential for productiveness and utility. In intimate relationships, the effect is principally noticeable by the absence of conflict and friction: nothing dramatic in its effect, but extremely helpful over the long pull because it lubricates any joint undertaking and allows things to come off smoothly. In less personal partnerships, this supports long and successful mutual undertakings, partners who manage over time to remain friends and coworkers and not fall victim to small annoyances and irritations. The composite *square* between Sun and Mars is a difficult aspect in any partnership because the partners will stimulate each other to counterproductive behavior. The probable cause of this is a below-the-surface irritation and annoyance created by the coming together. Even when the individuals are strongly attracted to each other or drawn by other more harmonious links, they somehow manage to upset each other. Continuing contact is like a barely audible but grating background noise, bearable for a while, but ultimately causing the individuals to strike out in unfocused anger and seemingly unwarranted harshness toward each other or toward the world which they share.

The *trine* between the Sun in one chart and Mars in another is perhaps the ideal link between these two strong and assertive sources. The normally placid and free-flowing trine works its calming effect on the planets, and efforts of the individuals fall neatly into a harmonic pattern which is both pleasing and reassuring to both. The Sun person will find the Mars person's way of dealing with things quite sensible and well-paced, asking nothing of the Sun person which they are unwilling to give and offering only an agreeable additional note in the chord. The Mars person will enjoy the approval of the Sun person and absence of any conflict or criticism in the Sun person's attitude. This often produces a quite clearly sensed physical response, with the Sun person simply enjoying the physical presence and aura of the Mars person. Almost anyone blossoms when admired and the Mars person should show their best and most attractive self, both physically and in a personality sense, under the warm and approving eye of the Sun person. In an active and vital way, this aspect is a major contributor to day-to-day compatibility. The *quincunx* between Sun and Mars in the composite chart is most typically visible in bad timing and mismatched urges, although it can show itself as a divisive and separative influence, causing the partners to minimize the shared ares of their lives. In an otherwise positive and harmonious relationship, it only requires an extra measure of sensitivity to each other's moods and desires. In a partnership with less powerful links (i.e., one based largely on self-oriented objectives such as sex or profit or advantage), the compromises required become, over time, corrosive and resented. If a relationship is punctuated by angry and frustrated outbursts which start, "How come you always...," it is likely that this quincunx is at play. The Sun/Mars *opposition* can have two quite different effects, depending on the individual personalities involved. If the partnership is characterized by one dominant and assertive personality and one rather passive, shelter-seeking one, the individuals can work well enough together without challenging each other over territorial pre-eminence. In this sort of situation, the relationship will have clear-cut leader/follower roles and the partners will be content with these. If, however, the relationship is a more balanced one, this opposition can result in a stalemating kind of confrontational interplay. There will be a constant tone of locking horns over any mutual effort, debates over priorities and directions which most often result in a frustrating kind of brooding paralysis. At best, in a peer relationship, this aspect requires a large measure of patience and willingness to negotiate a balance between the individuals and their personal needs. At worst, it can cause a build up of suppressed anger and frustration which will eventually be expressed violently, typically in the form of a nasty, bitter parting or divorce and occasionally in murder.

Sun Aspects To Uranus

Synastric With this *conjunction* in overlaid charts, the liberating effect of Uranus is typically clearly felt. The Sun person will respond to the Uranus person with unusual openness and without the normal cautiousness which typifies many initial human contacts. In fact, the Sun person may be so candid and to the point that the interaction will have to survive an initial period of "Hey, slow down a bit," response from the Uranus person. Nonetheless, the Uranus person will usually find the Sun person a stimulus to release normally repressed impulses (e.g., best identified by the natal house position of Uranus) and feel a strong link with the Sun person as a person with whom they can really "let go." The *sextile and trine* between Sun and Uranus takes much of the stuffiness and rigidity out of a relationship, allowing the individuals to express enthusiasms and responses without fear of being laughed at or teased. The Sun person, even if normally reticent or reserved, will find themselves babbling on about some interest and the Uranus person usually will enjoy the serendipitous discovery of another human who treats them as a confidante and worthwhile audience. These aspects are a wonderful antidote for the all-too-common loneliness and isolation of modern urban life. The *square* is a volatile overlay aspect between Sun and Uranus. Most often it is the source of arguments and disputes which seem to take on a life of their own and get blown out of proportion. Likely the Sun person will find something about the way the Uranus person goes about things which demands a corrective lecture; this is not one of the more welcome responses in another human with predictable exasperation from the Uranus person. The Uranus person will be pushed to extreme ranges of their natal personality characteristics, responding with anger, hurt feelings, sarcasm or a punch in the nose. In an otherwise harmonious interaction, this may only result in banter and needling, but if there aren't some strong counterbalances in other links between the individuals, the nitpicking and criticizing element of the response will dominate. The *quincunx* seems to create a quality of mystified disapproval between the individuals with each wondering what in the world possesses the other to have such an incomprehensible vision of life. Most often the result is just a nose-in-the-air avoidance of each other, but if the individuals are drawn together by other strong links, there will be a lot of unhappy conversations which begin, "If you would just...." The *opposition* between Sun and Uranus creates an ambivalent response based on superficial conflict of attitudes but an unconscious approval or envy of the other person's ability to act out things which are repressed by the other. At best, the individuals provide a kind of surrogate release for one another, letting each fulfill some difficult to reveal need through the other. At worst, the discomfort of realizing that one has a need which can't be openly expressed (and, as a result, just lies there and bugs you) is projected onto the other person in the form of huffy disapproval. There is nothing quite so annoying as seeing someone else do something which you want to do but are afraid to try.

Composite The composite *conjunction* between Sun and Uranus is a lively one, tending to make the partnership a catalyst for striking out on new avenues of self-expression. The partnership is characterized by an especially free and open bond between the individuals which encourages each to express to the other what particular aspirations they may have. With such freedom, the partnership itself can become a vehicle for the individuals to at least reach out for these goals with the assurance that they have a relationship on which to rely if things go awry. The composite *sextile* brings a quality of upbeat cheeriness to the relationship with each partner stimulating and invigorating the other. Because this aspect makes it possible for the individuals to share and articulate their feelings and responses to the passing days, they will come to rely on each other as safety valves and sounding boards to relieve frustrations and petty angers. Over time, this ease of release of tensions and stresses through sharing can lay a strong foundation of friendship and trust. The Sun/Uranus *square* in the composite chart introduces a quality of tenseness and hair trigger responses to the interaction. Being together seems to heighten the nervous stress in the individuals and while this may release itself in quick, thrusting exchanges, it is hard to settle back and relax into the partnership. This is not an insurmountable obstacle to a lasting interaction, but even with more tranquil links the partners will have to find a lifestyle and pattern of contacts which allows each to have a high level of personal freedom of action and privacy. Without these regular opportunities to get away and rest, the relationship becomes so volatile and charged that the individuals find being together exhausting.

The *trine* is the least unsettling of the composite contacts between Sun and Uranus, allowing the partners to indulge themselves in their own particular forms of individuality of expression without abrading the other. In fact, this aspect tends to bring together individuals who share similar outlets and attitudes because they find it comfortable to be with someone with whom they do not feel odd or out-of-step. Interests or attitudes which might be seen by others as a bit weird or offbeat or eccentric seems quite sensible and normal from within the relationship and the partners find themselves looking out at the world wondering why their shared behavior is met with surprise or uncertainty. Clearly, if "*I* think it's right and *you* think it's right, then it must be right!" The *quincunx*, while not a strong aspect, can require the partners to be particularly tolerant of the whims and passing impulses each experience and want to indulge. Unlike more harmonious aspects, the partners will tend not to share these impulses in a jolly simultaneity but rather find that one is suddenly moved to act, while the other is perfectly content to remain at rest. A fair amount of selflessness and willingness to go along with these whims is required even if the urge is not shared. In the more extreme situations, the partners simply do not have a common ground of unconscious needs and find being carried along with each other's sudden impulses too trying and stressful to appreciate. Given reasonably relaxed and tolerant personalities, this is no great problem, but if the individuals are stolid and deliberate souls, being jerked around by each other can cause a lot of resentment.

The composite *opposition* has both the virtue and risk of linking two versions of the same world view in the individuals. Usually this results in a balancing of attitudes and expressions which brings an equilibrium to the partnership, keeping either partner from swinging too far into either over-optimism or depression. If the individuals, however, are very similar in their personalities and motivations, the effect can be to exaggerate the swing of the pendulum. The partners then can motivate each other to extremes of attitudes and positions, making each more strident and one-sided in their response to life than either would be outside the relationship. Situations where an individual appears to be driven to excesses and extremes by the interaction can have its roots in this interaction. More commonly, however, the effect is simply that the relationship provides a continuing stimulus to expand and realize the potentials within each natal chart.

Sun Aspects to Secondary Planets

Aspects made to Sun by the remaining planets play a limited role in the early stages of a relationship and have their effect in a slow, accumulative way as any interaction evolves. They can serve to reinforce the early responses and reactions between the individuals, adding more complex and interesting harmonies within the relationship, or they can erode away the early enthusiasms as their effect gradually reveals discords below the surface. All these aspects reveal their true meaning as the individuals mesh the components of their personalities and function together. With aspects to these secondary planets, the initial lubricant of aspects made by the major planets may or may not be sufficient to allow this blending of actions of the more subtle secondary aspects. In a very real sense, these aspects to secondary planets by Sun fall into the category of "time will tell" and, because of this, are important in assessing the individuals will respond to each other after the initial rush of a new relationship has passed.

Sun Aspects To Saturn

Synastric The *conjunction* between Sun and Saturn has a curious effect in a relationship. It tends to make the response of the Sun person more serious and intense, with a pervasive quality of "meaningfulness" in the way in which they deal with the Saturn person. It is almost as if there isn't any room for lightness or superficiality in the relationship. The Saturn person will respond to all this within the context of the other, more powerful links. If the initial response is strong, then there will be a reassuring quality to all this seriousness, a conviction that it all just isn't fun and games with no purpose. If, however, the initial interaction is a more casual one, the tone will be a bit glum and unpromising. If the relationship does evolve into a complex interaction, this aspect provides a solid (if less than lighthearted) underpinning which gives durability and stability to the relationship. The *sextile* and *trine* bring a solid sensibleness to the relationship, a practicality and willingness to see in the other person something beyond sexual attraction or romantic fantasy. These aspects often occur where there are differences between individual ages or backgrounds which might otherwise inhibit a good relationship, but are, in this particular instance, overcome because of the rational and useful benefits which can be derived.

The *square* between Sun and Saturn is a very depressive link because it tends to pit two quite discordant qualities of personal structure against each other. The individuals will see each other as rigid and unfeeling in terms of what each considers worthy of caring about and, as a result, will tend to develop a quiet but deep disapproval of each other. The *quincunx* between Sun and Saturn seems only to produce a sense that the individuals want different things from life, an unrelated and somewhat unblendable match-up of lifestyles and goals. This is a minor aspect which is easily offset by other, more harmonious links, but it may inject a small but continuing wedge into a relationship which keeps it from ever achieving complete accord in such areas as which subculture is the most desirable to become a part of or what sort of social attitudes are most "reasonable." Individuals who are generally compatible, but argue over politics or social issues reflect this aspect's effect. The Sun/Saturn *opposition* has a quashing effect, shutting off the natural and comfortable expression of each personality. Not uncommonly, this link so distresses the individuals that they exaggerate the very tendencies which bother each other, almost taunting each other with displays of behavior which are unconsciously calculated to "stick it to" the other person. Also not uncommonly, this produces anger and sarcastic reactions, a less than ideal basis for a continuing relationship.

Composite Aspects from Sun to Saturn in the composite chart have a rather tight focus, the composite houses within which the planets fall being the area of mutual activity primarily influenced by the aspect. The effect of Saturn is to give sharp definition and structural integrity to activities within that house, but with the more harsh aspects, this passes over from a useful quality of clear focus and consistent application to unbending determination and lack of flexibility and adaptability. The *conjunction* introduces a sense of inevitability to the partnership: the conviction that the partnership must survive and be pursued almost without regard for the consequences. The purpose of this dedication is usually indicated by the house in which the conjunction occurs. While this may give a deep sense of purpose to the partnership, it may also narrow the range of relationship and keep it so tightly directed toward some single goal that over time the partnership becomes more of a burden than a pleasure. The most difficult thing about this aspect is the haunting sense that the partnership has some "fated" role to play in the lives of the individuals, but an inability to either define that role or a compulsion to force a definition on it which may neither be achievable or reasonable. Perhaps the best advice with this aspect is to lighten up and let the partnership find its own way without too strong direction. The *sextile* and *trine* are welcome aspects in a composite chart for their stabilizing influence and the strength they add to the foundation of the partnership. They function much like gyroscopes, pulling the relationship back into a balanced relationship with the forces acting on it when those forces want to push the partnership off its course. In general, the houses in which the Sun and Saturn fall in the composite chart will indicate the solid contact points with reality on which the partnership can depend when it experiences storms and turmoil. The *square* suggests a serious confrontation between the partnership's aspirations and the way in which the partners are most likely to seek a secure foundation for themselves. The blending of personalities is severely hampered by a fundamental disagreement on long term goals and rewards achievable through the coming together of the individuals. This is such a restrictive aspect that it is unlikely to even occur in functioning relationships since this disparity is clear even in the earlier stages of the relationship. If romantic and sexual drives initially overwhelm this very basic discordancy and the individuals do try to form a partnership, it is very probably going to founder on this problem. The two people simply define the way in which they want to build a life mode so differently that it is very unlikely that the two can ever reach any sort of compromise. However attractive another person may be, if they impose upon us a lifestyle and plan for the future which irritates us or makes us insecure, we will ultimatlely back away from the relationship.

The *quincunx* has an "either/or" influence, typically requiring the individuals to make hard choices within the relationship for it to function well. The houses involved will suggest the areas of the partnership's function which force this ambivalence, the difficult mutual decision which the partners must make between two partnership goals or contents. While not usually an unmanageable aspect in a relationship, the finding of the unavoidable compromise indicated by this aspect does require more than normal compassion and goodwill between the partners. Without this capacity to accept the limitations imposed by this aspect, the partners will ultimately tend to blame each other for whatever had to be sacrificed to preserve the relationship. The *opposition* can produce a slow-building but very corrosive problem in the partnership. While it may appear initially to the individuals that they seek the same things from the relationship, there may be a slowly developing sense that the *way* in which that goal is to be achieved conflicts. One partner is likely to look to the partnership itself as the source from which that fulfillment is derived while the other views the partnership as a mechanism to draw that fulfillment from the outer world. For example, if the opposition occurs in the 4th and 10th houses, one partner may look to the home and family and the tight circle of contacts that involves as the primary source of satisfaction to be obtained from the partnership, while the other may view the partnership as a foundation on which they can establish themselves in the world at large and draw from that much more populace and generalized arena the basic value of the partnership. The obvious separative effect of this opposition can then, over time, draw the individuals apart as each is increasingly required to find their life satisfactions alone rather than as a shared experience.

Sun Aspects To Jupiter

Synastric The amplifying and enlarging influence of Jupiter is most evident in an overlay which produces a *conjunction* between Sun and Jupiter. The Sun person becomes more voluable and generous under this influence, reaching into the most agreeable and warm corners to offer to the Jupiter person the best. The Jupiter person finds a glow of friendship and openness in the Sun person and usually seeks out this sunny spot in which to bask. There is a quality of eagerness and anticipation which grows from this overlay and, if there are other links to draw the individuals together, the prospect of spending time together is positive and happy. The Sun person may tend to overdo a bit and the Jupiter person's self-image may enlarge somewhat beyond modest limits, but it does no great harm for either and the warmth is welcome in a generally cold and indifferent world. The *sextile* and *trine* contribute the same sort of pleasure, but in more low-key and balanced form. With these aspects, the individuals are more likely to make an equal contribution of generosity and kindness with the result that neither finds themselves consistently the giver. The feeling is one of easy companionability, an excellent environment to explore whatever else may be percolating in the interaction. The most pleasant element of these aspects is the near absence of concern the individuals have for keeping score. Each is willing to do their part and more in sustaining any relationship, regardless of form or intimacy, with the result that both feel fortunate to know each other.

The *square* between Sun and Jupiter heightens the self-indulgent and over-reactive side of this aspect. The Sun person may not be able to restrain a tendency to exaggerate or overstate responses and the Jupiter person may be tempted to capitalize on this overreaction as a means of meeting some rather selfish ends. While not an entirely negative aspect, it does have the potential for inflating the importance and relevance of the interaction out of proportion and amplifying the self-gratifying drives. The *quincunx's* influence is primarily to unbalance the give/get element in the relationship, usually placing the Sun person in jeopardy of being inequitably used by the Jupiter person. While this is largely an unconscious response by the Jupiter person and does not necessarily suggest any deliberately callous or selfish motive, nonetheless, the interaction between the individuals will tend to fall into this pattern. It is a rare human who, when confronted with another person who seems congenitally incapable of resisting a wide range of demands, is able to remain entirely altruistic and unselfish. If you find one who can, hang onto them. The *opposition* between Sun and Jupiter in an overlay has great potential for one of those delightfully successful exchanges of complimentary qualities. Typically, the individuals find that they receive the sort of support and encouragement they most need and are, happily, able to offer the same kind of feedback. In the good sense of the word, this is a "bartering" aspect, an invitation often implicitly stated as "you scratch my back (or whatever) and I'll scratch yours." The only downside of this aspect is that, like a very, very good bargain, it can tempt individuals to make a commitment beyond their real needs. Sometimes it is hard to keep the overall value of a relationship in perspective when it seems to be so easy and comfortable and supportive. As nice as that may be, it takes more than this "old sweater" quality to warrant a full commitment... but, of course, it will do nicely until the "real thing" comes along.

Composite The Sun/Jupiter *conjunction* in the composite chart will give an extra punch to joint activity associated with the house(s) in which it falls. This conjunction typically indicates the particular element of the partnership which will grow over time into the central focus of the relationship and the most positive form of impact the individuals will have on each other. Usually it is via the window of opportunity suggested by Sun/Jupiter house in the chart that the partnership can achieve its greatest fulfillment and success. These may be strictly personal "successes" of the sort that comes from a relationship which never fails to provide companionship and warmth or, in the more worldly houses, may suggest the way in which the partners can work together to achieve more material forms of fulfillment. The *sextile* and *trine* are guarantors of a real friendship augmenting whatever else may evolve within the relationship. These aspects are welcome in any partnership because they provide a durable bond of harmony and compatibility which will remain even if more intense romantic/sexual drives slowly drift into familiarity and repetition. In less personal relationships, they provide a link of integrity and unselfishness which cannot help but enhance any joint effort. The *square* has an exaggerated effect almost certain to result in some form of overreaction or extreme behavior triggered by the interaction. This may be as harmless as overspending on gifts or exchanging vows of never-ending dedication after the first date. The effect, however, can be more damaging if it takes the form of expecting too much of each other and the relationship. The houses in which the Sun and Jupiter fall will suggest the form of the excessive expectations which can grow under this composite aspect... and the probable area of disappointment and unwarranted expectations. The overall effect is usually for the individuals to overcommit to the relationship without looking carefully at its real value and potentials.

The *quincunx* suggests a mismatch of expectations in the partner's perception of the purpose of the relationship. It is probable that each individual expects certain things from the partnership which will not be forthcoming from the other and this unrealized hope can create an atmosphere of either guilt over "failing" the other person or a resentment of the impossible demands made by one member on the other. Despite being only a minor aspect, this link can introduce a hard-to-solve problem into a relationship since the very expectations which played a role in initiating the relationship become the source of the disillusionment. Unless the partners show almost superhuman rationality and adjust those expectations, this aspect will be like a speck of dust under the eyelid, slowly irritating the individuals into red-eyed anger with each other. The *opposition* can have a positive influence in the partnership provided the individuals are dealing with each other essentially as peers and can settle into a relatively balanced division of responsibilities and activity. In this situation, the effect is to enhance the ability of the partners to support each other in the tasks they must individually undertake, to be the faithful bulwark which such a trusted ally is needed. If, however, the partnership is not a reasonably balanced one, the effect can be to exaggerate this imbalance and push the individuals to even more extreme expressions of the imbalance. The real danger with this aspect is a form of negative reinforcement which the individuals unconsciously offer each other, seemingly encouraging bad judgments, risk-taking or even self-destructive behavior. The opposition will not make good people bad or, by itself, trigger stupid behavior. If, however, those potentials already exist in the partners (particularly if there are harsh aspects between Uranus or Neptune and the inner planets in the natal charts), the partners may make these potentials for negative behavior more likely to be expressed. When people seem to be "bad influences" on each other, this aspect is common cause.

Sun Aspects To Mercury

Synastric Sun/Mercury aspects initially play a lesser role in the way in which people respond to each other, largely establishing a sense that the behavior of the other person is or is not comprehensible and rational. The *conjunction* formed by an overlay of charts will create a response in the Sun person that the Mercury probably thinks clearly and sensibly and goes about their life in a rational way. The Mercury person will feel comfortable with the Sun person's style of expression and general perspective in life. The *sextile* and *trine* increases the Sun person's conviction that they will be understood if they attempt to communicate their ideas and attitudes and that the Mercury person will generally agree with those ideas. The Mercury person will find the Sun person to be someone with whom daily routines can be easily shared without having to make major adjustments in the Mercury person's normal approach to those tasks. The overlay *square* tends to produce argumentativeness and friction over what should be inconsequential issues. The Sun person will respond to the Mercury person as "wrong-headed" and lacking in common sense, while the Mercury person will probably see the Sun person as rigid and intolerant in their thinking. The *quincunx* leaves both persons feeling that there probably isn't much in the way of common ground in world view or approach to life and, even if the individuals are drawn together by other links, each will continue to wonder if any sort of meeting of the minds is possible. The *opposition* may heighten the tendency between the individuals to challenge each other intellectually or get into occasionally lively discourses on matters which involve the relationship, but usually this adds only an increased capacity to communicate and a strong verbal link between the individuals. The Sun person will typically fall into the role of defining the problem and laying out the "right" solution, with the Mercury person playing Devil's Advocate. Most of the time, this is a healthy quality in any interaction, reducing the opportunity for misunderstandings... assuming neither has a proclivity for throwing things.

Composite The only significant aspect which can be formed between Sun and Mercury in the composite chart is a *conjunction* and it is so common that, in relationships which have reached a stage in which a true partnership is being considered, this aspect is more notable by its absence than its presence. As with Sun/Venus composite conjunctions, if the initial calculation produces an "impossible" opposition which is adjusted to a conjunction in the composite chart, this aspect takes on a more male/female polarity. The normal conjunction only enhances the capacity of the partners to communicate in the way that like-thinking people can usually manage. With the above "adjusted" conjunction, the communication has a more complementary quality with the partners using each other as counterpointing backboards off which ideas can be bounced and responses returned. In many ways, this is true "conversation" since each is responding to the other's gambits rather than the regretfully common situation where people simply take turns talking and close their ears when it is not their turn.

Sun Aspects to Neptune

Synastric A Sun/Neptune *conjunction* seems to put a rosy glow around any response, causing the Sun person to see the Neptune person through the sort of diffused (and potentially distorting) light used in photography to hide the flaws of a subject. The influence with this aspect is not inherently worrisome since it helps to reduce unnecessary criticality and to have the partners deal with each other in terms of the best qualities of each other's personality, but there is always the risk of a misjudgment of character or the ignoring of a significant quality bearing on the relationship. With this aspect, the Neptune person will come to realize they are not being dealt with entirely realistically. Whether this becomes a device for the Neptune person to manipulate the Sun person or only a welcome relief from having to always be at one's best depends entirely on the natal characteristics and other linkages involved. The *sextile* and *trine* have a very subtle effect, softening the interaction between the individuals and causing the Sun person to be more forgiving and tolerant in dealing with the Neptune person. The Neptune person will usually appreciate this undertone of noncriticality and feel more at ease in exploring other potentials of the relationship. The *square* creates an unconscious feeling of distrust and uncertainty in the Sun person's response, a persisting feeling that, somehow, the Neptune person will not play it straight in the relationship. The Neptune person, while not consciously aware of any negative urges, still may unknowingly mislead the Sun person about their intent. If there is any tendency in the Neptune person for ego-inflating game playing and self-indulgent flirtation, this square will tend to bring that quality to the fore. The *quincunx's* influence is so nebulous and deep in the unconscious that it, at worst, it probably only adds a small measure of confusion and poor communication to the interaction. The *opposition* between Sun and Neptune is, perhaps, the most evident of the aspects, causing the Sun person to unconsciously develop over-romanticized attitudes toward the Neptune person. The Neptune person is drawn to the fantasy-fulfilling romantic qualities of the Sun person, the paradigm realization which might be achieved through a relationship with that person. The real risk with this aspect is that both persons are responding not to the reality of the other, but rather to some stored image of an idealized "perfect" person. Alone this aspect causes no great difficulty, but in the context of a more fully operative romantic/sexual interaction, it sprinkles the whole relationship with fairy dust... and can leave both lost in the woods wondering what mind-drugging magic got them there.

   Composite As with all planets in a composite chart, aspects influence the ability to achieve some workable agreement on a partnership's function within the areas indicated by the house in which the composite planet falls. In appraising Neptune aspects in the composite, one must first look to Neptune's composite house as the area of partnership activity which each of the partners unconsciously believes will be fantasy/dream fulfilling if the partnership is pursued. The composite Neptune house suggests what part of each individual's life will be open to wish and hope realization through the relationship. Within the context of that house, a Sun/Neptune *conjunction* causes the individuals to behave toward each other with heightened romanticism and almost superhuman tolerance. As far as the partners are concerned, the simple existence of the relationship far outweighs in value any disappointing failures in the performance of the individuals because of the house-related fantasy realization it provides. Obviously, the significance of this aspect has to been seen in the total context of the partnership. In an honest and compatible relationship, it is a soothing balm in times of temporary turbulence. In more self-gratifying and narrow interactions, it clouds the judgment and allows the partners to rationalize away the flaws in the relationship in the interests of purely self goals. The *sextile* and *trine* function like ballbearings in the relationship, making what otherwise might be the little irritations of sharing space and life seem much easier and less annoying. The partners find it easy to forgive each other's little omissions because, compared to what life would be without the partnership, these minor events seem unimportant. The *square* probably causes the most grief when it occurs in the composite chart, principally because the purpose each individual sees the partnership playing in their lives is at odds. The individuals simply see the objective of the partnership in different terms and march to different drummers. The houses in which Sun and Neptune fall with this square give some clues to this divergence, but likely this square sets up a very difficult to resolve misunderstanding between the individuals about the basic nature and purpose of the relationship, one which will likely haunt it throughout its duration. The *quincunx* here is not especially significant in a partnership, perhaps only adding to normal need in any relationship for the individuals to modify and reduce their expectations to make the partnership work. It can occasionally cause the unpleasant result of persons finding that forming the partnership cost each of them too much sacrifice of their dreams and hopes, a slow-evolving but corrosive quality in a relationship. The *opposition* has an influence similar to the conjunction and, more often than not, actually helps the partnership achieve a higher level of satisfaction because of its complementary quality. It keeps the individuals from too much competitiveness and struggling for the same air space. This aspect works best in a strongly polarized or male/female relationship and will cause difficulty and confusion only in those partnerships where there is a struggle for dominance and control of what goals the partnership should have.

Sun Aspects To Pluto

Synastry Aspects in an overlay of charts which bring Sun and Pluto into contact link the formative influence of Sun with the entropic effect of Pluto, the personality-building force with the inevitable breakdown of any complex structure as a prerequisite for new growth. There is a natural enmity between these forces, an instinct for self-preservation which usually shows itself as either a determined warding off of the influence or, in more combative personalities, a "call to arms" kind of aggressive confrontation. As a result, the *conjunction* and *opposition* usually result in a hostility between the individuals. Typically, this simply results in the people avoiding each other, but if there is a strong romantic/physical attraction, the response may be much more volatile. It may make good theatre to have a fiery contest arise between the main actors in a romance, à la *The Taming Of The Shrew*, but in real life it is painful and dangerous. With either the conjunction or opposition, the Sun person will see the Pluto person as a threat to their basic identity and someone who is moved to control and dominate them. The Pluto person will often be surprised at the strength of the Sun person's enmity which, as far as the Pluto person can see, is unwarranted by any action on their part. In the face of this seemingly unjustified hostility, the Pluto person will strike back, sensing the potential vulnerability of the Sun person and the self-doubt which the Pluto person causes in them. If violence and anger is mixed with sexual greed, the results can be rather ugly. The *sextile* and *trine* are much more salutary overlays, allowing the individuals to respond to each other as possible rejuvenating influences in their lives. The Sun person may see the Pluto person as a catalyst for some change they may wish to make in their life and the Pluto person will easily accept this role as natural and worthwhile. The *square* may actually cause an entropic breakdown in the individuals if they persist in being around each other. The Sun person may undergo some rather negative life changes catalyzed by the Pluto person's influence, and the Pluto person may become obsessed with gaining control over the Sun person for some deep, unconscious need. Normally, the early hostility will prevent this from happening, but with strong romantic or sexual links, the results can be very damaging, breaking long followed patterns of behavior and bringing about major upheavals in personal lives. The *quincunx* is so minor an influence that it will probably not be noticed. As part of a complex and strong group of linkages, it probably only slightly increases the possibility of the Pluto person dominating and controlling the relationship in a deeply unconscious way.

Composite In general, aspects between Sun and Pluto indicate how revolutionary and life-altering the partnership may be for the individuals with the house(s) involved suggesting in what area of activity these upheavals may occur. The *conjunction* fairly clearly indicates that one of the purposes of the partnership is to bring about some major changes in the lives of the individuals with the relationship itself as the catalyst. The conjunction indicates that these changes will be "revolutionary" rather than simply "evolutionary" and may create some turbulent times for the partners. The *sextile* and *trine* indicate the life-altering effect of the partnership will take more stable and gradual form, but will nonetheless result in the individuals making significant changes in their life patterns as a result of the relationship. The *square* will make it difficult and confrontational for the partners to make such changes and create a rather hostile and angry form of dealing with changes required by the partnership. The *quincunx* will tend to place one person in a position of dominance, forcing the other to conform to changes within the partnership which they might not otherwise choose to make. The *opposition* will be visible as an influence largely by the recurring stalemates and paralyzing disagreements it can cause within the relationship. The partners are impelled by the relationship to make some revolutionary changes in their lives, but seem to be eternally polarized in what form those changes should take. In the end, the partners will feel trapped and limited by the partnership and often strike out at each other in frustration and anger.

ASPECTS TO MOON

The Moon, as with all the major components of the natal chart, has many functions ranging from establishing the intuitive qualities of the personality to defining those life ingredients which bring us contentment and peace. In synastry, the Moon's principal role is, in a broad sense, that particular feeling we have for others which operates outside logic or practicality. In its purest form, it is like the unqualified and all-forgiving love of a parent for a child, with all the blindness to flaws and failures and bottomless willingness to continue to support and believe in the child regardless of what is returned to the parent in the form of gratitude or appreciation. The dominant theme in Moon-based responses is that they come without a price tag. They are not rooted in hope for some fulfilling return to be derived from the relationship as a result of any contribution we make. Moon responses flow out freely and without reservation, seemingly independent of probable result or value to be derived. Because of this, these responses are sometimes so nondiscriminatory that they become like the blindness the mother of a delinquent child has to the child's awful behavior. When we talk about being "moved," of having our emotions aroused to some level which impels us to cry, laugh, feel fear or unaccountable glee or depression and to cling to obviously unsound attitudes and appraisals despite the realities which exist, we are talking about Moon responses. In synastry, these entirely irrational but deeply felt reactions to other humans derive from Moon linkages. In themselves, these links contain no element of romance or sex or any other component of a male/female interaction. They are as asexual as our affection for a pet or a grandparent or a favorite piece of music, and, in the same sense, as selfless and uncritical. Precisely because of this quality, they play an important role in human interactions since they provide the impetus to kindness, generosity, tolerance, loyalty and all the other qualities which makes us secure and grateful in a relationship.

Moon Aspects To Venus

Synastric Moon/Venus overlays which produce aspects bring together the two least assertive and demanding qualities in the personalities, with the result that they play a rather passive role in relationships. Despite the importance of both of these planets in a relationship, in aspect, they have a surprisingly modest impact much like adding chocolate syrup to ice cream; the combination is delightful and enhancing, but doesn't change the essential character of either component. The *conjunction* will create in the Moon person a particular strong willingness to express feelings of kindness and generosity in a form which will reinforce the Venus person's sense of their own value and worthiness. The responses will be aimed not at flattering, but rather to openly recognize the best qualities in the Venus person and ignore those less perfect. The Venus person will usually respond with appreciation and warmth, valuing the Moon person as a forgiving friend and someone with whom an enduring bond of affection can be achieved. The *sextile* and *trine* create such a gentle and undemanding harmonic between the individuals that neither are aware of any effect except that they get along well. This amiable interplay is rooted in a shared response to those things which bring a feeling of beauty and emotional fulfillment and make us happy. The sextile produces kind of matter-of-fact good natured responses often filled with humor or gentle needling. The trine's is more clearly emotionally based and is typically expressed with a greater emphasis on loving and tender exchanges. Either aspect will pour oil on just about any kind of troubled water. This *square* arouses the emotions in both individuals, but the Moon person is the one likely to experience hurt feelings from unintentional and well-meaning acts by the Venus person. The Venus person will not find it easy to understand the emotional needs of the Moon person and, while motivated to try to meet them, will often become frustrated by this consistent pattern of unconscious missteps and errors in coping with the feelings of the Moon person. The *quincunx* provides little in the way of common responses to the joys of life, with the Moon person unable to grasp why the Venus person finds such pleasure and beauty in such odd things. The Venus person will tend to interpret this absence of common emotional responses as evidence of the Moon person's lack of sensitivity, a rather self-serving conclusion since the problem is only that the individuals are *different*, rather than either being intrinsically insensitive. The *opposition* between these rather passive personality elements loses some of its often vitalizing quality, giving a somewhat serious tone to the responses. The Moon person will feel a sense of attunement with the Venus person, but it will have such a familiar coloring that it lacks any invigorating effect. The Venus person will not disagree or object to the Moon person's emotional reactions, but the relationship will have a low intensity "old shoes" quality. With livelier links elsewhere, this is a stabilizing influence, but it does little to enhance the emotional fulfillment of either person.

Composite Aspects in the composite chart between Moon and Venus have the same tranquil easiness as the synastric aspects, with the result that they seem to play a less apparent role in relationships than would be expected. The *conjunction* does seem to enlarge the capacity of the partners to share emotional experiences and the house in which this aspect occurs normally suggests the kind of activity within which the partnership finds its most full emotional development. Certainly, the relationship will be characterized by an unusually high degree of concern for the feelings and pleasures of the partners and an ability to compromise comfortably in achieving these. Over time, even the most compatible persons will develop interests which may not necessarily be shared by the partner, but with this conjunction, the individuals find ways to accommodate each other's tastes and preferences without any feeling of resentment or scorekeeping. The *sextile* and *trine* actually seem more invigorating for the partnership, with the individuals opening doors for one another into new areas of enjoyment. The houses involved often suggest how this will occur as the partnership evolves and the basis of what really is best defined as loving friendship will blossom. The *square* creates a high level of emotionality and a strong need for the partners to express these feelings within the relationship. It may cause a measure of excess and extreme in these expressions, but if you can tolerate a large bill from the florist or exponentially increasing game of who can give who the fanciest and most expensive present, it does no great damage. Sometimes the other side of this aspect shows itself, with a soap opera script of recurring emotional scenes complete with weeping, and hand-wringing... but teary making-up and resolves to "never let this happen again." All depends on whether or not one enjoys this extra dash of melodrama if this is a plus or minus in a partnership. The *quincunx* suggests a lack of emotional bonding in the relationship and a rather abrasive pattern of having to give in to one another over some strongly felt issues. The probable result is a slow growing feeling that, whatever else the partnership may provide, it is not a source of contentment and companionship. Obviously, this bodes ill for an intimate relationship since it forces the partners to look elsewhere to fill a fundamental need which each rightly feels should be filled from the partnership itself. The composite *opposition* is a surprisingly useful aspect in the chart, allowing the partners to play very fulfilling roles for each other. The effect is much like those happy combinations of hot dogs and mustard or pizza and pepperoni, with the sum being greater than the parts. Whatever each individual lacks or finds difficult to express emotionally, the partner compensates for and together they manage to get more pleasure and joy out of life in tandem than either could alone.

Moon Aspects To Mars

A reasonable argument can be made that aspects between Moon and Mars have a greater impact on human interaction than any other group of aspects. We begin with the premise that people enter into a relationship as a way to fill some personal need, to fulfill some want or hope, and the root of such needs and hopes are principally in the Moon placement in the natal chart. Then the powerful aggressive nature of Mars, with its energy directed to reaching out and taking from the world what is desired, cannot help but give great urgency and depth to the interaction when Moon and Mars are in aspect. This is particularly true when a male/female romantic relationship is involved because these aspects link forgiving and supportive elements of a personality with the drive for mastery and self-gratification... qualities which are present in the charts of both men and women in fundamentally equal measure despite a cultural inclination to believe otherwise.

Synastric The usually strong and influential *conjunction* loses some of its normal punch in this overlay aspect, principally because the considerable emotional energy which it generates is unchanneled and tends to use itself up without purpose. The result is like a great pot of steaming water without a device to capture and direct all this potential energy toward some objective. The Moon person will feel a strong emotional response to the Mars person, but find difficulty in knowing how and with what purpose it is best expressed. The Mars person will tend to take any initiative in the relationship, but often is so dominant and aggressive that the Moon person is discomforted. The *sextile* and *trine* between Moon and Mars in the overlay work much more successfully together, giving each individual a way to express their responses without conflicting with the other. The Moon person will sense the needs of the Mars person and find ways to respond to those needs with generosity and compassion. The Mars person will see the Moon person as a natural objective toward which all the energy of the planet can be directed and the release of emotional pressures which are created can be lavished. Both persons will find the interaction a context in which those drives normally constrained by self-protectiveness or fear of ridicule or rejection can be freely expressed, with the result that a powerful emotional bond can develop. The *square* will tend to influence the less generous and compassionate side of the emotions aroused, making the self-gratifying and indulgent contents of the relationship come to the fore. The Moon person will tend to use the Mars person as an emotional dumping ground for anxieties, complaints and frustrated hopes, seeing the Mars person as a device to relieve these depressions and disappointments. The Mars person's least attractive tendencies to try to control and manipulate the Moon person will reveal themselves, resulting in a pattern of jerking the Moon person around the emotional spectrum largely for the ego-fulfillment of the Mars person. This overlay aspect brings a great deal of heat to a relationship, but most of it is self-oriented. The *quincunx* brings two such inimical qualities into contact that the effect is like matter and anti-matter meeting, repulsion being the most likely result, but explosive self-immolation always is possible. The individuals demand such unwanted responses from one another that the principal product is anger and resentment. The *opposition* brings a crackling, confrontational quality to the responses, the sort of interplay which prompts the observation that the line between love and hate is a thin one. This is not necessarily a negative response, only one which stimulates the individuals to be particularly aggressive and demanding in what they ask of each other. The Moon person will often be so emotionally overwhelming in dealing with the Mars person that the relationship seems constantly blanketed by an overheated force field allowing no let-up or relaxation. The Mars person's demands on the relationship can become so forceful that they contain an element of threat or, at least, the potential that if they are not fulfilled, the Mars person will react with explosive frustration. Much depends here on the natal personality qualities of the individuals. Whatever the characteristics of the signs in which these planets fall in the natal charts will be exaggerated by this opposition and the individuals will be required to cope with these powerful expressions.

Composite As with all factors in the composite chart, the structural similarity in the form and depth of emotional energy which exists in the two individual natal charts is revealed by composite aspects formed by Moon and Mars. Particularly with such potentially powerful aspects as can be formed by Moon and Mars, it is important to remember that aspects in the composite chart reveal how well the natural way in which the individuals express their various personality qualities blend in contacts between the individuals. The composite *conjunction* indicates a basic similarity in emotional energy expression which allows the individuals to pour out their feelings for each other with an absolute assurance that the way in which these emotions are communicated will be understood and accepted. The result of this aspect is typically a feedback kind of amplification of emotions with responses of one individual being brought up the scale of intensity by the expressions of the other. The partnership then is usually marked by a high level of free-flowing emotional interplay and a strong sense of fulfillment in this part of the partnership. The *sextile* and *trine* are a more measured but still warm and easy harmonizing of emotional expression between the individuals. If the partnership is a complex romantic/sexual one, these aspects make both the timing and character of intimacy work very well and the partners will rarely do things which disturb, embarrass or annoy the other in pursuing emotional fulfillment. In a less complex interaction, at the very least, the partners will find that they respond to events around them in a similar way emotionally, feeling a comparable joy or anger as a result of such experiences. This sort of harmony makes any mutual activity much freer and open and contributes to an underlying harmony in any endeavor. The *square* here is quite difficult for the partners because they tend to respond so differently to shared experiences and feelings. It is hard to sustain a partnership when individuals find that they constantly "feel" differently about things. The result of this aspect is, indirectly, an increasing level of irritation and annoyance and produces responses such as, "Not now! I have a headache," or "Oh, stop! I'm trying to watch the ball game." In the end, the emotional energy of the individuals is so discordant that anger and bitterness become a constant undertone in the relationship. The *quincunx* often will set the stage for the emotional dominance of one partner over the other, a recurring confrontation in emotional needs which rarely allows for a happy compromise, but rather requires one partner to lay aside their needs to fulfill the needs of the other. In a balanced relationship, this may only take the form of "taking turns" with each partner alternately yielding to the other, but with some overall equitable result. More commonly, however, one partner is sufficiently dominant and forceful in demanding that "we do it my way" that the long-term result is only one of the partners deriving a sense of emotional fulfillment from the relationship. The *opposition* always links the mirror-image expressions of the same personality quality, tending to polarize and exaggerate whatever that potential may be. With Moon and Mars, the composite opposition links the passivity and yielding quality of Moon with the demanding, aggressive nature of Mars and typically results in raising the level of intensity in the expression of both these qualities: a tendency to go to extremes in emotional interplay. With normal, relatively stable personalities, this only creates particularly passionate exchanges. With less stable people, however, the effect the partners have on each other will drag out of dark corners any repressed (and, therefore, probably not entirely healthy) urges and turn them loose within the relationship. Appraising the result of this aspect then requires a careful appraisal of the natal charts with particular concern for any harsh aspects to Moon or Mars which may occur in those natal charts. In all Moon/Mars aspects, we are seeing the overt expression of emotions (which is what the word "passion" means) and, with the opposition, this translation of emotions into action reaches its most intense level.

Moon Aspects To Uranus

Perhaps the greatest barrier to human interaction is the fear of openly expressing one's feeling and emotional responses to another, particularly if those feelings are being energized by that particular person. Obviously, such openness invites some potentially very crushing reactions from the other person such as rejection, amusement or ridicule. If we could bottle and market the emotional energy which goes into "saving face" and protecting oneself against rejection in the normal intercourse between humans, there would be no need to worry about a fuel shortage. Aspects between Moon and Uranus are, fortunately, powerful unconscious sources of motivation to set aside this self-protective-ness and to "lay it on the line." Without these aspects, most relationships would take much longer to get past the fencing and probing stage and onto more substantive ground.

Synastric With an overlay *conjunction*, the Moon person will feel a surge of emotional response to the Uranus person which rarely can be repressed or left unrevealed. Even if the Moon person is not capable of directly expressing this feeling, their actions will reflect this percolation of emotions and be detected by the Uranus person as a kind of invitation to respond. The Uranus person may seem to be the one who takes the initiative in such a situation and, in fact, may make the first overt effort, but actually they are only responding to the subtle signals projected by the Moon person. What form this interchange takes and where it leads depends entirely on the overall links between the individuals, but they will not pass in the night without taking notice of each other. The *sextile* and *trine* in the overlay seem to ease the fears of the individuals in reaching out to each other and make the open expression of response less frightening. The Moon person will not feel the typical concern over allowing another person to penetrate their protective shields and often find themselves rattling off their life story to the Uranus person. The Uranus person will respond to the Moon person with an unusual degree of interest and curiosity, feeling an impulse to get to know the Moon person and find out more about what makes them tick. The *square* introduces a more compulsive quality to the responses of the individuals and a tendency to overreact. The Moon person will be prone to sudden and impulsive emotional acts which root in their own frustrations or repressed emotional needs. This may take almost any form, but the likely quality of these actions will be indicated by the natal chart of the Moon person and the aspects formed to the natal Moon by the outer planets. The Uranus person will seemingly be compelled to try to trigger these responses in the Moon person, sensing the potential of these unexpressed emotional needs and unconsciously behaving in a way to encourage them. The result of this overlay square is usually an ambivalent stimulus/conflict interaction that makes the responses and behavior of the individuals unpredictable and often unstable. The *quincunx,* while minor in effect, can trigger some unconscious fears in the Moon person and cause them to respond to the Uranus person as something of a threat. The Uranus person, sensing this, may well take a devilish pleasure in worrying the Moon person and without really consciously meaning to do so, use this reaction for a kind of ego-satisfying game. The *opposition* between Moon and Uranus seems to have the effect of releasing some of the most deeply repressed (and often rather dark) impulses in the individuals. Those secret emotional corners everyone possesses are tapped by this opposition and the Moon person will feel the impact of the Uranus person in that form. The Uranus person will sense this curious response in the Moon person and be motivated to probe for these dark corners. What the result of all this will be is, of course, a matter of the natal potentials of the individuals and the other links involved; but with this synastric opposition, some atypical behavior will tend to emerge with the Moon person providing the scenario and the Uranus person the initiative and direction.

Composite As with all composite aspects, the impact of a Moon/Uranus *conjunction* does not reveal itself until the individuals have decided, at some level, to experiment with the relationship; that is, it does not create "attraction" per se, but when that initial attraction does exist and brings the individuals into contact, this conjunction can have an extraordinary effect in brushing aside barriers to opening up to each other. The emotional exchange between the individuals rushes almost too rapidly up the scale and, before either individual fully grasps the full import of the relationship, a level of emotional involvement is established. While this may be magnetic, it can be so intense that it overwhelms a more balanced judgment of the real value of the relationship. Nonetheless, this can be a powerful stimulus in a partnership, allowing the individuals to release emotional frustrations and derive the therapeutic calm which can come from finding someone with whom one can share innermost feelings. The house in which this falls will usually indicate the channel through which the individuals will express this unique emotional vent. The *sextile* and *trine* allow the blending of emotional energies and impulses in a happy, light-hearted way, opening an avenue for the individuals to find whatever value the relationship may have without a feeling of guardedness or any need to hold back feelings and responses. This effect persists as long as the partnership is functioning and cannot help but add to the pleasure and relaxed quality of any relationship where the individuals turn to each other for reassurance and emotional security.

The *square* between a composite Moon and Uranus heightens the emotional interplay between the individuals, but tends to bring different personal objectives for the partnership into conflict. The houses occupied by the composite Moon and Uranus will often indicate the areas of the relationship which are difficult to reconcile and which may be the root of emotional distress for the individuals. In any circumstance, this square creates an unconscious tension and touchiness in a relationship which will, from time to time, relieve itself in emotional outbursts and confrontations. It is not an unmanageable aspect in a partnership, but one can expect a pattern of periodic emotional upheavals between the individuals, the consequences of which must be appraised in light of the overall relationship and the natal personalities involved. The *quincunx* will tend to exaggerate any tendency for one of the partners to emotionally dominate the relationship, inviting a kind of tyranny of emotional crises as a tool to control the partnership. Alone, this aspect has only a minor undertone impact, but in a high-intensity relationship or one involving emotionally demanding and florid personalities, it can set the stage for a growing quality of selfishness and inability to find common ground in the fulfilling of the emotional needs of both individuals. The *opposition* will, more often than not, bring together emotional impulses and energies which counteract and negate each other. The feeling will be that of being squashed emotionally by each other, of not being allowed to freely express oneself because of the unconscious responses of the other person. Gradually this concern for encountering negating responses will cause the individuals to be more and more cautious in openly expressing their feeling to each other with the obvious result that neither will perceive the partnership to be one in which they can find some relief from the anxieties and frustrations of their lives. This "wet blanket" effect is hard to cope with in relationships and requires a very high level of self-awareness and sensitivity in the partners to prevent it from becoming a limiting and deadening factor in the partnership. Without that awareness, in time the individuals will look elsewhere for more positive and supportive responses to their emotional expressions and needs.

Moon Aspects To Saturn

Synastric Aspects formed by Moon and Saturn link two expressions of what is fundamentally the same human need: the inner fulfillment of self through evolving a life mode which brings contentment and a sense of realization of potentials. With Moon, this usually is sought by responding to those things which give us emotional satisfaction and tranquility of spirit. The Saturnian thrust, however, tries to build a life structure within which we feel secure and protected, an identity and worldly recognition which assures us of our place and status. Synastric aspects between Moon and Saturn tell us how the individuals appraise one another as vehicles or allies in achieving a fulfilled self; in one sense, a rather self-oriented measurement of how well the other person fits into our general life plan. Sometimes these aspects are described as having a "fated" or "karmic" quality. Likely this feeling derives from a sense of how the other person harmonizes with our own self-defined "destiny." The *conjunction* creates a response which, while usually clearly felt, may cause doubt in the Moon person about the openness of the Saturn person to the soul-freeing acceptance of life which the Moon person believes is the path to contentment. The Saturn person may be seen as struggling too hard and aggressively for that which the Moon person believes can only come through open-hearted patience and serendipity. The Saturn person, for similar reasons, may see the Moon person as too passive and lacking in the drive to achieve these ends. The result then of this conjunction is ambivalent; the individuals sense a shared aspiration, but suspect that each would be restricted or held back in achieving that aspiration by the other if a bond is formed. The *sextile* and *trine* create a response which is reassuring and promises a capacity to blend aspirations. The Moon person draws confidence and a sense of security from the Saturn person's personality and will likely perceive them to be a stalwart ally in seeking what the Moon person desires from life. The Saturn person draws the warmth and affection of the Moon person as a balm for the harsh demands of competing for what is sought in the world in general. The result is a quiet confidence growing out of the contact which gives both persons a measure of will and courage to get on with their life quests. The *square* raises doubts about whether what the individuals seek from life is really harmonic, particularly in the area of each person's aspirations to express their potentials. It is almost as if these inner visions of completeness somehow work against each other and may not be able to coexist in a close relationship. The Moon person will sense the instinctive disapproval and lack of attunement in the Saturn person and often have their self-confidence shaken by the Saturn person's unconscious responses. The Saturn person struggles with a feeling that the Moon person's goals are irrelevant, even frivolous and, even if drawn by other links to the Moon person, will usually not be able to repress a sense that the Moon person is seeking superficial and unimportant ends. The *quincunx* leaves both persons with a feeling that they would probably have to surrender something vital within their own life scheme to accommodate to each other. The Moon person will feel that the Saturn person would force them to repress some important mode of emotional expression or release which seems necessary for a happy and fulfilled life. The Saturn person will sense in the Moon person emotional needs which are foreign to the Saturn person and would cost them a high price to try to fulfill or even tolerate. There is, with this aspect, an almost "anti-karmic" response, a sense of unbridgeable gaps in the life needs of the individuals. The *opposition* may well be the most magnetic of the Moon/ Saturn aspects if the contact is between male and female or between other personalities which fall at the extremes of the aggressive/passive spectrum. The response is that the other person is capable of providing the counter-balance needed to sustain and complete the circle of life required, the perfect wife to the career-oriented achiever or the stable provider for the self-obsessed creator. This aspect is an expression of the adage that "behind every successful man is a supportive and sustaining woman." Laying aside the gender issue, it recognizes that great achievement requires a total dedication to a goal, leaving much else in life unattended. If, however, one has a partner to see to those unattended portions of a partnership, the result is then a more balanced and fulfilled life. The individuals will then respond to this aspect with a sense that they make a highly complementary tandem capable of rounding out each other's lives. Occasionally, the response is just the opposite: that they are headed in entirely different directions and would only stalemate each other. The reaction depends entirely on the qualities of the natal personalities involved, in particular, the balance of assertiveness and structural confidence each individual has in themselves and what they hope to accomplish with this energy.

Composite The blending of Moon/Saturn energies, while not playing a major role in the early relationship, over time will mean a great deal in determining how satisfactory the partnership is to the individuals. Partnerships are usually entered into initially for largely self-gratifying reasons of a rather immediate nature, but in the long term, partnerships are successful because they support the individuals in fulfilling their own life hopes and perceived potentials. The time comes in any partnership when the individuals look beyond it for a wider realization of dreams and begin to appraise the relationship in terms of how useful the partnership is in accomplishing those aspirations. It is at this point that the blending of Moon/Saturn energies reveals itself. The composite *conjunction* suggests a successful blending of energies in that the individuals provide each other with considerable stability and shelter as each seeks to achieve their individual goals. By itself, this conjunction tends to so stabilize the interaction that, without other more enlivening links, the partnership may suffer from over-seriousness and a lack of spontaneity, but given those other releases of the lighter sides of the partnership this aspect should give the partnership considerable durability. The one real danger in this aspect is that it ends to lock the individuals into roles, roles which later may not match the maturing and evolving personalities. This aspect makes it more difficult for persons in a long-term relationship to alter their relationship to each other as circumstances within the partnership change. Often marriages which come apart after the children have flown the nest and individuals are required to find new alternatives to the old parental roles will show this composite conjunction. The *sextile* and *trine* function so quietly and beneath the surface that the partners are hardly aware of their impact. These aspects are excellent examples of the fact that compatibility is usually more a matter of the *absence* of conflict than the presence of particular factors. The partners simply do not interfere with or make more difficult the achieving of aspirations each has and find it easy and comfortable to encourage and support each other in these endeavors. Probably no composite aspects offer better hope for a hassle-free, non-confrontational relationship than these and, if anyone ever tells you that they and their partner "never fight," the roots of that amiable acceptance of each other's needs and wants will likely be in this interaction of Moon and Saturn. The *square* between Moon and Saturn in the composite chart is sometimes an unsurmountable barrier to a fulfilling partnership. Partnerships usually don't come apart because of some single, dramatic negative event, but rather from an accumulation of minute irritations and annoyances. This square typically makes the whole process of sharing space and hopes much harder for the individuals and gradually there is a piling up of little grudges and resentments against the day in which one or both slam the door yelling, "I can't stand this anymore!" If you asked either what it is they "can't stand," they would be hard pressed to give a clear, concise answer... but, beneath this irritation is the cumulative fact that they have reached a point where they just "can't stand" the other person. Not a happy result of time spent together, but a rather predictable result of this aspect.

The *quincunx,* while minor in its influence and quite tolerable in a good relationship, does tend to require more compromise between the partners in the finding of emotional fulfillment through the partnership. Its most likely effect in an otherwise satisfactory relationship is that the individuals will require an unusually high amount of independent activity to which each turns for some large amount of life satisfaction. As long as each is not threatened by this pattern, it works well enough. Only if one of the partners is deeply insecure and lacking in a durable self-image does this become a problem since, in this situation, the individual relies too heavily on the partnership itself for their emotional security to be comfortable with the other person finding a large part of their fulfillment outside it. The *opposition* between Moon and Saturn in the composite chart occurs with very high frequency in those relationships which seem to be immune to time and travail, particularly in male/female relationships which survive geographic separation or the comings and goings of other relationships. The underlying dynamic here is an unconscious sense that the individuals can "count on" each other, relying on the fact that no matter what happens, the other person will always be there with a sympathetic and interested response. Perhaps more than any other aspect, this opposition earns the title "karmic" for Moon/Saturn links because the bond seems beyond time and circumstance. It is not uncommon for individuals who share this composite link to feel that they shared a relationship in an earlier incarnation or that, regardless of other circumstance, will be bound together "forever." What role this opposition plays in the overall partnership is a matter of the structure of the entire pattern of linkages, but no matter what may evolve, this feeling of a timeless and unshakable bond will exist.

Moon Aspects To Mercury

The principal influence of Moon/Mercury aspects is to link the unconscious and often esoteric emotional needs of Moon with the rational and pragmatic qualities of Mercury. The translation of the highly subjective aspirations of Moon into some tangible, real-life substance relies to a large degree on Mercury's influence, both in the natal chart of the individual and, when another person becomes one of the avenues for realization of these hopes, in the synastric and composite links. These aspects then give us some insight into what channels may exist to make the emotional needs of the individual part of their real-world existence in conjunction with another human being.

Synastric *Conjunctions* between Moon and Mercury usually indicate that the Moon person is stimulated to articulate hopes, feeling that these aspirations will be understood in an ungarbled or unmodified way. We gradually come to know that what we say is often so modified in its interpretation by the different perceptions and experiences of others that our real meaning is lost on them. With this aspect, the response is that such an unintelligible translation will not occur and that the Mercury person will grasp the often diffused outlines of our dreams and be sympathetic with them. The Mercury person will respond to the Moon person as one with whom they might share common perceptions of what constitutes the "good life" and a satisfactory lifestyle. The *sextile* and *trine* have some of the same effect with the individuals responding to each other as persons for whom no difficult modification of life mode would be required. The interaction is less apparent and not so openly articulated, largely because there doesn't seem to be any need to say to each other, "Now, let's be sure we agree on this before we proceed." The assumption is that, at least as far as how one might make a happy and fulfilling life, there is already an unspoken agreement. The *square* often creates a response in the Moon person that if they reveal their hopes and dreams, the Mercury person either will not agree or not really understand. The Mercury person will be constantly trying to relate what the Moon person reveals to their own set of perceptions and finding the Moon person's aspirations confusing and ill-defined. There is an ongoing sense on both sides of "Yes, yes, but what do you mean by that?"... not the best basis for a relaxed and satisfactory interaction.

The *quincunx* seems to virtually eliminate useful communication between the individuals when an issue of shared activity arises. The Moon person will feel a need to conceal or repress any ideas about life fulfillment to avoid getting a blank look and a puzzled shaking of the head from the Mercury person. The Mercury person will sense that being around the Moon person would require a constant adjustment in the way they respond to the world around them, an adjustment which feels unnatural and forced to the Mercury person. It is not so much disagreement or disapproval which permeates this linkage as it is the inability of both to relate real life experiences, situations and events to whatever unconscious emotional need exists in the individuals. When one wants to attend the ballet and the other a boxing match and neither understands the roots of these preferences or the objections, it is an example of this sort of linkage. With the *opposition*, the essential pragmatic neutrality of Mercury is most apparent. The Mercury person finds it relatively easy not only to understand the emotional needs of the Moon person, but also to act in a way which buttresses these needs. The Moon person will respond to the Mercury person as one on whom they can rely to bring cohesiveness and practicality to the shared aspirations. The difficulty with this link is that it tends to encourage the Moon person to become too much the dreamer and lean too heavily on the Mercury person to give some substance to these dreams. The Mercury person may come to feel forever burdened with the task of giving tangible form to the Moon person's hopes, but may not be receiving the same sort of support in return. In the context of a balanced and equitable interaction, this response will not be a serious problem, but if the Moon person is too ethereal and other-worldly natally, the Mercury person may feel that any interaction would be too difficult to bring down to a practical functioning level.

Composite Because neither Moon nor Mercury is a strongly assertive force in the personality, their blended energy in the composite chart will be prone to take the path of least resistance in expressing itself; in this context, the house(s) of the composite chart in which these fall. To the degree that these houses work well together, the partnership will use the area(s) of life activity suggested by the house(s) to create a shared ongoing life mode fulfilling for the individuals. A Moon/Mercury *conjunction* has such a mundane influence that its contribution may be overlooked in a partnership. It may not seem vital in the early stages of a relationship for the partners to come to an easy and almost unconscious accord on where and how to live out the ordinary routines of the day, but over time this kind of effortless agreement goes a long way toward sustaining a relationship. With this conjunction, such simple yet basic questions of what sort of environment or dwelling or decor suits will not generate discord between the partners. The individuals will typically be so closely attuned in these ordinary areas of life that they will hardly even be aware that such issues cause difficulties for others. The focus of the shared processes of living will likely be indicated by the house in which this aspect occurs, particularly as a common goal toward which the individuals can combine their efforts best to achieve a satisfactory life mode. The *sextile* and *trine* indicate a similar uncomplicated and effortless blending of efforts toward achieving a contented daily routine, differing largely only in that the individuals will follow different yet harmonious personal avenues in their daily life activity, paths which parallel and are mutually supportive in creating a satisfactory life mode for the partnership. Again the houses involved suggest the blending of activity which provides the framework for the support of the partnership.

The *square* will introduce a quality of contentiousness in daily routines, a persisting difficulty in finding a mode of living which allows both partners to be content and satisfied. Career conflicts, differences over where and how to establish a base for the partnership, even philosophic or religious differences can emerge from this square. The houses involved usually indicate the focus of the contention and the divergent areas of activities which the partners find hard to blend. The *quincunx*, a very minor influence with these planets, nonetheless can indicate that one of the partners may have to regularly defer to the other in style and mode of the relationship's operation. This can create an "either/or" situation for the partnership in which one individual may have to sublimate career ambitions or preferred lifestyle for periods of time to make some partnership goal achievable. While not deadly to relationships, over a long period of time the partners need to be conscious of this influence and work to assure neither feels they have made all the compromises. The *opposition* between Moon and Mercury has the curious property of allowing persons with greatly different preferences in basic lifestyle to nonetheless arrive at some sort of workable arrangement in a partnership. It often even suggests that this is part of the reward of the partnership, the great difference in this particular element of the relationship which allows each individual to follow their own path of daily life, yet appreciate and enjoy the very different content of each other's world. Curiously successful relationships between ballet dancers and police officers, TV personalities and reclusive researchers, concert pianists and gardeners, etc., are examples of this sort of partnership. Each seems to provide something in the daily life of the other which, at a purely practical level, could not be had without the partnership and with the result that both individuals feel their lives are more complete and fulfilled without having to make major sacrifices in their main life themes.

Moon Aspects To Jupiter

Where Moon/Saturn aspects link basically similar needs with two different forms of expressions of that need, Moon/Jupiter aspects link two fundamentally *different* needs which share similar modes of expression. In synastry, Moon typically seeks emotional fulfillment and a sense of security through stable relationships. Jupiter drives, on the other hand, invest a relationship with the capacity for evolution and growth, an ever-renewing and invigorating energy to find new ways to derive pleasure and excitement from human interaction. These energies, nonetheless, tend to reveal themselves in similar style, infusing the interplay with upbeat emotional tones, expansive acts of generosity and kindness and a pervasive warmth and closeness of approach. Aspects then between Moon and Jupiter bring surging emotional energy and an outreaching openness to relationships, the results of which may either provide the basis for enduring warmth between the partners or, on the negative side, over-emotionalism, excesses in self-indulgence within the relationship or the exaggeration of any instability in the natal personalities.

Synastric With the *conjunction* in an overlay, the Moon person will respond to the Jupiter person with considerable emotional openness, and find it almost irresistible to perform little acts of giving, uttering the most warm compliments and generally being much more unreserved in their expression of their affection for the Jupiter person. The Jupiter person will find in their response to the Moon person a release from the normal social constraints and a freedom from any tendency toward self-protectiveness which would otherwise keep other humans at a safe distance. The basic tone of the interplay is to let down the emotional barriers between the interaction and feel much more at ease and secure in letting each other know what feelings are being stimulated by the contact. The *sextile* and *trine* in the overlay produces a less intense and more easy-going response between the individuals, with the Moon person finding the Jupiter person someone with whom they can "let down their hair," share their dreams and aspirations and be generally much more at ease with them than with other humans. The Jupiter person will find that the Moon person stimulates capacities for hope and optimism and will turn to the Moon person as a supportive resource in times of doubt or discouragement. The *square* will tend to exaggerate the particular qualities of the signs in which these planets fall in both natal charts, with the Moon person being unconsciously motivated to show the least attractive emotional qualities of that sign. In some situations, the Moon person will seem almost unable to control expressions of emotional qualities which grate on or anger the Jupiter person and the more this occurs, the more exaggerated the behavior appears to become. The Jupiter person, confronted with a form of emotional expression with which they are not attuned, will tend to berate the Moon person or become very pompous in pointing out how "foolish" the Moon person's behavior seems. With this square, the interplay is not cool and detached, but rather characterized by heated exchanges and emotional confrontations. The *quincunx* links two forms of behavior which cannot be simultaneously expressed with any feeling of harmony. The Moon person's emotional response to the Jupiter person seems not to make any sense to the Jupiter person and leaves the Jupiter person wondering what ever prompted the Moon person to behave in such a way. The Moon person will usually misinterpret the actions of the Jupiter person, attributing meanings to the actions of the Jupiter person which are not, in fact, the intent of the act, but rather what the Moon person would *want* the intent to be. The whole interplay gets more and more confusing and frustrating and, even with strong positive links elsewhere, this tone of not really "understanding" each other at an intuitive level will persist. The *opposition* has considerable potential for driving each of the persons to the poles of behavior suggested by the natal chart Moon and Jupiter potentials. If the Moon person has a rather reserved emotional quality (i.e., Moon in Earth sign), the response to the Jupiter person will be to become even more extremely reserved, which is exactly the opposite of what the Jupiter person seeks. The Jupiter person, sensing this retreat to the polar extreme of the other person's Moon sign, will redouble their efforts to derive what they want from the interaction. The result of this link then is often a feeling of great emotional pressure and demand within the interplay, a quality which is sometimes magnetic, but over time, is wearing and likely to exhaust the individuals and cause them to seek more relaxed relationships elsewhere.

Composite The composite *conjunction* indicates a very powerful emotional reso-nance between the partners, an emotion heightening blend of energies which infuses the whole relationship with an extra measure of affection and desire for emotional closeness. The form in which this energy will be expressed is usually indicated by the house in which this aspect occurs in the composite chart, but wherever it falls, the partners will be unusually open and warm in their expression of appreciation and generosity toward each other. While not, in itself, a romantic or sexual aspect, this conjunction has such a sweetly invigorating pull that it can carry a partnership beyond the range suggested by other links, overcoming circumstantial barriers and differences. Whatever else may occur, the individuals will retain a feeling of positiveness and warmth about the relationship which will not disappear even if the relationship falls short of early expectations. The *sextile* and *trine* blend the composite energies in ways which allow the partners to draw on each other as sources of renewal and encouragement in getting on with life. Very often, this combination of energies is quite instrumental in aiding the individuals in achieving material and worldly goals since it is a great antidote for discouragement and anxiety. There is a reassuring and supportive exchange between the individuals which sends each back out into the world refreshed and restored, a very valuable gift in grappling with a world which is, at best, indifferent to our aspirations, and often seemingly determined to block us in achieving them. The *square* heightens the more negative emotional exchanges between the partners, with a lot of nagging and complaining being the more common outcome. The partners seem at times to be acting more out of spite and resentment in dealing with each other than out of affection. Despite this, the bond may be very strong and the partners may spend their lives in a kind of endless emotional combat, an activity which to others seems absurd, but to the partners provides some kind of emotional fulfillment. Certainly the partnership will never be calm and quiet, but only if the individuals show a predilecton for violence or extreme emotionalism in their natal charts is this square a real threat to the partnership. The *quincunx* suggests less of a complementary exchange of energies than a kind of "alternating current," with the partners taking turns in giving emotional support and sustenance to the other. Given other positive links and a measure of generosity of spirit in the natal charts, this pattern is not difficult to manage in a partnership. If, however, either personality has a tendency toward self-centeredness or "score-keeping" in relationships, this may result in a kind of carefully monitored and less than altruistic form of generosity between the individuals, with each making sure they "get their share." The *opposition,* while giving a lot of emotional power to the partnership, will often result in excesses within the relationship which cause difficulties. The blending of energies is such that the good judgment of the individuals if often negated when they put their heads together. The life activities in which these poor judgments will most likely occur are suggested by the houses in which the planets fall, but the result of this composite opposition is usually some ill-advised over-extension of the partnership. The root of this seems to be that the partners encourage the most unrealistic aspirations in each other and feed on each other's over-optimism. Hopefully one of the partners has some arithmetic aptitude and can, now and then, get the check book back in balance.

Moon Aspects To Neptune

Neptune has perhaps its greatest illusion-created impact with aspects to Moon since Moon is usually the seat of one's dreams of emotional and personal fulfillment. At best, these aspects soften the edges of any image, making the individuals (particularly the Moon person) less critical and more accepting. At worst, the aspects can create entirely false and illusory hopes for a realization of dreams through the other person. Since Neptune in the natal chart suggests the areas of life (indicated largely by the natal house in which Neptune falls) in which the individual finds the greatest difficulty in stabilizing and actuating their individual aspirations, aspects between Moon and Neptune seem almost inevitably to contain an element of overexpectation and almost desperate hope that the other person will fulfill some long held fantasy. As a minor ingredient in an otherwise positive overlay or composite interaction, this is a rather sweet and forgiving harmonic, but if it is one of the major ingredients in the interaction, there is great potential for disappointment and the raising of false hopes.

Synastric The *conjunction* evokes a deeply felt emotional vulnerability in the Moon person, causing them to feel that there is some boundless "good" in the Neptune person which, despite any evidence to the contrary, can be trusted. The Neptune person will seem to see beyond the surface of the Moon person, finding virtues and values not generally appreciated by most people. The overall effect of this overlay conjunction can be a rather nice blindness to any flaws and quirks in each other. Hopefully, both individuals warrant this trust and faith. The *sextile* and *trine* create a response somewhat more realistic, but nonetheless very forgiving in tone. The Moon person will recognize the less-than-perfect qualities of the Neptune person, but not be troubled by them or find them reasons for rejection. The Neptune person will be motivated to seek out the real essence of the Moon person and show considerable tolerance in dealing with superficial barriers of defensiveness or suspicion while probing for this discovery. All in all, the effect is generally, "I like you, warts and all!"... a useful basis for interaction of any sort. The *square* in an overlay generates less positive fantasies, creating in the Moon person an unconscious sense that the Neptune person can be an object through which some less than healthy personal dreams can be realized. The Neptune person will tend to respond to the Moon person as someone who is vulnerable to being manipulated through illusion and will feel an unconscious motivation to use the Moon person's fantasies against them. With the square, tenderness is replaced by subtle deception, both in terms of preying on each other's fantasies and self-deception about the real motivations for the interaction. Oddly, the *quincunx* often engenders strongly sexual fantasizing, not because the other person is particularly sexually attractive, but because they seem seducible. The Moon person will sense unconsciously that there is a sexual undertone to the Neptune person's response and be tempted to capitalize on that response. The Neptune person will respond to the Moon person as one whose normal defenses are somehow weakened by the interaction and have some difficulty in resisting a predatory urge. The *opposition's* most common influence is to establish a strong unconscious undercurrent in the interaction which seems to flow toward a seemingly "natural" partnership. For no evident reason, the Moon person will feel drawn to the Neptune person as someone with whom a bond should be established, even if the circumstances of the contact would not usually engender such a response. The Neptune person, probably without consciously meaning to do so, projects an aura of seeking such a bond. Those unusual situations where one falls in with a stranger and seems almost immediately to form some sort of very personal and deep linkage often root in this opposition, a linkage which, despite its unusual beginning, will persist for a long time.

Composite The composite *conjunction* blends two rather passive and gentle qualities with the result that the partnership will be sheltered from many of the more harsh conflicts which can arise between individuals who spend time together. The effect is largely to make the partners more caring, patient and forgiving of each other, sometimes to a degree which really is not in their own self-interest. Nonetheless, such an element in a partnership is usually a positive thing, preventing those annoyances and irritations which can often erode less tolerant relationships. The *sextile* and *trine* also give the partnership a measure of tolerance and acceptance, based less on being blind to the difficulties which arise than on simple good-natured patience and humor. The general tone is, "He/she may be a nitwit sometimes, but he/she is *my* nitwit!" The *square* has the rather unfortunate effect of causing the individuals to misread the real import of the partnership. Each will tend to find in the partnership what they want to find (and thereby justify their involvement) rather than seeing what really drives the interaction. Often this square appears in partnerships which are sustained for such very narrow forms of gratification as sex, security or status and permits the individuals to conceal this from themselves adequately to persist in the partnership well beyond the time its real value and content would justify. The *quincunx* is a minor influence, perhaps adding only to the potential for manipulation and selfish use of each other for personal fulfillment. Much here depends on the houses in which the Moon and Neptune fall in the composite chart and what charade these may suggest. The *opposition* has an effect similar to the conjunction with greater emphasis on bonding the individuals in a romantic/sexual relationship. Too often, however, with this opposition in the composite chart, the partnerships are relating to a fantasy person each has formed in their own mind, rather than to the real individual with whom they are involved. Up to a point, this only adds romanticism to the partnership, but carried too far, the individuals may suddenly find themselves confronted with the real personality of the partner when the relationship comes under some stress and wonder how they ever deluded themselves so thoroughly.

Moon Aspects To Pluto

There seems always to be an ambivalent quality to responses generated by aspects between Moon and Pluto, not only because these are rising from deep in the unconscious, but because such aspects bring together essentially inimical forces in the personalities.

Moon seeks its fulfillment in emotional closeness, generosity of the spirit and the kind of personal contentment which is derived from a strong sense of stability and tranquility. Pluto's remote and faceless force for entropic change, coldly destroying what exists to prepare the way for something new and more vital, threatens this Moon hope for predictability and stability. Yet, human discontent also roots in unmet Moon needs, and the prospect of sweeping all away and seeking out new fulfillments makes Moon's response to Pluto's potentially darkly magnetic. There is always something disturbing and unsettling about Moon/Pluto aspects; the degree to which this stirring of deep inner feelings manifests itself in action depends on the natal characteristics of the individuals. Tentative and fearful persons will suppress these feelings and go on their established way, but those people who have a strong self-image and emotional power will respond with some pattern-breaking energy. Under any circumstance, these aspects are destabilizing and force the individuals to reevaluate how fully their emotional needs are being realized.

The *conjunction* is probably the actual cause for actions by the Moon person who later sadly explains, "The Devil made me do it!" The response is often obsessive in nature and the Moon person feels irretrievably drawn to the Pluto person by a tidal flow far below the rational surface which the conscious mind cannot easily resist. The Pluto person will have a relentless attachment to the Moon person, feeling an unconscious need to penetrate the personal life of the Moon person and somehow influence the course of that life. Whether this takes a positive regenerative form which benefits both individuals or, at the other extreme, carries the individuals to the black reaches of obsessive domination of spirit is entirely a matter of the natal potentials and links to the overall synastric pattern. Usually this interaction resolves itself without any major upheaval, establishing only a profound emotional bond, but when the unfortunate coming together of a violent, highly dominant personality and a passive, shelter-seeking one contains this overlay aspect, it can be very dangerous. The *sextile* and *trine* cause responses so subtle that they are hardly consciously noticeable. The Moon person will feel a sense of refreshing reinvigoration in dealing with the Pluto person, a perception that the Pluto person may bring something new and interesting into their lives. The Pluto person will see the Moon person as a vehicle for self-discovery and exploration of elements of themselves previously dormant. These responses are, however, so harmonic that both will probably characterize their response to each other as simply that which one feels when we meet an "interesting" person. The *square* in the overlay is often a bit scary, particularly for the Moon person. Some very deep and carefully controlled urges start banging on their cages in the Moon person's psyche when they contact the Pluto person and most humans would just as soon keep the padlocks firmly in place on these hidden images. Deep down in the remote corners of the Pluto person's inner self, there is a sense that the Moon person might be vulnerable to manipulation and dominance, to that urge which exists in all humans to gain control over some part of their world. If there are romantic/sexual links between the individuals elsewhere, this can take on a very sulphurous quality since not only do most humans want, at times, to exercise complete control over their world and not have to account for their use of this control, most also sometimes wish to abandon themselves to external control and absolve themselves of responsibility for what results: in blunt terms, the emotional forces which drive sadism and masochism. This overlay aspect is not, of course, going to pervert anyone's personality or behavior by itself, but if that potential exists in the natal chart, then this overlay aspect may well trigger such behavior. Since no one is entirely immune to these forces, at the very least, this aspect will stir up whatever may be tucked away in some dark recess of the mind.

The *quincunx* adds a disquieting tone to the responses, with the Moon person feeling an unconscious emotional discomfort in the presence of the Pluto person, a vague feeling of foreignness and threat. The Pluto person will likely sense this absence of emotional harmonics and dismiss the Moon person as one who does not share common needs. The atmosphere is largely of persons who, whatever else may bring them together, would not find a kindred spirit down deep in the soul and, therefore fail to link successfully. The overlay *opposition* can be a truly disturbing interaction, arousing the same sort of emotional responses as one feels when confronted with something terrifying yet intriguing, perhaps the reason we go to horror films is to be frightened, disgusted... and transfixed. The Moon person will feel that they are standing at the entrance to a dark and mysterious cave within which may lie all sorts of ghastly but fascinating terrors, a thrills and chills sort of intrigue. The Pluto person may be stirred into a difficult-to-manage kind of obsessive fascination with the Moon person, a compulsion to "do something," the focus of which will be determined by other links between the charts. Usually these compulsive links resolve themselves in manageable ways, with the individuals not abandoning good sense even if they may elect to explore a little of this ambivalent fear/ fascination... but not always. There is always an undertone of dark, mindless violence in this aspect and, with the wrong combination of personalities, it can get out of hand.

Composite Whether or not the composite Moon/Pluto *conjunction* plays a significant role in the relationship depends on whether either individual has strong angular natal aspects to Moon from the outer planets. If this significant natal potential in the unconscious exists, then this conjunction between Moon and Pluto in the composite chart will typically give the partnership a quality of revolutionizing the lives of the individuals, of using the partnership to bring about major change in life patterns aimed at emotional fulfillment. The emotional impact of the partnership on the individuals will be not only profound, but very binding, making it difficult for the individuals to free themselves from the relationship if they later want to do so. If, however, the natal Moons are largely unaspected, this composite conjunction will only lend a higher level of emotional intensity to the partnership, intensity which neither individual typically feels in their normal interplay with other humans. The *sextile* and *trine* will stabilize the emotional content of the relationship, making it easier for the partners to weather difficulties and to fall back on the partnership for support when outside events and influences upset their lives. Perhaps the best result of these harmonic aspects is that the relationship will continue to evolve at an emotional level and, as the individuals mature, they will be able to retain a paralleling pattern of behavior, not growing apart in terms of what each defines as life-enriching and satisfying.

The *square* is not a happy aspect in the composite chart, often being a source of deep resentment, emotional distress between the partners and, in some situations, that peculiar element in some relationships in which one of the partners actually carries a fear of the other. Because the blending of energies is fraught with emotional discord and confrontational elements in the very areas of life where a close partnership ought to provide a tranquil haven and stability, the partners will struggle to maintain some sort of balance in the relationship. Often even minor events or actions will trigger violent disagreements and the partners will have low thresholds of tolerance for each other's efforts to fulfill needs. The root of this discord will probably revolve around the composite houses in which Moon and Pluto fall and the divergent kinds of course corrections and life alterations the individuals wish to impose on the partnership. In the end, the most likely result is that the individuals will sadly conclude that they are on different life paths and neither will have much peace if they try to tread the same one. The *quincunx* adds a bit of difficulty to finding agreement on where the partnership is going, a rather small influence which is meaningful only if there are other, more significant discords (i.e., harsh aspects between Moon and Mars or Saturn in the composite chart). This minor aspect doesn't seem to help much in keeping a harmonious emotional balance in the relationship, but it does no great harm either given positive links elsewhere. Probably the only noticeable result will be a need from time to time, for one partner to sublimate some emotional need of their own to make possible the realization of the other partner's hopes... not an unreasonable thing to ask in an otherwise good relationship. The *opposition's* influence on a partnership is rather hard to predict without seeing it in the context of the overall relationship. It introduces an element of emotional dependency and a blending of energies which places great emotional demands on the individuals, but how they will respond to this depends, of course, on what kind of personalities they are. If there is a need for and a capacity to respond to this intense need for emotional interplay between the individuals, this may be a powerful binding force in the partnership, one characterized by two persons who seem never to be apart or functioning as independent souls. If, however, one or both of the partners find this "fly paper" quality intrusive or too much hassle, this can be a source of irritation and annoyance. One or both will eventually scream "LEAVE ME ALONE!" and flee to get a little emotional peace. Whatever the result, the powerful polarity of this opposition will add both depth and intensity to the emotional properties in the partnership and neither will feel either ignored or unimportant to the other... even when, at times, they might want to be.

ASPECTS TO VENUS

With Sun and Moon, we have been examining the broader, aggregated responses which arise between individuals, those which can take many forms and have a variety of objectives in relationships. With Venus, the focus is narrower and more targeted to fulfilling the need which exists in all humans to find beauty and pleasure in life, to experience and even be an intimate party to something or someone who produces that sensation of joy, of transcendence, of taking us out of and above the plainness, imperfection and hollowness of everyday experiences. In a very accurate sense, we do not really "like" individuals who arouse this response in us, nor do we feel a sense of compatibility with or affection for them. In some ways, we don't even deal with them as human beings, but rather as cherished and valuable discoveries of rare content which somehow conform to our inner paradigm of beauty and excellence. Because these individuals, when we find them, seem so unique and rare, so unlikely to be replicated, we are willing to make considerable sacrifice to be in their presence and to feel the rush of happiness and fulfillment they seem to generate in us. More often than we like to admit, the people who create this response in us are less valued as friends or companions than as addictive stimulants of feelings we want to experience and reexperience within ourselves. This is, of course, a lovely aromatic ambience which adds a romantic dimension to the relationship: a powerful binding force because they are so valuable we will show extraordinary patience and tolerance in dealing with them. This sense of their preciousness is why we characterize love as being "blind," not in that we fail to see the flaws in the other person, but rather that we will rationalize them and blind ourselves to them deliberately as the price we must pay to keep them in our lives.

In synastry, then, the ultimate consequence of aspects to Venus are, in large measure, a product of the broader, more general relationship. If these aspects occur within the boundaries of a compatible relationship, with positive elements of true affection, they convert that fundamentally good interaction into a lovely, joy-filled romantic interplay. If, however, these Venus aspects are the primary linkages between individuals or exist in the context of a broader interaction which is filled with conflict and discord, they will "lead us down the garden path" of unrealistic expectations, painful and disappointing experiences and failed romances. Perhaps no greater challenge faces us than when we are confronted with such a situation in synastry since any attempt to advise and alert someone to the potential disappointments in such a limited interaction must breach the barriers of their most cherished fantasies and profound responses. Nonetheless, an appraisal of these Venus aspects which fails to relate them to the overall character of the relationship avoids the real purpose of synastry: the raising of the sort of questions which will cause us to reexamine our own feelings and expectations in what will hopefully be more realistic and enduring terms.

Aspects made to Venus by the planets from Mars outward to Pluto then engender a perception of beauty and perfection of a *particular sort* indicated by the aspecting planet, a rather specific matching up with specific inner paradigms formed in our own charts by those same planets. These aspects determine, then, in what way the other person is especially valuable to us and the kind of actions we will take to assure ourselves of that so we can continue to experience that specific pleasure with them. Romantic love has many possible components and these aspects give us some insight into what particular romantic formula is operating in any individual relationship.

Venus Aspects To Mars

Synastric Overlay aspects which link Venus and Mars are almost entirely sexual in content and the *conjunction* is undoubtedly the most potent in their impact, although not necessarily the most likely to prompt sexual initiative. The Venus person will find the Mars person a personification of physical sexual attractiveness, of pure sexual beauty and archetypically the kind of person with whom the primal mating and procreative drive is most strongly aroused. The Mars person's response is much like an animal reaction. They sense the availability of the other person and, given other links which create attraction for the Mars person, they will move to take advantage of this opportunity. Sometimes, however, the conjunction creates such a biological turmoil in the individuals, particularly the Venus person, that it can't find any easy and comfortable avenue for expression. It is almost too pervasive and disorienting to be kept in perspective and get the rather simple and basic act of sexual joining organized. Without other more general compatibility links, the individuals may just writhe in anticipation, but find it impossible to deal with the simple task of locating a bed. The *sextile* and *trine* make all this much easier and, while not initially triggering such a powerful sexual response, this overlay seems much more comfortable and natural. The response of the Venus person is, with the sextile, so unguarded and guileless that the Mars person feels no nervousness or unease in accepting the invitation. With the trine, the Venus person will tend to be more passive and express their interest more in the form of a projected tractability than an overt sign of interest, but with either aspect, and given any other links which attract the individuals to each other, getting it all together is no great problem. The *square* will certainly arouse sexual interest, but of a more combative and challenging nature. The Venus person may be tempted to tease and flirt, but somehow still manages to communicate that there is also doubt and guardedness in their response. The Mars person will probably feel some sexual anger and resentment despite an element of attraction and take cover behind some form of studied indifference or elaborate arrogance. The interplay is highly charged sexually, but probably best left at the posturing and strutting stage without great expectations for culmination. The interaction is too self-oriented and self-gratifying to offer any likelihood of a long-term romantic/sexual satisfaction. Within the small orb of the *quincunx*, this Venus/Mars overlay can have significant sexual content. The Venus individual will feel that their particular style of sexual expression would somehow not please the Mars person, or at least that the Venus person would have to modify and sublimate their normal behavior in a sexual relationship. The Mars person will likely feel that, while the Venus person would be an attractive partner, the relationship would be less of a joint venture as a "your turn/my turn" process in which each accommodates the other, but little mutuality would emerge. With strong links elsewhere to bring the individuals together, they will be willing to give it a try, but this feeling of not being able to fully understand and respond to each other's sexual needs will probably persist. The *opposition* between Venus and Mars in an overlay is a mixed blessing. It probably works best if the Venus person is the female and the Mars person is male. In this instance, the compensatory nature of this linkage seems to fit the sexual psyches of the individuals in ways which allow each to offer the counterbalancing and resonant responses the other wants without forcing unnatural role-playing. If the situation is reversed, with the male being the Venus person, there will be a quite noticeable sexual response, but very often the individuals are left in a state of inaction because any potential interaction would seem to impose on each roles which neither really enjoys. Appraisal of the responses and capacities to cope with these behavioral traits requires a careful look at the natal characteristics of the individuals with an eye to how well the Venus person can accept the "giving" role and the Mars person the role of initiator and "getting" partner.

Composite The important thing to remember with Venus/Mars aspects in the composite chart is that they exist only in potential and will only come to the fore if there are stronger, more compelling links to bring the partners together. They will not trigger a sexual relationship in themselves; they will only cause the individuals to sense that if a partnership is undertaken, the sexual content of it will be influenced by these aspects.

Another factor which influences the outcome of any composite Venus/Mars aspect are the house(s) in which the planets fall in the composite chart. The blending of Venus and Mars energies occurs within a context of the mutual objectives in the partnership and the basic roles and purposes of a romantic/sexual interaction suggested by these houses. Such interplay between individuals has complex roots and a great variety of objectives beyond just self-gratification. While we may not like to recognize this, the give and take of love and sex does usually have some purpose behind it, some particular outcome the partners hope to manage when they form the partnership and make physical and emotional intimacy a part of it. Not all houses are "naturally" associated with love and sex and, in those instances where the houses in which the planet falls in the composite charts are not usually linked with romance and sex, the quality of the intimacy will seem less selfless and simple, more vulnerable to the "let's make a deal" syndrome. The *conjunction* creates a great feeling of shared needs and offerings between the partners, an atmosphere in which the individuals not only intuitively understand each other's needs, but anticipate and respond to each other effortlessly. Perhaps the only negative with this conjunction is that there are a few surprises and new discoveries to be made as the partners come to know each other romantically and sexually. While these aspects pretty much assure that sexuality within the relationship will not create misunderstandings or anxieties, it does have some potential for sameness and unimaginative, ultimately uninteresting patterns of intimacy. The *sextile* and *trine* link similar and harmonic energies which are just enough different to be captivating, but compatible enough to sustain interest. Romantic physical closeness will come easily and comfortably to the partners and usually with an undertone of good humor and perspective. With the sextile, great openness and reciprocity will emerge in this very personal area of the partnership with neither likely to feel that the other is not doing their share. With the trine, the blending of energies is so smooth and effortless that the partners hardly feel any sense of having to "work at it" or adjust their own styles and responses to match the partner. It can, in fact, come so easily and naturally that, after a time, the partners take it for granted and sometimes fail to appreciate the rather uncommon nature of this blending. In that sense only, the trine between the composite Venus and Mars can suggest a tendency for the partners to wander, unconsciously seeking the darker, more confrontational side of romantic sex with other partners, a classic exercise in not fully realizing the value of something which comes too easily to us.

The *square's* impact in a partnership, for better or worse, depends on the context in which it occurs, on the overall nature of the partnership. Within a healthy, open and harmonic relationship, it keeps romantic/sexual intimacy invigorated and intense, with little likelihood of either party becoming bored. This element of any relationship is always, to some degree, a greedy game of self-gratification and the square heightens the level of demand made by each partner on the other. If the sexual content of the partnership is, therefore, the primary fulcrum on which it rests and the remainder of the relationship is not harmonic and strongly linked, the square gives sexual gratification too large a role in the partnership. The individuals may well find it difficult to spend time together without constantly demanding "highs" from each other, a scenario which will exhaust nearly anyone and wear out the value of the relationship rather quickly. The *quincunx* suggests a less than ideal matching of styles within the relationship, one in which considerable modification and repressing of individual needs must occur for the partners to share intimacy. Since most partnerships will eventually produce a dominant partner, ultimately the quincunx suggests that that partner will dictate the tone and style of intimacy and the more passive partner will be required to meet that demand, regardless of whether or not it is a satisfying mode for them. How bearable this will be over time is largely a matter of the quality and content of the overall relationship, but it does not promise particularly happy results from the more intimate aspects of the partnership. The *opposition* will be a powerful and magnetic force in the sexual content of a partnership, largely because it polarizes the behavior of the individuals, drawing out the most extreme expressions of physical needs. Assuming these full-blown expressions of individual needs are compatible, the opposition contributes a highly colored passion to the relationship, a drive to act out fully the inner drives and urges. If, however, the individuals are driven by essentially inimical needs, the quality of intimacy becomes a sort of warfare between the partners with constant struggling for control and dominance. With the opposition in the composite chart, there is always the possibility of the sexual side of the relationship straying out of manageable forms and becoming perverse, violent or humiliating for one or both of the partners. This is, of course, not the most common result, but almost certainly whatever usually repressed urges exist in the individuals will be more likely to come out of the closet with this aspect.

Venus Aspects To Uranus

Aspects formed between Venus and Uranus influence the responses of the individuals to each other in terms of the customary mating rituals and "proper" forms of interaction dictated by both the society in which they live and the self-protective cautiousness which roots in all human's anxiety about failure and rejection. Usually the presence of significant aspects between Venus and Uranus causes the individuals to alter their normal mode of behavior in dealing with another human to whom they are attracted and be more willing to openly express their interest. Venus/Uranus aspects do not, in themselves, create attraction or romantic response, but rather make other responses triggered by links between the inner planets more likely to be openly revealed, and some things even compulsively expressed with a cavalier disregard for convention or consequence. The reputation these aspects have for "unconventional" interactions is less a matter of oddball match-ups of individuals than it is initiating and continuing the relationship in a very impulsive and sometimes in foolish ways, ways which resemble an individual jumping off a cliff and asking on the way down how far they have to fall.

Synastric The *conjunction* usually creates in the Venus person a very intense and penetrating awareness of the Uranus person, an impact of presence which cuts through the fog of other preoccupations and rivets the Venus person's attention. The Uranus person can hardly miss being stared at and being followed around the room by an unswerving gaze and will unconsciously weigh what to do about this. Given a modicum of attraction, this situation will brush aside the typical probing and testing and get to the meat of the issue. The impact is more than a little disorienting and both individuals will be moved to make quick judgments about each other from which to proceed, judgments which are just as likely to be inaccurate as sound. The *sextile* and *trine* create a less enthralling response, but one almost as likely to open the doors quickly to communication. The Venus person will feel the impulse to reach out for contact and will usually be quite open and gregarious in their response to the Uranus person. The Uranus person, unaccustomed like most humans to anyone else being friendly and openly responsive, will typically warm up to this opening and feed back what seems appropriate. Whatever the other links between the individuals suggest as potential, the exploration of these potentials will get off to a fast and furious start. The *square* has a more challenging quality and can engender that not uncommon response in the Venus person of seeing the Uranus person as one who is causing entirely too much chemistry for comfort. The Venus person may throw up an arrogant "just go ahead and try, you..." mask and, of course, the Uranus person will usually dive right in and return fire. The result is usually something like the old premise in romantic novels that individuals who immediately start fighting as soon as they meet will certainly wind up in love at the end of the book. Perhaps they will, but they'll have to work their way through a lot of thorns and thickets to get there with this aspect because this square will continue to create a prickly atmosphere. The *quincunx* likely will cause a fundamental misunderstanding at the outset with the Venus person reading the Uranus person's motives incorrectly and the Uranus person wondering why the Venus person is behaving in such an odd and apparently unwarranted way. This overlay aspect won't prevent a relationship from developing, but there will be repetitions of this inaccurate understanding of who wants what and why, an ingredient which will probably make any evolution of a personal relationship vulnerable to coming unglued over rather insignificant events. The *opposition* between Venus and Uranus in the overlay will likely cause the Venus person to respond to the Uranus person as a threat to destabilize things. Since persons to whom we are indifferent pose no threat to our emotional state, we worry only about those folks for whom we feel a response, yet who somehow make us unsure and vulnerable. The Venus person will be "upset," at the unconscious level, by the Uranus person and, not really knowing why, will throw up protective barriers. The poor Uranus person will wonder if their slip is showing or their fly is unzipped and struggle to grasp what's going on. Because there is a strong impulse to link up inherent in this aspect, the individuals may get past this early disorientation because of other connections between the charts, but the early stages may be almost comedically defensive and muddled.

Composite The Venus/Uranus *conjunction* sometimes is characterized as a "love at first sight" phenomenon, but it is more accurate to see it as a blending of romantic and impulse energies which indicate that whatever the overall quality of the interaction may be, the individuals will find it especially easy to get right to it. The essence of this conjunction is that the individuals find in each other the intrinsic value and personal qualities to justify jumping in and testing the waters. Whatever form the partnership takes (and this conjunction does little to dictate that form, only to open the door for experimentation), the partnership will retain its willingness to seek out the fully realized potential which may exist. In fact, the individuals will come together in a way which almost compels that realization. The *sextile* and *trine* seem to minimize game-playing and indirection in the partnership, keeping it free of foolish over-cautiousness and self-protective behavior. The partners are out front with each other and the blending of energies causes each to be relaxed and free in quickly expressing their feelings for each other. For some less obvious reason, this also seems to engender a lot of giggling and tickling, a truly cosmic phenomenon. The *square* may make it seem to the partners that there is justification to quickly form a partnership, but the nature of this square is what gives "impulsiveness" a bad name: poor anticipation of the consequences of an act. The partners are actually being motivated by quite different and usually discordant impulses and, as a result, are vulnerable to a Keystone Kop kind of colliding interaction. The blending of energies triggers such different compulsions in the partners (see the involved houses for a clue to where this conflict might originate) that they wind up feeling anger and disappointment with each other's behavior. At the base of this misfiring is probably a greatly differing definition of pleasure and happiness, especially those little unplanned but happy incidents which give humans unexpected joy. It's hard to enjoy a partnership when the individuals do not share similar pleasures and recreations and the square between Venus and Uranus make the result rather likely. The *quincunx* seems not to be particularly important with these planets, contributing only a certain inability to understand each other's impulses and unconscious urges. The result will likely be a mutual feeling that the other person has some odd and uninteresting tastes and preferences for using the hours available for fun and games. The *opposition* probably comes closest to earning the reputation that Venus/Uranus aspects have for bringing together some unusual and seemingly unblendable combinations. This composite opposition is often the binding force in love affairs, even marriages, involving people who seem to have little in common in the way of personality types, worldly interests or careers. The personalities blend in a way that, despite these outward differences, the individuals find very private and personal harmonies which are strong enough to make other divergences seem unimportant. Perhaps these apparent mismatched qualities will prove unimportant, but when partnerships are formed with this opposition as a key element, it puts a very great strain on the cohesiveness and durability of the relationship. Nonetheless, if the links between the charts (and especially the composite chart) show positive and harmonic bonds, the apparent superficial differences between the individuals (i.e., career interests, cultural backgrounds, age, etc.) will turn out to be irrelevant and the unusual combination will function successfully. This aspect has made poor prophets out of many a friend or parent as they sat glumly in the wedding chapel and predicted dire things ahead for the partners, not knowing that the "odd couple" had this opposition in their composite chart to make it all work out well.

Venus Aspects To Saturn

On the surface, aspects between sweet and romantic Venus and glum old rigid Saturn might seem inevitably to indicate something less than wonderful, but that really is not the case. Venusian romanticism often flourishes in the sturdy, protective shelter of Saturn's solid good sense and predictability. As exciting as wild, irresponsible romances may be initially, the stability and substance which can arise from these aspects give relationships staying power and security. Saturn will, of course, have something of a restricting influence on Venus. Whether that is a valuable and stabilizing influence or the origin of frustration and anger depends both on the aspect formed and the natal qualities of the individuals. As always, the house(s) involved suggest in what venues of living this influence will be most felt by the individuals. Beyond these mundane considerations, there is also the "kronos" side of Saturn, the quality of timelessness and, metaphysically, of links which reach beyond this temporal point on the Universe's continuum, if you wish, "karma" or a quality of "fatedness." Not uncommonly, aspects between Venus and Saturn create an unconscious sense of déjà vu, of past contacts or loves, and for those who believe literally in reincarnation, the feeling of lovers reuniting.

Synastric The *conjunction* between Venus and Saturn is perhaps too strong a link to be positive, too much grey weight to place upon Venus. The Venus person will feel the presence of the Saturn person quite profoundly, but usually find the granitic power of the Saturn personality too inflexible and restraining to see much of the positive side of such a response. The Saturn person will look upon the Venus person as someone who engenders great seriousness of purpose, but may be so heavy-handed or grave in their attitudes that their behavior becomes a cross between an intrusive parent and a monkish auditor. This aspect creates a strong bond, but one from which both parties seem to struggle to free themselves. The *sextile* and *trine* deliver the most balanced and welcome responses in an overlay. The Venus person will feel a strong sense of trust and confidence in the Saturn person, a conviction that the Saturn person is reliable and sensible. While not the most exciting response to another human, if the Venus person has any degree of maturity and life experience, then this perception of another human is valuable and not dismissed lightly. The Saturn person will often respond in a parently and protective way and, while the behavior may be more of grave courtesy and concern, it rings of genuineness and durability. These aspects appear rather commonly in interactions which bridge age and generation gaps and, while not in themselves suggesting a romantic/sexual relationship, if other links create this sort of response between the individuals, these aspects are very supportive of such May-December relationships.

The *square* creates the most negative responses in the individuals, revealing all the unpleasant connotations of rigidity, restriction and latent paralysis of spirit. The Venus person will sense that the Saturn person would inevitably bring only boredom and sameness into any relationship and would find little to share in seeking the joy and pleasure in life. The Saturn person will tend to see the Venus person as shallow and frivolous with immature aspirations and foolish perceptions. Almost certainly the individuals will find reasons to be elsewhere. The *quincunx* in a synastric overlay usually has a minor influence in the responses of the individuals, creating only a vague discomfort in the Venus person and feeling of detachment and indifference in the Saturn person. The exception to this occurs when there are strong romantic/sexual links elsewhere in the charts. When this atypical situation exists, the Venus person may enter into an intimate relationship, but feel a vague and free-floating fearfulness about the Saturn person. The Saturn person will unconsciously have to cope with the occasional emergence of a cold and detached quality in any intimacy. This is an odd and hard-to-describe quality, not overwhelming, but still present. If either individual shows natal indications of emotional instability, low self-esteem or a touch of simple cruelty in their charts, it can be a factor in a close relationship–with less than attractive consequences. The *opposition* has perhaps the most evident quality of karmic linkage, the feeling of fatedness in the responses of the individuals. What that "inevitability" may seem to be is established by other links in the overlay, but the sense of cosmic bond will be felt by both individuals. The Venus person will respond as if some invisible hand is directing them, drawing them along toward some unseen but specific objective under the influence of the Saturn person. The Saturn person will respond sometimes as a guru-like guide, but also sometimes with a more manipulative and dictatorial tone. More often than not, both individuals find this rather unsettling and unpleasant and break the link, mostly out of uncertainty of where it leads. With powerful attraction links elsewhere in the overlay, however, this sense of flowing with fate is hard to resist and one or both will yield to it. What the result of all this may be requires an analysis of the overall relationship, but if there is much to suggest a fully involved interaction, this opposition becomes like a steel cable between the psyches, flexing with the relationship as it evolves, but forming a tough, seemingly permanent bond.

Composite Venus/Saturn aspects in the composite chart influence the capacities of the partners to give substance and reality to those shared hopes and dreams which add up to enjoying life and harvesting the hoped-for fruits of coming together in a relationship. In a very fundamental way, these aspects suggest how the individuals can blend their energies to "succeed" in the broad sense of the word. The house(s) involved indicate the paths and openings most likely to be followed by the partnership: paths cleared or blocked by the harmonics of this blending. The *conjunction* is a powerful force in the composite chart, giving a clear and well-defined focus to the central reason the partnership exists (principally indicated by the house in which it occurs). The individuals may, because of their own independent responses, try to direct the partnership away from this focus point, but the partnership will inevitably veer back to this heading. Whether this suits either or both of the partners is a matter of synastric motivations which initiated the relationship, but the influence is largely inescapable and, therefore, must be accepted if the partnership is to function. It may sound simplistic, but the *sextile* and *trine* suggest the individuals make "good partners"; that is, they can work well together to achieve things through the partnership which might be otherwise unavailable. The blending of energies brings together reasonable combinations of aspirations (again suggested by the house in which the planets fall) and, by and large, the partners can manage to realize a fair amount of these aspirations working together. These aspects won't inspire any intense romanticism or passion in a relationship, but they get the bills paid and the lawn mowed...or whatever else the individuals set as goals for their relationship.

The *square* will have the opposite effect, making it hard for the individuals to reach an agreement on where the partnership should direct its efforts. The individuals seem to cancel out each other's best efforts and, as a result, the partners come to see the relationship as a barrier to achieving individual aspirations. This grows out of a basic lack of commonality in defining what makes the good life and "success" and, no matter how much love and affection may exist in the relationship, over time this self-defeating undertone will do some real damage to the partnership. The *quincunx* requires an unusually high degree of compromise in the partnership, a willingness to accept and work for things which perhaps are important to only one of the partners. In a strong, harmonic overall relationship, this is manageable and some sort of balance can be achieved, but it will be a difficult problem creating resentment and self-pity if the bonds are narrow or weak. Partnerships formed largely for sexual gratification, profit or fulfillment of romantic fantasy will falter in the face of the considerateness and generosity required by this aspect. The *opposition* creates a curious, but often workable form of blending of energies, one characterized by the adage, "You scratch my back and I'll scratch yours." The partners do not so much share aspirations for the partnership as they individually seek objectives which complement each other and, therefore, satisfy each individual. The career-absorbed husband with the wife wholly committed to being a homemaker and mother is an example of such a dichotomous yet successful complementarity. Relationships which seem all "one way" to the outsider, and, therefore, unattractive, still can satisfy the needs of the partners. When the opposition occurs in the composite chart, this polarity will be hard to avoid. Whether its welcome and comfortable or a pain in the neck is something the individuals have to decide over time. Surprisingly, many decide they like it.

Venus Aspects To Jupiter

These rather benign aspects play a useful role in overcoming the inevitable self-centeredness of most humans in a relationship. It is quite normal and fundamental to human nature that we cannot deal with anything outside ourselves except in terms of ourselves. Other humans, events, situations, etc. are all seen with ourselves as the central reference point and in terms of what value and consequence these external phenomenon have on us. Links between Venus and Jupiter do not change this basic human trait, but do make it possible for us to also view these external events from a perspective outside ourselves, in the case of human interactions, to also recognize and respond to situations in terms of how they effect another person who is important to us. The influence of these aspects then is to contribute a quality of generosity, kindness and sensitivity to a relationship or, in some cases, to become so deeply caught up in the presumed perspective of the other person that we overdo and wind up trying to live the other person's life for them. Jupiter can introduce the potential of the Big Daddy or Stage Mother response, with one person so moved to take charge of the other's life that the result is less than happy.

Synastric The Venus/Jupiter *conjunction* opens the hearts of the individuals to each other, creating a sense of warmth and desire to please the other person. The Venus person will respond to the Jupiter person as a benign and kindly personality in whom a significant measure of trust can be placed. The Jupiter person will find their normal critical faculties are diffused and that when dealing with the Venus person, an unusually high degree of tolerance and acceptance is possible. The *sextile* and *trine* show up largely as a strong feeling of simply liking each other and a sense that the interaction is well lubricated by goodwill and friendliness. The Venus person will "see" the pleasing qualities in the Jupiter person and tend to not be deflected by any of the less attractive qualities displayed. The Jupiter person will make a genuine effort to reach out to the Venus person with open acts of friendliness and concern and feel confident that the Venus person is deserving this effort. The *square* creates an unconscious anxiety in the Venus person that the weight of the personality of the Jupiter person may be too overwhelming to cope with. The Jupiter person will be prompted to go too far and be too effusive in expressing their feelings for the Venus person, often to the discomfort of the Venus person. With this square in the overlay, there is a tendency to overreact in the early stages of a relationship with excesses in behavior which are hard to retreat from if the relationship later settles down to a more normal tempo. The *quincunx*, while subtle in influence, can create a strong sense of obligation in the individuals. The Venus person may feel that somehow they are always in debt to the Jupiter person for any kindnesses or warmth, an ambivalent reaction since, while these kindnesses are appreciated, no one enjoys a chronic sense of "owing." The Jupiter will offer the best of themselves, sometimes without any clear reason to do so. The end result is often a bond of loyalty, but one based on an unconscious and essentially impersonal quality of obligation rather than of any conscious admiration for each other. The *opposition* in the overlay introduces the most evident quality of Jupiterian largess, the most apparent expression of the beneficent and expansive quality of this planet. The Venus person will unconsciously perceive the Jupiter person to be a source of good things, an open-handed and open-hearted person whose basic response is to offer support and sustenance to the Venus person without demanding much in return. The Jupiter person will be moved to step in the guardian role, almost "adopting" the Venus person and assuming responsibility for their well-being. At best, this can be a marvelous exchange of needs and fulfillments, but obviously it can be distorted if the motivations of either person are too self-oriented. How this opposition fits into the overall relationship and what its impact will be depends on the natal qualities of the individuals. By and large, the worst that can happen is that both will look back and wonder why they invested so much for so little, but more likely the influence will be for the good and add a happy quality of selflessness and absence of any tendency to worry about "keeping accounts" in an emotional and material sense. The other person will always seem worth it.

Composite None of the composite aspects between Venus and Jupiter seem to do much harm and usually add to the warmth and openness of the partnership. Their primary influence is to measure how balanced and reasonable the blending of the pleasure-seeking and expansive energies in the personalities will be. The *conjunction* indicates a very upbeat and fun-and-games quality to the partnership with a sharing of pleasures and perhaps a considerable emphasis on value of the partnership as an avenue for exploring the joyous side of life. The composite house involved will suggest the focus of this blending and, while it has the potential for excess, nobody seems to mind the cost later. The *sextile* and *trine* are very relaxed and effortless aspects, allowing the individuals to find rewards in the simple, daily processes which can be shared. Perhaps no aspects contribute more to the ability to find in the ordinary events of living adequate rewards to make a relationship work and to keep the little irritations from being important and corrosive. The *square* adds a rather harmless effusiveness and enthusiasm to the relationship with the partners blending their energies with great energy and assertiveness. The only concern here would be that any tendency in the individual natal charts toward over-doing, over-spending or the like would be aggravated by the way in which the individuals influence each other. In the context of an otherwise solid relationship, the only result will probably be a running battle with credit cards and car payments. The *quincunx* is hardly noticeable in most situations, suggesting only the potential for an imbalance of contribution and over-dependency of one partner. This effect, however, is not likely to be a major consideration in the partnership unless other, stronger links suggest such a one-sided and imbalanced interaction. The *opposition* is a very lively composite aspect and perhaps the only one of the Venus/Jupiter aspects which emphasizes the romantic and deeply moving potential of this polarity. The energies blend in a way which draws out of the partners the most dramatic and sweeping expressions of warmth and closeness, keeping florists, jewelers and candy makers in business and being the only acceptable excuse for people giving each other disgusting pet names. This can, of course, be overdone to the disadvantage of the checkbook and those who must endure all this goo from the outside, but for persons who need and enjoy these harmless theatrics, it allows the easy expression of these urges.

Venus Aspects To Mercury

Venus/Mercury aspects are subtle and quiet in their influence, but that does not mean they are without importance. A maxim of both art and music is that the space between the notes or, as in the extraordinary simplicity of Japanese painting, the unpainted areas of the canvas are perhaps more important to the creation than the more evident notes and brush strokes. In human relationships, most planetary interplay provides the musical notes or brush strokes, giving the relationship its principle image, but within those boundaries are large expanses of time and space in which, in a literal sense, nothing much is happening. The individuals are going about their individual business, seeing to their own needs, but if a relationship exists, the bonds of that relationship still surround them. Venus/Mercury aspects give some insight into how these "white spaces" of human relationships will function, how well individuals can function in a relationship out of bed, working independently or just wool-gathering while the other person reads. Many relationships work well enough when the individuals are intensely involved with each other, but when long periods of slack occur, the individuals experience restlessness, irritation and boredom, a response which may cause them to see the relationship as wanting. Mercury/Venus help prevent these sorts of gaps in relationships.

Synastric A *conjunction* in this overlay establishes a strong intuitive link between the individuals, heightening nonverbal communication and a sensitivity to the moods of each other. The Venus person will feel this link as almost knowing what the other person is thinking. The Mercury person will be particularly well equipped to understand the state of mind of the Venus person and respond with empathy and sensitivity. The *sextile* and *trine* are more important because of what they tend to prevent than anything they initiate. With these aspects, the Venus person will respond to the Mercury person as someone who understands them and, therefore, requires no great effort to be with and to communicate the ebb and flow of feelings. The Mercury person will, in fact, have this sense of what is going on inside the Venus person's psyche and not experience confusion or uncertainty in coping with these tides. The result is the absence of misunderstanding and inappropriate responses to each other, responses which might be very annoying or discouraging without these aspects. The *square* is ambivalent in its effect, introducing a challenging and confrontational tone to the interaction, but yet still based on a degree of understanding each other. If the remainder of the interaction is tranquil and compatible, the Venus person will feel only that the Mercury person is incessantly probing into the mind and spirit, questioning and curious. If there is not this basic harmony of responses, the Venus person will feel challenged and confronted by the Mercury person, a feeling probably justified since the Mercury person will tend to respond with an almost compulsive need to puzzle out the Venus person's motives and needs. The *quincunx* tends to limit the ability of the individuals to communicate, especially at the nonverbal or intuitive level, requiring a continuing demand for clarification and explanation of each other's thinking and feeling. The Venus person will feel pressure to explain and justify, and the Mercury person will have a sense of the fruitlessness of trying to ever grasp the workings of the Venus person's mind. The *opposition* of Venus and Mercury in the overlay is curious and often amusing in its effect. The people really are operating on very different wavelengths, yet this often has a positive impact on the relationship. The Venus person will respond to the Mercury person as a stimulus, waking up interests and ideas in the Venus person which, while external in origin, somehow do not seem foreign or irrelevant. The Mercury person will feel a tug from the Venus person's personality to stretch out their own mind and interests and will be motivated to engage the Venus person in some shared activity. The "push/pull" quality of this opposition in the overlay is sometimes a bit demanding on the individuals, requiring the expenditure of considerable mental and emotional energy, but the result is usually a livelier, more vital relationship which finds an unusually wide range of things to do and enthusiasms to share.

Composite In a partnership, the blending of Venus and Mercury energies especially reveals its impact since presumably the individuals are spending large amounts of time either literally together or linked by some mutual accord when they are apart. The composite *conjunction* indicates an intuitive linkage which is almost uncanny in its intimacy. The individuals seem to ebb and flow on the same tide, sharing highs and consoling each other in lows with almost effortless closeness. The primary value of this aspect is obvious, the ability to derive the greatest pleasure from the ordinary goings-on of life. Its downside is equally obvious. The psyches of the partners blend in such a harmonic resonance that the rhythms of life are amplified. This negative side is not a major factor if the individuals are relatively stable personalities. Only if one or both personalities fall natally at the extreme ends of the emotional scale will this be much of a problem. The *sextile* between Venus and Mercury in the composite chart has the rather unglamorous but very helpful effect of the individuals' simply not annoying each other as they go about the routines of living. Neither partner is inclined to be upset over the way the other stacks the canned goods, hangs up the clothes or drives the car. This might not seem all that important, but more partnerships have come apart over an accumulation of repressed annoyances over little things than because of a single, big explosive event. A well-known marriage counselor once observed that more marriages failed over hair left in the sink or leaving the seat up on the toilet than because of infidelity, an outcome which this pleasant little aspect does much to prevent (including infidelity).

Since the maximum separation possible between Venus and Mercury is approximately 76 degrees, these are the only meaningful aspects which can be formed by these planets in the composite chart. The minor *semi-square* aspect might add a touch of argumentativeness to the partnership, but nothing of great importance. As with Venus, where the unadjusted calculation of the midpoints results in an impossible opposition between Venus and Mercury and this is adjusted to a conjunction in the composite chart, the effect appears to emphasize the male/female polarity of the "conjunction." The blending results in a complementary interactive bond no less strong than the true conjunction, but less vulnerable to amplifying the highs and lows of the interaction.

Venus Aspects To Neptune

Some astrologers argue that any close link between Venus and Neptune is potentially worrisome because these bring together a perceived sense of beauty and excellence with illusion and fantasy, an invitation to over-romanticize and exaggerate the worth of another human. A more charitable argument is that all humans have worth and beauty, but these attributes are only visible to a relatively few other humans and Neptune provides the special "sight" necessary to find and appreciate these virtues. On balance, the more positive aspects seem to contribute a sweet blindness to the flaws and foibles of the individuals involved and do much to make close and continuing contact less vulnerable to eroding away the initial attraction between people. Only the more harsh aspects are likely to create serious problems of false images and unreal dreams and need to be carefully appraised in assuring the relationship is based on rational assumptions.

Synastric This *conjunction* has, for all its inherent strength, a surprisingly gentle impact. The Venus person will feel a certain soft warmth and uncriticality toward the Neptune person, seeming almost unable to respond with other than a tolerant smile and reassuring tone. The Neptune person will respond to the pleasing image of the Venus person, finding beauty and value in what is perceived to be the "inner" person, regardless of whether a perception of physical beauty is created. This conjunction usually results in the individuals wishing the best for each other and being willing to speak up in defense of the worthiness and deserving qualities of the aspected person. The *sextile* and *trine*, contrary to their normally less potent impact, seem with Venus and Neptune more likely to stimulate the individuals to convert their perceptions of each other into an active interaction. The Venus person is likely to find great charm and "presentability" in the Neptune person, a feeling that being with the Neptune person somehow surrounds them with a lovely aura of beauty which is evident not only to them, but to others. The Neptune person is likely to find real beauty, in a physical sense, in the Venus person and, if there are other romantic/sexual links, these aspects often result in an intensely romantic feeling. Perhaps no other aspects offer so much magic of an enduring sort to a relationship. They are free, in themselves, of any self-gratifying interest and contain only an enduring appreciation of the other person's qualities, qualities which often are not visible or appreciated by the world at large. The *square* is, regretfully, a potential troublemaker. This aspect stimulates the fantasies resident in everyone's imagination and impels the individuals to see each other as instruments with which to realize those fantasies. The result usually is that the individuals are really interacting with a self-created fantasy than a real human being. What form these fantasies take is a product of the individual natal charts, but it can be assumed that the Venus person will feel a desire to yield themselves to the Neptune person and use that person as a device to escape reality. The Neptune person's fantasies will be more to the point, with a desire to "possess" the Venus person as one might a lovely work of art, a mechanism to enhance the Neptune person's own self-image and gain some evidence of their own self-worth. This synastric link is not strong enough in itself to cause great difficulty, but in the context of stronger romantic/sexual bonds, it leads the relationship off into an unreal fairyland made of self-serving illusion, a path almost certain ultimately to cause disillusionment and even humiliation. The *quincunx* is a fleeting but still present influence with its primary influence involving the stimulus of any fantasies which relate to frustrations and repressed resentments. The Venus person will respond to the Neptune person as someone who somehow might free them of the restraints and disappointments in their life and allow them to float freely above the turmoil. The Neptune person will feel the press of any inner resentment over a lack of control over their own life and find in the Venus person a potential for release of these through some form of manipulation or control. Not usually a very meaningful synastric link in itself, it can show itself if either individual suffers from a significant number of repressed guilts or fears and, because of other stronger links, the two people are drawn into a relationship. It is not necessarily harmful even in this circumstance, but there will be an undertone of "using" each other to escape the trials and disappointments of life. The *opposition* has the strongest male/ female polarity, drawing the individuals to the extreme ends of this scale in the way in which they deal with each other. A normally assertive person may find themselves very passive and yielding if linked by this aspect, or a typically reserved and guarded personality can become quite aggressive in responding to this linkage. The Venus person will feel a sense of the melting of the usual defenses and protections in dealing with the Neptune person and an atypical willingness to express whatever they may be feeling. The Neptune person will sense this vulnerability and openness and be released from anxiety over the potential for being rejected. The synastric opposition does not, in itself, make the individuals "attractive" to each other, but rather seems to eliminate the usual barriers to acting on whatever attraction is generated by other aspects.

Composite One of the more common reasons to form a partnership is to increase the chances of realizing whatever scenario the individuals have erected as a definition of "the good life," the fulfillment of dreams and hopes in whatever form the natal charts are inclined to define these dreams. Venus/Neptune aspects in the composite chart offer some insight into how successfully the individuals will blend this questing energy for fulfillment, particularly as this relates to pleasure, the joy of moving and beautiful experiences and simple self-gratification. The *conjunction* suggests a quite close and harmonious accord on what particular life contents will give the greatest satisfaction and pleasure to the partnership, those often being indicated by the house in which the conjunction occurs. To the degree that a partnership benefits by a mutual enjoyment of the same forms of pleasure, in or out of bed, this aspect indicates there will be strong commonality of responses and the partners will not have to look outside the partnership for a major part of their individual recreational companionship. The *sextile* and *trine* may not result in such a common definition of a pleasing and satisfactory life content, but it makes the combining of dreams and aspirations easy and, not uncommonly, quite productive. With such aspects, the individuals are more likely to seek out gratifying activities which complement or even support each other and, quite often, actually enhance each other's pleasure in their own particular pleasure pursuits. If you are looking for someone to accompany you on the guitar while you tootle your recorder or do the upholstery work while you repair the engine of your prized classic car, these are the aspects to look for.

The *square* is a misleading and devilish aspect in a composite chart because it tends to result in the partners creating unachievable aspirations for the relationship. The energies of the chart blend in a way that the individual evolves hopes for the partnership which somehow are contrary to the situation in which it operates or are unrealistic in terms of the personalities of the individuals. The end result is usually a persisting sense of frustration over unfulfilled hopes and a feeling that the partnership will never "get it together", in many cases, the partnership itself will never quite be able to be realized and the individuals may go on for a long time never finding a way to create a true partnership in the form they fantasize. The *quincunx* tends only to unbalance the efforts of the partnership in seeking pleasure and joy from life, giving a greater emphasis to one partner's preferences than to the needs of the other. If you see a wife sitting glumly in a boat while the husband is immersed in the joys of fishing, there is likely this little annoying quincunx in the composite chart. The *opposition* indicates that the partnership itself is the dream realization object, the major element in the scenario which the partners come together to realize. In a sense, this is the old "rose-covered cottage" plot in which all problems are solved by forming the partnership and everybody lives happily ever after. While this rarely actually occurs, at least the blending of energies in the composite chart gives it a better chance than normal. Assuming the individuals have realistic expectations and there are stronger, more meaningful links elsewhere in the chart (particularly the *absence* of any really difficult and stressful composite links), there is no reason to assume that the partnership will not meet at least a major part of the expectations. Certainly there will be a strong appreciation of the value of the relationship which emerges from this opposition. Only if the individuals are seeking to escape reality via the partnership or are motivated by entirely self-interested motives without genuine concern for each other is this opposition likely to lead to difficulties.

Venus Aspects To Pluto

Pluto's association with death and regeneration and the impersonal qualities this implies makes links with Venus's intensely personal and intimate energy take a curious turn. In responses to another person, Venus needs typically focus strongly on the special "identity" that person has and finds unique beauty and value in that identity. With aspects from Venus to Pluto, however, the Venusian need which is operating appears to require either the detachment from that special identity or even perhaps the sublimation or destruction of it. Pluto is often associated with violence. In human terms, Pluto is associated with such acts as rape or murder which, by their nature, require a detachment from the persona of the victim. Venus is too gentle and giving a force in the personality to take this form of response, but the drives which are aroused and the value placed on the other person run much deeper in the psyche and touch the unreasoning, primal needs, needs which do not shock or surprise us in nonreasoning animals, but which we find somehow disturbing in humans who are supposed to be "above" such motivations. Romantic/sexual obsessions, uncluttered lust and powerful base-of-the-spine responses (figuratively and literally since the most primitive and unevolved elements of the brain actually are in the spinal cortex) are triggered by Venus/Pluto aspects. These are really more instinctive than reasoning, more a part of the procreative drive to perpetuate the species than abstract love and, ultimately, less related to the aggregate personality complex of the individuals than to some primal core quality. Standing alone, these aspects are only a deep bass chord in the response just barely within our audible range; but with other more conscious and powerful links, they add the same quality to the harmony, a profound cosmic resonance that is felt in the gut rather than the mind or heart.

Synastric A *conjunction* in the overlay will be felt by the Venus person as a subconscious penetration into the inner self, almost like an involuntary tensing of the muscles in the stomach. It is not necessarily a "threat" response, but there is awareness that the Pluto person somehow is reaching them at a level immune to good sense and sound judgment. The Pluto person will tend to fix on the Venus person with an often hard to control need to move in and encompass that person. Normally this is sufficiently disturbing for the individuals that their conscious mind steps in and counsels careful reappraisal, but both know they somehow "got to" each other. The *sextile* and *trine* are less unsettling and would probably be characterized by the individuals as a "turn on," a keenly felt but entirely manageable impact. The Venus person will unconsciously begin a general assessment of the Pluto person, asking if there is anything beyond this initial, rather uncomplicated response to warrant pursuing the matter. The Pluto person will be less passive, reaching out openly for an indication that the Venus person is responsive. This really is a human version of what nature film makers like to characterize as the "rutting season" and "receptivity." In the majority of situations, that's as far as it goes (assessment), but with other links which give the interaction broader value, it's yo-ho-ho and off to bed we go! The Venus/Pluto *square* in the overlay arouses the less attractive qualities in both planets, the self-gratifying urges of Venus and the strong urge to possess another without regard to their feelings or desires in Pluto. Lust is the least desirable form with the Venus person feeling only a sort of mindless need for sexual gratification and the Pluto person a strong desire to "use" the other person in an impersonal and dominating way. Again, by itself, it only rumbles in the gut without much likelihood of producing anything other than a tendency to stare, but with other links, it adds a touch of anger and detachment to any intimacy. The usually minor *quincunx* is felt somewhat more strongly with Venus and Pluto because it is, by its nature, an aspect which requires the sublimation of one thing to another. The Venus person may feel a deep vulnerability to the Pluto person, an inability to say "no" if caught in a situation which exposes them to this potential. The Pluto person will likely sense this vulnerability and find it erotic and tantalizing. Of course, the individuals will tend to retreat from this disturbing response if there are not other significant links, but if there is a strong romantic/sexual bond, this aspect will likely manifest itself in an imbalance of dominance and passivity in any intimate relationship.

The *opposition* is perhaps the most disturbing of all the Venus/Pluto aspects in the overlay. If the Venus person is a self-confident and assertive personality, they will feel a strong sexual tug and at least explore its potential. If, however, the Venus person is easily frightened or lacks self-confidence, their own response will scare the hell out of them and they will run for cover. Either way, the Pluto person is obsessively drawn to the Venus person and will pursue that obsession to its logical end. There is too much primal anxiety in this opposition to make it pleasant, but it is hard to ignore and its ensnaring quality is musky and dark. It, more than nearly any other aspect possible, ought to come with a "handle with care" label.

Composite This is not a very elegant way to see these Venus/Pluto aspects in the composite chart, but nonetheless the most accurate way: these aspects indicate what harmonics exist between the deep, lusty needs of the partners and how successfully they can, within the partnership, fill that need for each other. They do not, in themselves, create lust, but they influence how the partners, in the grip of these drives, respond to and answer each other. The *conjunction* blends two virtually identical forms of such energy. The individuals will be able to be entirely open and unrepressed in responding to each other, but this aspect can make the partnership too centered on this element of the interaction. It also may, over time, limit variety and imaginativeness since neither brings unique individual needs or inspirations to the partnership. Nonetheless, in romantic, sexual partnerships, it gives a sturdy, rather uncomplicated sexual base to the relationship. The *sextile* and *trine* are exciting and innovative blendings, with each partner comfortable with the other, but willing to introduce new and revitalizing avenues of side trips which are almost certain to be acceptable and pleasant. The most attractive quality of these aspects is that the intimate sexual side of the relationship, while important, will be kept in perspective and retain its good humor and humanity. Perhaps the only shortcomings of these aspects is that they cause a lot of giggling and squealing. The Venus/Pluto *square* in the composite chart intensifies the intimate physical element of the partnership, but tends to turn it more inward, focusing on the self-gratifying side of the intimacy. The energies do not blend smoothly and comfortably despite their intensity and the partners are reduced to looking to their own gratification with little regard for each other. The "you get yours and then I'll get mine" quality persists and this will, over time, have a separative and anger-producing effect. A lot of self-help books on the subject will be consumed and something which should not have to be discussed and analyzed will be subjected to endless scrutiny. Eventually, one or both of the partners will be exhausted by all this and go elsewhere, a sad result because neither could really do much about the fundamental conflict and lack of harmonic blending of energies involved. The *quincunx* is not a serious barrier to intimacy, but the partners will have to understand that their needs differ in significant ways. Provided there is the love and goodwill to respond to each other's unshared needs, the result can actually be rather nice: reassuring each other that there is an honest desire to please and willingness to stretch a little to do so. In a less than sturdy relationship, however, one of the partners will get tired of yielding to the other and, to some degree, either withdraw from the intimacy or lose enthusiasm for it. The *opposition* is a wild and woolly aspect, causing the partners to push out to the extreme ranges of their capacities for physical intimacy. Whether this only rattles the china or gets out of hand and turns violent and dangerous is entirely a matter of the natal potentials of the individuals. This aspect in the composite chart indicates that the full potential, for good or bad, of each of the partners' capacities for passionate expression is triggered by the intimate interaction. Usually this is only aerobic, but one should be aware that if either partner is unstable or prone to extremes, the contact between the individuals will heighten this tendency. Whatever the result, this is a powerful blending of energies which links the deep sources of urgency and demand in the partner's natal personalities.

ASPECTS TO MARS

With Mars, we see the polar opposite of Venus's giving, appreciative qualities, the focus of energy on the "I WANT" side of this polarity. Standing by itself, Mars is only an unfocused reservoir of this energy, its style colored by the natal sign in which it falls and its directionality by the natal house. In synastric interaction, contact with the other chart provides the acquisitive drive of Mars with a clear, stronly-felt objective on which to affix itself. Aspects made to Mars by the outer planets stir the unconscious needs and wants in a personality and, in synastry, the other person whose chart is aspecting Mars becomes the object which will satisfy these unconscious needs. In appraising synastric aspects to Mars, it is especially important to see all such interchart aspects within the confines of the natal potential of the individual. Even the strongest and most powerful synastric aspects will not substantially alter the capacity of the individual to aggressively seek out what they want. A shy and uncertain person natally will, despite any potent interaction with another chart, remain that same person in the way they deal with the individual who is causing the response. In fact, when confronted with unusually strong Martian responses, such a reserved person is likely to be disconcerted by them and go through a meltdown of confusion and anxiety rather than openly respond to them. A natally assertive and confident person, on the other hand, will come storming out in pursuit of their goals even if the aspects made to their Mars by the other chart are rather minor. The natal Mars potentials are what ultimately motivate overt behavior in individuals, behavior which causes others to place them on a scale of aggressiveness, self-confidence and power of personality. Synastric responses will not fundamentally alter that natal pattern of behavior no matter how numerous or powerful.

In synastry then two thoughts need to be kept in mind in analyzing Martian potentials. First, the synastric links will not fundamentally alter the way in which a person behaves toward other humans. A placid personality with low emotional energy will remain so in a synastric interplay and, regretfully, a violent or unstable personality will also. We would be fooling ourselves to believe that synastric links will bring about any basic change in the behavior patterns of any individuals. The other idea to remember is that there is a tendency to judge the depth and significance of another person's behavior on a scale based on our own personality. If we are shy and guarded in our responses and we are dealing with a person who is very openly and aggressively pursuing us, there is a quite understandable tendency to give great weight to that behavior, to relate that to our own rare and uncommon manifesting of the same sort of behavior. Similarly, if we are open and unguarded in our dealings with others and we face a response from another which is seemingly very reserved and self-protective, we will be tempted to assume a lack of interest in that person based on what such behavior would mean in ourselves. It is necessary to lay aside any yardstick for appraising someone else's behavior based on our own personality (a very common trap in astrology) and appraise the probable Martian responses in terms of the natal potentials of that other individual.

Mars Aspects To Uranus

Uranus is sometimes characterized as an influence which is unpredictable and prone to bringing about surprising and unsettling effects. Once having defined its influence this way, we are relieved of having to speculate about what impact it will have; which is a nice safe way out of really tackling this planet's influence, but something of a cop-out. Actually, in synastry, Uranus is much better defined as an influence which frees us from the self-imposed restraints which all humans, consciously or unconsciously, set up around themselves and allows us to respond in ways truer to our actual motivations and urges. This is "eccentric" (a departure from the norm) only in the sense that we usually are so anxious about how others will interpret our actions, fearful about some ill-defined consequence of our action or just victims of habit patterns that our responses are grooved down well-worn and presumably "safe" channels. The Uranian influence in synastry is really nothing more than a willingness to cast aside these binding concerns and respond without regard for the potential disapproval or rejection which normally strangles our interaction with other humans.

Linked with Mars in either a synastric overlay or in the composite chart, the Uranian influence allows us to overtly act out impulses which are created by the other, more personal responses with greater freedom and with less concern for protecting our precious ego images. In themselves, these Mars/Uranus links do not create any particular type of response (i.e., compatibility, affection, love, etc.), but only open the doors to the other feelings we have. In fact, the Uranian tone is so essentially detached and unconcerned that the real mechanics behind our responses is a kind of "what the hell" attitude, an indifference to the consequences which, under other circumstances, might worry us. Of course, this can sometimes get us into trouble if we are too willing to yield to these influences, but in human relationships, it seems far more often unnecessary barriers and preset requirements block open interchange between people. The probable behavioral consequences of Mars/Uranus links are not that difficult to predict either. The Mars person will behave within the framework of the natal sign and house in which Mars falls and so will the Uranus person...but with a greater likelihood of openness and initiative. With these links, people behave as they would *like* to behave rather than as externally imposed customs and norms prescribe and we see a clearer, more revealing pattern of behavior inherent in the natal personality, patterns which otherwise might not show themselves until much later in the interaction.

Synastric The *conjunction* in the overlay seems to have less impact than one would expect from such a normally potent aspect. Mars is already a fully charged battery and the additional energy provided by Uranus floats on the top of this reservoir of assertiveness as useful but not necessarily required fuel. The Mars person will feel a greater freedom to express whatever they may feel about the other person and the Uranus person responds within the framework of the Uranian natal potential, but the exchange may not seem to have any particular place to go. In the end, the most likely consequence is a mutual feeling that here is someone who is unusually easy to be around and candid. The *sextile* and *trine* are more likely to engender some sense of objective role image, a feeling that here is someone with whom one can actively cooperate to get to some goal formed by other aspects between the charts. The Mars person will be stimulated by the Uranus person's presence and feel an urge to reach out and include the Uranus person in their plans. The Uranus person will likely see the Mars person as a personality with whom they can release some drives usually not shared with others. The general effect is at least a willingness to explore the potentials of the interaction without going through a lengthy preliminary feeling-out process. The synastric *square* typically opens the lines between individuals who might otherwise see each other as "not my type." While this initial appraisal is often right and the two individuals may not be generally compatible, this square does allow each to look past the surface and discover what value may lie beneath in personalities they might otherwise dismiss out of hand. The Mars person will be surprisingly drawn to the Uranus person, wondering why this particular person interests them when other similar-seeming souls do not. The Uranus person will be attracted by the off-center character of their own response, fascinated by the very foreignness and unusual quality of the exchange. The risk with this aspect is, of course, that we sometimes suspend the wisdom of our past experience in defining what is good for us in human relationships, but with some reasonable care, this aspect can give us some interesting detours from our main course. The *quincunx* has a curious sexual undertone in its influence, introducing the quality of true "exoticness" in the response. The Mars person may feel an impulse to find out "what it would be like with *that* sort," (i.e. a partner who might usually not be likely to interest them). The Uranus person, like all humans, will have some rather bizarre and eccentric fantasies in the inner recesses of their unconscious and the Mars person will cause these little devils to start pushing on the door to get out. Not a strong motivator in itself, if this little quincunx coexists with more powerful and personal links, it contributes a twisty little kink in the interaction, the ultimate impact of which will depend, of course, on the natal needs and qualities of the individuals involved. The *opposition* in the overlay seems most evident in its impact with male/female relationships which not only bring together two unlikely individuals, but also give the interaction itself an unusual form. People who are typically unable to form real friendships with members of the opposite sex may find this aspect present in the rare exception to that rule. The Mars person will feel an urge to reach across the common barriers to human interaction and form some sort of a bond with the Uranus person. The Uranus person will tend to be very impulsive and quick-responding to the Mars person without much regard to the odd and atypical quality of the interaction. The phenomenon of a "Marian the Librarian and the Travelling Salesman" sort of link is characteristic, but the fully evolved form of the interaction will depend more on other linkages between the charts. This opposition only makes initiating such off-the-wall relationships possible.

Composite Mars/Uranus aspects in the composite chart are very common in relationships which get off the ground and take some recognizable form for the obvious reason that the urge to act and the timing and form of the impulse translate that urge into reality link in a way which allows the individuals to "get it together." The *conjunction* in the composite chart is a powerhouse link with the partners experiencing an unusually high level of simultaneity in impulses, a great boon to any two people who want to get something done. What that "something" is depends on the overall pattern of links between the individuals and, in particular, the house in which this conjunction falls, but whatever that may be, the individuals will fall very easily into acting out their mutual impulses with little likelihood of bad timing, misinterpreted signals or confusion.

The *sextile* and *trine* make spending time together effortless and a real pleasure because the individuals generally want to use their energies in compatible ways and find doing so with each other free of much of the compromise and sublimation required in most human interactions. There is a spontaneity and free-flowing quality to the partnership which makes it great for fun and games, but also quite good for more serious cooperation. The individuals do not chafe on each other and there is often a very high level of teamwork and coordination with these aspects. Whatever active and outwardly oriented efforts the partners put forth usually works out well–great for doubles partners, dancing and trying out waterbeds. The *square* between Mars and Uranus is often present in proto-partnerships, those that tried vainly to get something going but failed. This blending of energies creates a strong sense of intense urgency in the interaction, but of a confrontational and demanding nature. The would-be partners often want something of each other, but these wants diverge in such a way that the interaction deteriorates in flashes of anger and bitterness. The individuals abrade each other no matter how hard they try not to and, in the end, find that their life rhythms and impulses butt heads rather than flow together. Too bad, they say, because there was something very electric in the interaction. Not many can, however, live comfortably with such high voltage. The *quincunx* is of minor influence, perhaps giving a pushy and selfish quality to the interaction. Because it is the kind of flowing together of energies which tends to turn off any initial attraction, it is uncommon to find it in composite charts of functioning partnerships. The individuals don't cooperate well nor do they seem to want the same forms of energy release and activity. When it does occur in an existing partnership, there will be this little tint of separative self-orientation in the partnership, not unbearable, but reducing the overall closeness of the partnership by forcing the individuals to limit the number of things they can do together happily. The *opposition* is not really a helpful link in a composite chart. The individuals are pulling against each other in response to their own individual drives to achieve and do. The result is very divisive, driving the individuals into more and more independent pursuit of their own goals.In time, each will question the value of a partnership which contains so little mutuality and cooperation and probably decide to either go it alone or find a more harmonious partnership. The initial attraction was based on this "oppositeness," a seemingly intriguing, but ultimately stressful bond. Probably the only way this aspect could work in a durable partnership would be if it was, from the beginning, an "arrangement" for purposes other than true blending of personalities. Not a very pretty set-up, but more common than many would like to admit.

Mars Aspects To Saturn

Mars and Saturn are sometimes seen as inimical forces with the outward-reaching and forcefulness of Mars confronting the granitic immovability and confining force of Saturn in a hostile and dangerous way, the irresistible force meeting the immovable object. This image is really overly dramatic and exaggerated, particularly in synastry, since it fails to recognize the positive value of Saturn's stabilizing and form-giving influence on the otherwise potentially undisciplined and unfocused energy of Mars. Perhaps the best way to see aspects between Mars and Saturn is as a strong, driving force being shaped and directed by a channeling influence, an influence which may only give the energy direction and consistency or may block, deflect or weaken its potential. In synastry, the influence of the Saturn person on the Mars person is to shape the overt behavior of the Mars person, for good or bad. The Saturn person, in exercising this influence, is responding across a broad spectrum from supportive guidance to rigid confrontation. The end product might be characterized as a measure of how freely the individuals can function in their quest for life satisfaction within the confines of the interaction.

Synastric With the overlay *conjunction* between Mars and Saturn, the weight of the Saturn restraint may be too confining and unrelenting to be truly helpful. The Mars person will sense this potential for being limited by the Saturn person's influence and wriggle away from the steely grip which the Saturn person seems to want to maintain on them. The Saturn person may feel a kind of "godfather" impulse to direct the life energies of the Mars person, but this will too often be expressed in a remote and impersonal way rather than with warmth and empathy. The *sextile* and *trine* between these muscular planets permits a much more tolerable and stabilizing influence. The Mars person will be less discomforted by the boundaries created by the Saturn person and often derives a sense of security from the moderating influence of these aspects. The Saturn person will feel compelled to play the role of navigator for the Mars person, using their influence to keep the Mars person generally on course, but not being strongly impelled to impose a specific destination. With these aspects, both persons feel a workable balance between bright optimism and sensible precaution can be managed. The *square* sets the stolid and inflexible perceptions of the Saturn person smack in the line of the rush of Martian energy, almost inevitably forcing some measure of confrontation and anger. At first, the natural aggressiveness and combativeness of the Mars person may respond to this as a challenge and determine to overcome the entrenched position of the Saturn person, but time will make this seem a useless waste of energy and the Mars person will turn away from the pointless battering for more rewarding paths. The Saturn person will have great difficulty in not succumbing to an urge to try to deflect the course of the Mars person into a path which, to the Saturn person, seems more sensible. In doing so, the Saturn person is almost forced into a rigid and unyielding stance and digs in to hold their ground. This obviously is not a very rewarding sort of interplay of personalities. Life makes too many such confrontations unavoidable so, when we have a choice, we walk away from those where the rewards are not worth the combat. The *quincunx* in this overlay often creates a feeling of unconscious threat and anxiety in the Mars person as if the Saturn person has the power of personality to take over control of the Mars person's behavior and warp it to their liking. Usually this is a worrisome feeling and will cause the Mars person to back away, but if the Mars person is natally (or even temporarily due to transits) uncertain of their life course and their own ability to find their way, the Saturn person may be accepted as a guru to whom the Mars person hands over a major degree of life control. The Saturn person will likely feel the leverage given them by the Mars person's response and act to establish this kind of directorial control. How significant this interplay becomes depends on the inherent strength of both persons and the remainder of links between them, but under most circumstances, this little aspect will find a way to alter the course of the Mars person's life for good or bad unless they quickly remove themselves from the influence of the Saturn person. The *opposition* between Mars and Saturn has traditionally been seen as one which sets up a struggle for dominance between the personalities. In some very intense interactions, this may be the response, but more commonly the effect is to drive the individuals away from a balanced center of the spectrum of behavior toward highly polarized roles. The Mars person will feel pressed to act more aggressively to pursue whatever the other linkages energize, but the Saturn person will feel an opposite compulsion to make negating counter-moves. The two persons become like chess players, thrusting and counter-thrusting with little real progress in any direction. Ultimately, the entire interaction becomes like digging a hole in loose sand and both players give up in frustration, too neutralized by the other to achieve much of anything.

Composite The blending Martian energy with the drive to achieve some stable life form in a partnership is often a major element in both the durability and sense of success the partners may achieve. The *conjunction* between Mars and Saturn in the composite chart will likely reveal its influence as an intensely goal-oriented, but not necessarily well-integrated relationship. The partners will find in the relationship the resources to drive hard for some mutually desired objective and, because of this single-minded focus, may well achieve it. This pouring of all the energy of the relationship into a single channel may, however, leave the remainder of the relationship undeveloped and, once the goal is achieved, the individuals may find they do not, in fact, have much of a basis for enjoyment of life on a broader stage. The house in which this conjunction falls will suggest what that specific goal may be and, from the other elements of the composite chart which are left uninvigorated by this concentration, one might speculate on where the partnership may not evolve. The *sextile* and *trine* promise a more balanced and stable joining of efforts and particularly suggest that the influence of the partners on each other will be productive and will serve to keep both individually on some useful and rewarding path. The primary influence of these aspects is to establish comfortable perimeters for the combined energies of the individuals which allow room for individual fulfillment of life goals without setting up unnecessary and unwelcome limits. The sextile and trine do not create much excitement or fervor in a relationship, but they give it strength and stability within which other more lively forces can play without damaging the stable foundations of the partnership. With a *square* in a composite chart, it is hard to imagine the individuals reaching a stage in a relationship where they would even try to create a blended partnership. There is a feeling which grows out of any close and continuing contact which leaves both individuals feeling that they could never reconcile their goals, never put together a winning plan for life or be happy with the same results. This aura of divergent paths makes the prospect of forming a partnership seem senseless since the purpose of such a partnership would be to enhance each person's chances of achieving the kind of life they seek. It is entirely possible that other factors may strongly attract and bond the individuals (sex being the most likely), but neither will ever be convinced that a fully evolved relationship and commitment would work. If they are compelled to try, it is probably either a function of immaturity or despair... and almost certainly will result in a disappointing and frustrating breakdown later. The *quincunx* is a subtle but potentially nasty little influence in the composite chart, most likely to reveal itself in intimate relationships. If the partnership is a romantic/sexual one, this quincunx can result in one partner seeking physical dominance over the other with all the unpleasant implications that entails. Mars always has its physical/sexual implications and Saturn its impulse to control and confine. This may only mean that the intimate physical relationship will evolve into a more extreme polarization of giver and taker, but if one personality is natally inclined toward trying to dominate (e.g., a Sun or Moon angular aspect to Pluto) and the other to yield up the responsibility for their own fate to another (e.g., Neptune angular aspects) this quincunx can deteriorate into aberrant forms of intimacies. This is not the typical result, obviously, but with this aspect, the people may be drawn together and bound by some form of this dominance/passivity interplay and, therefore, should guard against it being too central a force in the partnership. The *opposition*, like the square, sets up such a barrier early on in a relationship that it rarely occurs in functioning partnerships. The individuals simply work against each other, cancelling rather than supporting each other's efforts. Given other less than harmonious links, this can even result in violent outbursts of anger and sometimes even physical striking back, a reaction to the bottling up effect of this composite aspect. Most likely the individuals will sense this influence early enough that they will not attempt to form a real partnership and content themselves with whatever limited interaction they can tolerate to get what they seek from each other. Only if one sees marriage or other intimate commitments as an indoor form of bullfighting would this be a useful aspect in a partnership. Even then, the mortality rate would be high and the life expectancy of the relationship short.

Mars Aspects To Jupiter

Synastric The *conjunction* between Mars and Jupiter in the overlay links two highly energetic and outgoing elements of the personality. The Mars person will be stimulated to show the most positive and strongly emphasized qualities of their natal potential (especially as these are indicated by the natal sign and house) and hold back very little in showing whatever they may feel about the Jupiter person. The Jupiter person will feel a kindly and open response to the Mars person, accepting the behavior of the Mars person at face value and with the most charitable interpretation. This overlay aspect opens doors to the free expression of whatever other links are operating between the individuals. The *sextile* and *trine* lubricate the process of involvement with each other in an active sense. Perhaps the key idea with these aspects is "cooperation" in that the individuals can function well in tandem and generally not stress or irritate each other even in continuing close contact. The Mars person may play the role of the initiator, but there will be no sense of resentment over this from the Jupiter person. The *square* tends to exaggerate the expression of assertiveness in the Mars person, making them behave in a way which may cause the Jupiter person to feel that they are "coming on too strong" or being too selfishly demanding. The Mars person will not find it easy to understand the extreme responses (often negative) of the Jupiter person in the face of the Mars person's reaching out for contact and, in the end, will probably write off the Jupiter person as too self-oriented and ungenerous to be linked with. The *quincunx* is a troublesome aspect in an overlay between Mars and Jupiter. Everything the Jupiter person does seems to get a negative and suspicious interpretation from the Mars person, almost as if any Jovian generosity is somehow calculated to trap or influence the Mars person. With this aspect, the best and most honestly motivated actions of the individuals will come a cropper largely because an absence of parallel perceptions of what kind of behavior can be trusted in another. In terms of the normal active expressions of self, the two people just don't understand each other. The *opposition* most commonly has a counteractive influence with the behavior of the individuals seemingly neutralizing or nullifying each other. Mars and Jupiter are assertive and demonstrative influences with drives from both revealing themselves in the outward expressions of the individuals. With the opposition, the actions of the Mars person seem so consistently at odds with the normal behavior of the Jupiter person that the Mars person feels blocked and restricted. The Jupiter person's apparent resistance to the wants of the Mars person are so frustrating for the Mars person that they will redouble their efforts to squeeze out of the Jupiter person what is wanted in the way of response. The probable result will be a kind of paralytic confrontation of will with neither achieving what they want, but not really understanding why.

Composite This is a lively *conjunction* in the composite chart, linking two personalities who, by their natal character, are independently expressive and, in contact with each other, literally bubble and steam with a blended energy. The composite house in which this conjunction falls will suggest the focal area of the partnership in which this burst of energy will show itself, but whatever that may be, this will not be a flaccid and inexpressive interaction. The only real problem this conjunction can create is an overemphasis or overreaction between the partners in that composite house area, giving that particular element of the relationship more importance than the overall quality of the partnership warrants. It seems to give an extra charge to the behavior of the individuals when they are functioning within the partnership, so the target of all this active pursuit of the mutual goal becomes particularly significant. Hopefully, the house in which this occurs points to an objective which is supportive rather than counterproductive for the partners. The *sextile* and *trine* promise very productive and successful blending of efforts toward the goals of the partnership. In fact, these are the true aspects of a working partnership, people who are capable of blending efforts and energies for some common purpose. If we accept that all partnerships are, in some measure, formed to achieve something which the individuals believe are best achieved by combining talents and energies, then these useful aspects suggest the goals and, with these aspects, the most probable results of this blending of Martian energy and Jovian imagination and optimism. The *square* will trigger a substantial amount of enthusiasm and energy in the partners, but not always provide an objective which satisfies both individuals. This is an aspect of dynamic tension, a quality in a partnership which may either stress the individuals more than either prefers or hyperactivates them to achieve their individual objectives. The partners will not have much success in focusing the partnership on a single mutual objective, but perhaps the competitive and contentious effect the partners have on each other will stimulate each to greater achievements in their individual areas of endeavor. How successfully all this stressful behavior can be managed within the relationship will depend on the overall relationship. The *quincunx* will add a small problem of priorities within the relationship and a struggle over who is steering the ship. With two personalities with similar levels of self-confidence and assertiveness, this can be a nagging little irritant since "who's the boss?" will be a recurring issue. More typically, however, the natally dominant personality will direct the partnership's efforts and resources toward some goal perceived as mutually beneficial and the less demanding partner will accept this and go along with the plan. The composite *opposition* most commonly occurs in pairings of individuals already predisposed to self-indulgence and a tendency to undisciplined actions, so just as often the partnership only exaggerates this problem. This is a relatively harmless little quirk in an otherwise stable and balanced partnership, leading only to an occasional excess which can be managed, but it remains a potential land mine in less responsible relationships. Any tendencies toward overdoing or poor self-management in the natal personalities will be accelerated by the contact between the partners, each encouraging the other to step over reasonable bounds. The houses involved will suggest where the vulnerabilities lie for the partnership and what might be put at risk by mutual self-indulgence. Every excess comes with a price tag and, with this opposition, neither partner is likely to look at the price tag before committing the relationship.

Mars Aspects To Mercury

The principal influence of Mars/Mercury are to give impetus to communication between the individuals and to stimulate each of the persons to extend their minds and capacity for expression because of the contact.

Synastric The *conjunction* will trigger an initiative in the Mars person to reach out for verbal contact with the Mercury person and, in the presence of the Mars person's interest and openness, the Mercury person will usually respond by articulating what is perceived to be the common interests of the two persons. The most noticeable impact of this link in the overlay is the seeming inexhaustible capacity the individuals have for conversation, comparing ideas and responses and using each other as vehicles to bring to the conscious level for expression of feelings and attitude that might not normally be articulated. The *sextile* and *trine* are more relaxed and slower forming in their effect, but the individuals will find that whatever impulses bring them together will be easily translated into clear understandings. With these aspects, it is more likely the Mercury person will be the initiator of any communicative link with the Mars person's personality being both the stimulus to and often the focus of the communication. The Mars person may well use the interplay to aid in working out issues which are churning in their heads and come to rely on the Mercury person as a friendly and interested listener. The *square* often produces a rather aggressive and confrontational type of exchange between the individuals, appearing less like a friendly conversation than a heated debate. The Mercury person seems almost to sense that the Mars person operates from a different perceptual base and is impelled to challenge that life vision. The Mars person will, depending on other links between the chart, either rise to this rather barbed verbalization with a spirited defense of their own ideas or, if there are no other important links between the charts to motivate the Mars person, simply close the contact with a conversation-deadening cut. Even when there are strong positive links between the charts, the verbal interplay between the two minds will be intense and fiery at times. The *quincunx* sometimes leads to mind games between the individuals, with the Mercury person motivated to establish a kind of mental dominance over the Mars person by appearing more intelligent or better informed. The Mars person often finds this unsettling and, if doubtful of their own mental skills, threatening. This quincunx usually only leads to poor communication and one-way conversations, but if either individual is vulnerable to being jerked around mentally by a stronger intellect (perhaps by natal angular aspects from Neptune to Mercury), the Mercury person may play Svengali to the Mars person, leading them into some pseudo-intellectual or even metaphysical quagmires which are actually self-serving journeys for the Mercury person. Anyone who tells you "everybody is doing it!" is hoping for such a quincunx to make you believe that. The *opposition* will stimulate exchanges between the individuals, but over time will probably be more argumentative than harmonious. The Mercury person will feel an urge to try to persuade the Mars person to agree on any issues which bear on the relationship. The Mars person, in the face of the rather aggressive sales effort, will usually dig in and take a firmly opposing stance. Actually neither may feel as strongly as this interchange may suggest, but the face-to-face impact of this opposition is to polarize attitudes and impel the individuals to press for their own positions. This, of course, can operate within a very friendly and companionable environment and be only a source of ongoing stimulus like a long-lasting chess game or other amiable competitiveness at an intellectual level. This is the exception, however, since such polarization of ideas and attitudes will more likely cause discord between all but the most strongly attracted personalities.

Composite Composite links between Mars and Mercury reveal themselves primarily in the relative harmony individuals can achieve in responding to and dealing with the ordinary and necessary tasks of daily life with which any partnership must cope. The *conjunction* is, in a quiet and unobtrusive way, very helpful in a partnership. The individuals tend to respond to events and occurrences quite similarly and, as a result, will generally have little difficulty in agreeing on what to do about these situations. Since the apparent solutions to problems are mutually easily defined, dealing with problems and coping with the mundane demands of life as these affect the partnership are usually successful. The *sextile* and *trine* are helpful in another way for a partnership, with the partners having just different enough responses to the daily problems to individually contribute solutions which might not occur to the partners, but similar enough perceptions that agreement is possible. These aspects add a very imaginative and creative quality to the partnership which, in some circumstances, can be translated in significant worldly success. The individuals literally "think well" in tandem and become an exercise in the old axiom that "two heads are better than one." With the composite *square* between Mars and Mercury, the partners will have a difficult time coming together to deal with the partnership's tasks. The individual perceptions of how to respond to any problem are so different that the interaction often dissolves into argumentative cantankerousness. The relationship will be marred with recurring disputes over how joint resources will be used, what priorities should exist within the relationship and even where to go on vacation. In earlier times, such couples just banged each other on the head with a skillet, then got on with life. In our contemporary world, they will, no doubt, see a therapist, write a self-help book and appear on a talk show...but they still won't be able to achieve a peaceful and harmonious relationship. The *quincunx* has a barely perceptible influence in a partnership, becoming a significant element in the relationship only if the individuals are not generally intellectual peers. Normally, this little aspect only limits the areas of common intellectual interests and throws the relationship back on its affectional, emotional or romantic/sexual contents for its sustenance. In those exceptional, intellectually unbalanced situations, however, the dominant partner may have, in fact, entered the relationship in part because it allows them to play the authority figure and direct the life of the other partner in a tutorial way. For some persons, being someone else's supermentor and "straightening out their life" is a powerful aphrodisiac. The *opposition* between Mars and Mercury is such a barrier to agreeing on even the most elemental issues in a relationship that it is unlikely to appear in the composite chart of a functioning partnership. Each individual wonders how the other person can be such a blockheaded nitwit about so many things when it is obvious what the "right" view should be. This is not your normal, everyday basis for spending time together or developing much admiration and respect for each other. Even lust rampant on a field of centerfolds is unlikely to overcome this nonblending of Mercury and Mars energies and the individuals will wind up wishing each other the worst.

Mars Aspects To Neptune

Mars is not only the energy source for our capacity to reach out and take what we want from the world, it is also the muscle and sinew of our self-discipline. It is not happenstance that the word "martial" (which has the warrior aspect of Mars as its root) contains both the idea of bravery and physical aggressiveness, but also such currently out-of-fashion ideas as self-sacrifice and honor. In all the world's mythologies, the most honored and revered figures (if not the most loved or pandered to) were those like Tyr and Ajax and Parsifal who sacrificed themselves for the good of the whole... sometimes the whole tribe or society, but in the context of astrology, the whole persona. The power and vitality of Mars can be, and usually is, used for the good of the whole personality; people use their aggressiveness and courage in their own self-interest, but not without regard to the restraints of ethics and principles... usually. Sometimes the strength of spirit weakens, the restraints of ethics and morality crumble and what primitive cultures call "The Snake in the Mind" contorts itself to justify and rationalize the use of Martian strength in self-gratifying and almost mindless ways. The primal force which melts away the eons of civility and permits us the license to indulge our most primitive drives is Neptune. Linked with other, less volcanic planets, Neptune's influence can be sweet, unfettering and creative, but with Mars already standing with spear in hand, prepared to lunge, it can open the gates for our least elegant impulses. Such links do not, as with Pluto, trigger the animal violence deeply stored in our psyches, but rather numb the frontal lobes: the seat of judgment. Neptune is the solar system's oldest "mind-altering substance."

Synastric The overlay *conjunction* is perhaps less of a problem to cope with than the strong impulse it releases might suggest. The deep sense of being touched by another person at some primal level is present, but more a burst of diffused light than hard, cutting beam. The Mars person feels low octave rumbles in their physical innards almost like some distant but unidentifiable thunder. They are unsettled and perhaps a bit threatened, but not stampeded. The Neptune person senses vague images being released, but these are so unfocused that no clear scenario is seen. Both people feel each other's presence like the vibration in a floor as a train passes, but unless there are other, more intimate and immediate links between the charts, nothing much will happen. The *sextile* and *trine* float half-defined images of physical and soul-stirring gratification through the mind, a sense that the other person somehow would bring to our touch the most profound needs in us. With these aspects, the response is not that disturbing with the Mars person feeling much like a person standing in front of a bakery case, secretly envisioning themselves gorging on cream puffs. The Neptune person feels a shiver of physical response which starts somewhere in the lower brain and heads south. Deliciously private and mildly off-center, the interaction from these aspects is manageable and usually adds only a "hands in the cookie jar" enticement to whatever else may be present. A little manageable secret guilt can leaven any relationship. The *square* is the Devil himself... and not in formal dress. The Mars person will feel like their self-restraint and good judgment just settled into a position near the navel and nothing any higher up the spine is functioning. The Neptune person will find a not-so-small voice from the darkest corner of the persona saying, "I WANT THAT ONE!" With any lubrication from other, more powerful aspects, the individuals will slip down the slope and into a compulsive bonding. Standing by itself, this square will only rock the libido and bring blood to the cheeks, but with much else to sustain it, it is likely to lead to some sort of effort to realize the fantasies it engenders. The *quincunx*, if in tight orb and with some other strong aspects, is the least pretty response. It triggers the most mindless and berserk qualities of the Mars person, the urge to discard all restraints and pillage from the situation whatever is available. The Neptune person will feel a deep drive to possess and gorge themselves on the Mars person without regard to that person's human identity, a response which is the origin of the feminist complaint that women are seen only as "objects." Anyone who has, however, observed the audience for male strippers knows this is not a uniquely male response. The *opposition* kicks up a nice, healthy lust mixed in with more than a touch of romanticism and, as a result, isn't all that troublesome. Both persons feel a quality of "naturalness" about their responses, a wholesome, in-tune-with-the-earth rutting impulse that is difficult to feel guilty about. The Mars person will respond to the Neptune person almost instinctively as a natural partner in the oldest and most necessary game in the human survival process. The Neptune person will perhaps sense the essential goodness and uncluttered beauty of the procreative drive. Nothing much will come of all this unless other, more important links exist, but the individuals will enjoy each other's presence even if just in the abstract. It is much like digging one's fingers in good, rich soil. It's reassuring to feel its fertility even if we don't plant a seed.

Composite Mars/Neptune aspects in the composite chart suggest how harmonic the active fantasies of the individuals are and, more particularly, what the outcome might be of a combining of energies to realize these fantasies. Mars always contains some significant element of sexuality and these aspects do appear often in romantic/sexual partnerships, but the influence of Mars/Neptune aspects go beyond the rather uncomplicated scope of sexual fantasizing. Our fantasies and dreams provide much of our "fallback" motivation when real life fails to provide excitement or satisfaction and the pursuit of these imagined satisfactions often keeps us from giving up in the face of discouragement. The capacity of partners to share their individual rainbows to chase contributes much to a relationship's pleasurability and the partners' feeling of openness in articulating, and even combining energies to realize these dreams is one of the reasons the partnership is formed in the first place. Whether this joining of fantasies produces healthy and sustaining results or creates problems for the partners depends, of course, on the aspect and the composite houses involved. In a world saturated by TV with an almost infinite range of possible fantasy fulfillments, these Mars/Neptune aspects play a significant role in how successfully the partners blend their efforts to actively pursue and realize their dreams. The *conjunction* makes the open sharing of fantasies easy and uninhibited. This does not necessarily mean that the partners use each other as tools in achieving the scenarios they create, but the ability to reveal these dreams and, in doing so, understand their meanings, is a useful element in any sort of relationship. The composite house in which this aspect falls often indicates the common thread of shared images which the partners find attractive. This aspect won't create or sustain a partnership in itself, but in the context of a broader harmonic one, it contributes a special kind of secret intimacy and freedom. The *sextile* and *trine* suggest that the partners can actually help each other achieve some of the things about which they fantasize. The individuals each bring resources of mind and heart to the relationship which somehow legitimizes and makes feasible some of the aspirations which exist in both persons. It is not so much that the partners have the same dreams, but rather the components of each individual's scenarios work together to make a more complete and satisfactory result. These aspects suggest, perhaps more than any other, that the existence of the partnership itself sustains optimism and hope in the individuals and keeps them slugging away at life's frustrations without losing heart.

The *square* indicates a blending of energies which can create at least false hopes and, under certain conditions, really cause the partners to stray off onto some foolish and unrealistic paths. This aspect seems to have its greatest frequency and most damaging impact in romantic/sexual relationships. The unfulfilled romantic fantasies every individual carries in their imagination are triggered by this aspect when the individuals come together. Each seems to the other a living fulfillment of these unrealized dreams. Regretfully, each is usually playing internal mind games, creating an unreal "partner" and scenario rather than interacting with the actual personality before them. Unavoidably, there are particular persons who, just by their presence, trigger these self-deluding fantasies in us and we go deliriously off down the path in pursuit, but it won't work...really. The best we can hope for is a gradual and relatively painless realization that it was all a dream. The worst is that the very dumbest and irrational parts of our self will be revealed for all the world to see and the price we paid for this fantasy can be ridiculous or even tragic. The *quincunx* between Mars and Neptune in a composite chart can be the seed of some really humiliating and soul-crushing interplay if it occurs in an intimate relationship. There are very few humans who do not have, buried somewhere in their psyches, some unpleasant little scenarios involving another human in an intimate situation and, regretfully, this composite aspect can encourage the partners to act these out. It's a minor and subtle aspect which usually plays a small role in partnerships, but in the presence of other significant links which contain strong emotions and intense sexuality, this quincunx can have ugly results. Look closely at the natal predispositions in the individual charts and, if there are hard aspects from Saturn, Neptune or Pluto to Moon or Venus, be cautious. The *opposition* often indicates that the individuals themselves are the object of each other's fantasies: the "perfect lover" syndrome or some other manifestation of the human tendency to try to find in another human an idealized reality. While there is nothing inherently harmful in this if it occurs in an otherwise sound and compatible relationship, too often it causes the partners to blind themselves to the flaws in both the individual personalities and how these complex constructions blend. The strong polarity of this aspect gives it special pungency in male/female relationships and can hold people in a relationship built on very limited but intense fulfillment of some particular fantasy even if the partnership is not, in general, a productive or compatible one. There is an obsessional quality to the interaction this opposition triggers and the partners must guard against blinding themselves to real meaning of the relationship and paying too high a price for such a narrow return on their emotional and physical investment.

Mars Aspects To Pluto

Aspects between Mars and Pluto do not seem to play a major role in synastric interactions and the impact they do have appears so often to produce anxiety or stress it is almost easier to see them as principally valuable by their absence. Links which bring the very individualistic vitality and questing energy of Mars into contact with the cold and faceless force which deals with us as only one of the countless and meaningless collections of atoms in the cycle of the death and rebirth of the universe is never a pleasant experience. Pluto forces us to face our own insignificance and tiny finite span, a chore the ego-centered and chest-thumping Mars deeply resents. We don't really respond well to other humans who remind us of our own lack of importance and only in the sense that they help us retain perspective and perhaps to renew ourselves as a result of being reminded where we fit into the universe are they welcome. With all but the most gentle of aspects, we tend to back away from this insight. One of the primary reasons for establishing a relationship with another human is to make them a part of our emotional and intellectual support structure. Someone who insists on shaking and rattling that edifice on which our ego is suspended is not usually our favorite social companion, lover or friend.

Synastric A *conjunction* in the overlay usually produces a response that the individual can somehow play a role in resolving some problematic barrier in our lives. The Mars person will unconsciously be motivated to use the contact with the Pluto person to lever some change into being, drawing on any evidence that the Pluto person has an interest and awareness of them. The Pluto person may be motivated to step in and alter some element of the Mars person's life and to almost force a particular role or form on the Mars person. There is nothing especially personal or warm in all this (although obviously other synastric links can create such feelings) and neither person is likely to be even consciously aware this is all going on. Retrospectively, however, both will realize that they interacted in a way which probably brought about some change in both their lives. The *sextile* and *trine* take more sensitive and interested forms of expression, but will nonetheless remain subtle and impersonal. The Mars person may look to the Pluto person for some insight and support in dealing with the fluctuations in their lives with an unconscious sense that the Pluto person can and will be helpful in an impersonal way. The Pluto person responds with a kind of cosmic detachment to the problems of the Mars person, but not without interest and a willingness to offer an objective and nonjudgmental response. The *square* can trigger some unconscious hostility and resentment in the Mars person much as we feel a detached resentment toward unpleasant weather or bad news from overseas. The Pluto person will respond negatively to the Mars person's apparently unwarranted self-importance and high opinion of self. In extreme instances, with aggressive and hostile personalities, this can actually bring about senseless confrontations which just seem to materialize out of thin air. Most ice hockey players seem to come equipped with this built-in synastric relationship to the world. The *quincunx* only adds a touch of subtle unconscious fearfulness and self-protectiveness to the Mars person response, perhaps because the Pluto person instinctively feels able to dominate the Mars person. All this is operating well down in the unconscious of both persons, but it is felt and will usually result in a mutual backing off. The *opposition* may even cause a kind of titillating terror in the Mars person a bit like that which motivates people to take heart-stopping rides in amusement parks. While not a powerful synastric link, if it occurs in the context of strong emotional or sexual response, it can add a darkly attractive note to the interaction. Certainly the Pluto person will sense that they unbalance the Mars person in some obscure way and, if motivated by other aspects, may decide to use this advantage to achieve some end. Again, this is neither a warm or personal response, just an undertone of some subtle but powerful forces operating beneath the surface.

Composite The Mars/Pluto *conjunction* in the composite chart gives a penetrating quality to the way in which the partners interact. The blending of energies allows the individuals to get below the surface of the relationship and dig deep into each other's psyches. The result is that, over time, the partnership brings about some fundamental changes in the personalities due largely to their influence on each other. Neither inherently good or bad in its impact, much depends on the overall relationship and the natal personalities whether this results in healthy and useful casting off of old and tired components or brings out the less attractive qualities in each. If a partnership is formed, however, both individuals will be substantially modified in the way they attack life by this interplay. The *sextile* and *trine* seem to make it easier for the partners to combine their personal abilities in bringing about changes in their shared lives. Perhaps the most helpful result of these aspects is that when, as is almost inevitable in any durable partnership, things go awry and it becomes necessary to back off, pick up the pieces and cope with difficulties, the partners can and do help each other in this task. The *square* creates a deep-seated and hard to cope with unconscious hostility between the partners. This often is buried so deep and far below the surface of the relationship that it manifests itself only under stressful situations. When the partnership is, however, confronted with trials or difficulties, this hostility emerges in the form of explosive anger, vilification of each other and sometimes even in physical violence. Anger at this remote and impersonal level is the kind that festers for long periods without ever being openly expressed, but eventually it will come out... coldly and without compassion. Ultimately, it is too strong a barrier to real warmth and compassion to be tolerable in most relationships. The *quincunx* seems only to limit the capacity of the individuals to cope with stress in the relationship. The probable result is a tone of intolerance and unwillingness to empathize with each other when individual problems arise. The *opposition* is a separative influence which shows up largely only when something truly important and vital to one of the partners arises. In that situation, the partners seem unable to combine effectively to deal with the issue and, in fact, unconsciously may work against each other. It is almost as if the partners are trying to sublimate each other's egos and, under pressure, use "put downs" and sarcasm to squash the other's hopes and aspirations. This is an unfriendly and cold aspect which is unlikely to occur in functioning partnerships for obvious reasons. Who needs a live-in enemy?

ASPECTS OF THE
OUTER PLANETS

Outer planets, particularly Uranus, Neptune and Pluto, are often characterized as "generational" because they move slowly through the signs (i.e. Uranus requires about seven years to transit a sign, Neptune and Pluto up to twenty years). Not only do members of the same generation share the sign position of these planets, they also will often share any natal aspects formed by the outer planets. Even the signs and aspects of faster moving Jupiter (one year in a sign) and Saturn (about and two-and-one half years in a sign) are often shared by individuals who come into a relationship. Since the outer planets condition the unconscious motivations and aspirations of individuals, aspects between these outer planets establish "generational" attitudes, value systems, priorities and worldly perceptions. Differences in these natal factors produce "generation gaps" and, obviously, will play a role in the coming together of partners. We rarely choose a person for a close relationship if that person sees the world in very different terms than ourselves. The outer planets moving through the signs sometimes, however, contribute to the ability of persons of considerable age difference to form successful partnerships. This particular effect on relationships is discussed in more detail in Part III; however, it should be obvious that, given a large enough span of time, the movement of these outer planets will cycle back into harmonious blending of sign positions (i.e. the twelve-year cycle of Jupiter, for example, can provide a link between persons separated in age by these same twelve years).

The synastric overlays and composite charts, aspects between the outer planets, seem not to play any major role beyond this generational effect in the early attraction and exploration of compatibility between individuals. Only after a period of time, and then only if the individuals make a serious effort to form a durable relationship, do these aspects play a role in the partnership. More than anything else, they influence the ability of the individuals to establish and maintain a harmonious on-going agreement on life-style, philosophic and political values and priorities. Such foundational accord is usually not too important if individuals are only casually and socially involved, with disagreement cropping up only over questions of how to use recreational resources or on which kind of music to listen to. Over time, however, as partners begin to try to work in tandem to achieve some mutual goals, these life structure-forming aspects reveal themselves and influence the capacity of the individuals to achieve a sense of mutual success and fulfillment from the relationship.

Jupiter in Aspect to Outer Planets

Harmonious aspects such as the *conjunction, sextile* and *trine* from Jupiter to any of the outer planets tends to moderate and give positive energy to the impact of the planet. With *Saturn*, the effect is to enhance the ability of the relationship to stimulate steady, productive growth and achievement. With *Uranus*, the effect is to heighten spontaneity and capacity to find in the everyday events of life a greater shared pleasure and relaxation. With *Neptune*, Jupiter in harmonious aspect gives a rather agreeable shared capacity to "dream the same dreams" and find mutual satisfaction in fantasizing about the same aspirations, a very pleasant influence when two persons join their resources to seek fulfillment of personal hopes and dreams. *Pluto* in harmonious aspect to Jupiter appears to reinforce the conviction of the partners that, through the relationship, they can bring about things in their lives which they might not individually be able to achieve, a kind of "faith" in the positive value and worth of the partnership.

With *squares* or *oppositions* from Jupiter to the outer planets, slow-growing discords or a discouraging sense of underlying lack of real agreement over life goals may emerge in a partnership. With *Saturn*, these difficult aspects make it harder for the partners to find harmonious paths for each to follow in their careers or life roles. The choices each makes about how to realize individual potentials do not seem to blend well and even conflict and inhibit each other. With hard aspects to *Uranus* from Jupiter, the partners have a more difficult time managing their self-indulgent and impractical impulses with the individuals actually seeming to encourage each other to overdo. It seems almost as if the partners egg each other on to make fools of themselves. With hard aspects to *Neptune*, Jupiter creates a pervasive sense of dissatisfaction and discontent in the relationship. Somehow the individuals never seem to find it easy to establish a life-style or home base which lives up to expectations, and the partnership may be characterized by a pattern of many job changes, moves and impractical schemes to achieve some illusory end. *Pluto* in square or opposition to Jupiter can create a confrontational undertone to a relationship which reveals itself in a pattern of bickering, sarcasm and complaints. Partners who spend as much time "putting down" each other as being supportive and encouraging are showing some of the influence of these difficult aspects between Jupiter and Pluto.

Saturn Aspects to Outer Planets

Saturn's structure-giving qualities can be either enhanced or made more restrictive by aspects formed to the outer planets, but the ultimate influence of these subtle and unconscious aspects usually does not reveal itself early on. Slowly, over time, the partners come either to realize and appreciate the stabilizing influence of the positive aspects or feel the restraints of the hard aspects. A partner who, after fifteen or twenty years of marriage, describes the relationship as either one which made possible achievements largely because of the devoted support of the other person or, conversely, explains a divorce by citing that the other partner "never let me be myself and become what I could have become" reflects the impact of these Saturn aspects.

Saturn in *conjunction, sextile* or *trine* to *Uranus* seems to help the partnership stay on track, with a minimum of unproductive wandering up blind alleys and unsuccessful detours. The conjunctions, in particular, give a strong directedness to the relationship as if the individuals came together from the beginning to achieve some specific goal. The result may seem to others an almost obsessive slugging away at achieving a place or status or condition, the value of which may appear out of proportion to the energy required, but to the partners the joint goal is worth the effort. Positive aspects from Saturn to *Neptune* appear to have the opposite effect, relaxing a tendency toward compulsive behavior in the individuals, reducing the stress between the partners and allowing each to be more "laid back" in the relationship. With *Pluto,* these positive aspects will reveal themselves only if the partnership confronts situations which seriously threaten or assault it. Partners who weather deeply discouraging or heartbreaking events and come together under such stress to support each other show the deep but strengthening harmonics of these two planets.

With *squares* or *oppositions* from Saturn, the soundness of the partnership structure is undermined in subtle ways. With a hard aspect to *Uranus* from Saturn, the partners leave each other with the unconscious sense that major elements of their natural personality and modes of expression must be suppressed to avoid clashing with each other. If *Neptune* is in hard aspect to Saturn, it seems much harder for the partners to develop real confidence in the long-term promise of the relationship. A lingering feeling that "something will go wrong" will hover just below the surface which time will never totally mollify. Saturn square or in opposition to *Pluto* leaves a subtle little knot of unfocused anger buried deep in the relationship, a factor which may not prevent a partnership from forming and continuing, but adding to the difficulty of remaining tolerant and forgiving within the relationship.

Uranus, Neptune and Pluto in Aspect

The impact of these three outer planets in aspect to each other in synastric overlays and composite charts is so diffused and generational that their role is almost undetectable. In general, the only importance they may have is to aggravate or reinforce any negative natal tendencies of the individuals if the partners are approximately contemporary and a part of a generational group which had the misfortune to be born with hard natal aspects between these planets. Yuppies marry yuppies and interact with each other to increase the effect of the natal aspects which made them yuppies in the first place. Only where major age differences occur in a partnership and the individuals do not share these generational sign positions and aspects in their natal charts do these synastric or composite aspects seem to play any role in relationships. In such situations, it is well to look back at the natal charts and see if there are factors which cause either partner to feel alienated from their own generation or deeply insecure about their own abilities to attract and hold a partner (see Part III for more comments on this subject).

PART III

APPENDIX

A man gazing at the stars is

proverbially at the mercy of

puddles in the road.

Alexander Smith
Dreamtrop

Thoughts on Why
We Form Relationships
And Other Irrational Behavior

From the Fringe

It is not possible to spend over twenty years analyzing natal charts and the relationships of the persons symbolized by those charts without arriving at some conclusions about the dynamics which motivate all of us to seek partners. The material presented in the main body of this book falls within generally accepted theories and consensus of modern astrology (although a few parts may just barely squeeze in) and benefits from the accumulated labors of many to support the validity and reliability of the techniques and conclusions. In this final informal section, some purely personal (and not necessarily trustworthy) ideas are offered to the reader largely to stimulate further exploration and evaluation. These ideas and conclusions are not offered as proven theories or even as reliable guideposts; only as speculations which, to some degree, seem valid to me, but should be tested by the reader in the real world before being included in their own synastric work method. Perhaps the most trustworthy rule in astrology is that, since it is an intuitive art rather than an exact science and the product is no better than the aptitudes and insights brought to the art by the individual practitioner, the best test of what is "correct" technique is whether it works in the real world. Astrologers, of necessity, must experiment and explore until they find the particular methods which produce the best results for them. This life-long and sometimes frustrating learning and testing is unavoidable in astrology. The only hard and fast rule is that each serious astrologer must continue to explore new ideas and techniques. Once we stop this exploration and fall into repetitive application of the same old techniques, our insights and intuitive sensitivity not only stop growing but even seem to atrophy. These final 'thoughts then are offered to stimulate more and broader exploration and, hopefully, to open some exciting new paths to the reader along which they can make their own unique discoveries.

Where do our Paradigms Come From?

As we mature, we gradually develop inner, highly personal paradigms or personal models of the "perfect" partner. Normally we are only vaguely aware of these paradigms and could not articulate them clearly no matter how hard we try. Usually the best we can do is observe that some person we encounter is "my kinda guy" or "that's the way girls ought to look" and let it go at that. On rare occasions, however, someone comes along who seems to really hit the target bang on and we come totally unglued in the face of this personification of perfection. We may not be able to articulate our paradigms, but we can certainly recognize them when they come wrapped in the single package and stand before us seemingly effortlessly reducing us to jelly. What are the roots of these deeply felt and profoundly moving surges and can they be isolated and understood within the framework of synastry? Perhaps.

One seemingly promising path to understanding how these paradigms form as we mature lies in the interaction of the natal and solar charts. The "logic" is straightforward enough. If we see the natal chart as our life-long birth gift of potentials (and limits) within which our individual life experience, insight and wisdom play in developing our own personality, and we also see the solar chart as the projected self to which the world responds and makes demands accordingly, we begin to see the interaction between these two "selves" as the engine of our maturation. Most of us are constantly trying to reconcile what we *are* with what the *world demands of us*, trying to reconcile and come to terms with our natal chart versus our solar chart. As noted earlier in this book, some persons have a rather easy time of this. Their natal and solar charts may involve different signs and houses, but the two are fundamentally harmonious, and as a result, the world does not ask anything of them (based on the solar projection they send out) which is discordant with their natal capacities. Others of us, however, do not have such an easy time. The world demands of us qualities which are much harder for us to produce, and we are forced to find ways to cope with these external demands even if we did not enter the world equipped to respond easily to them. In general, the natal angle between Sun and Ascendant gives a broad guide to whether this reconciliation of the two selves will be painless and straightforward or difficult and stressful. Persons born very near sunrise have Sun and Ascendant in or near conjunction, and as a result, what the world "sees" is very much like the inner, natal person, making this reconciliation quite simple and uncomplicated. Those fortunate enough to have their natal Sun in sextile or trine with their Ascendant seem also to have an easy chore. What the world (and individuals within that world, including partners) asks of them is harmonious and easily managed. For the majority of us, however, the reconciliation is not so simple.

As noted earlier, we can reach a general conclusion about this life-long demand on individuals by comparing the qualities of their natal charts and their solar charts and arrive at some broad conclusions about how the persons will mature as they learn to meet the requirements of the society: in effect, how they will mature toward the solar personality, at least in an external sense. The question of the origins of paradigms evolves from this need to reconcile the two selves. There is, in my view, some evidence that the mid-points between the planetary positions of the natal chart and the solar chart may give us clues to the formation of these paradigms. Arguably, these mid-points symbolize the unconscious conclusions we reach about how we can most successfully and perfectly meet the demands of the outer world within the limits of our natal potential: in effect, a paradigm for our most perfect self. It is not a major leap then to assume that, once having arrived at a deep inner conclusion on what (for us anyway) constitutes "perfection," if we happen to chance upon someone who seems to have all or most of these "perfect" qualities, we respond with great enthusiasm.

Atypical Relationships and Relating Patterns

The great majority of relationships in our society conform, in a general way, to what we collectively define as "normal": heterosexual, conventional in expression and involving persons who are roughly contemporary and possess broadly similar background and experience. A percentage, however, do not fit this general pattern; and, while not strictly within the confines of synastry as a topic, it is worthwhile to consider some of the natal characteristics which appear to point to the forming of atypical and off-center partnerships. We can also speculate here about the factors in natal charts which produce a life pattern of unsuccessful, unfulfilling or even self-destructive relationships. These speculations will not, however, extend to homosexual behavior, which is both highly controversial in its astrological origin and a whole subject in itself deserving of its own book. These speculations about the ingredients of natal charts which might be interpreted as deflecting persons away from traditional and conventional relationships, are therefore limited to heterosexual relationships only.

The most common forms of relating behavior which might be defined as "atypical" would seem to be (1) those involving major age differences (perhaps twenty years or more) (2) the inability to play out the conventional gender role resulting in a kind of "role reversal" in relationships and (3) the recurring forming of self-defeating, humiliating or even self-punishing kinds of relationships despite many experiences with such partnerships (i.e., "Gawd, didn't you learn *anything* last time about getting involved with that kind of person?").

May/December Match-ups

After more than twenty years of chart analysis, the natal characteristics of an individual who tends consistently to fall into romantic/sexual relationships with persons greatly differing in age seem rather clear. The natal chart will usually reveal two clear factors: a series of difficult aspects from Sun and/or Moon to the outer planets (suggesting that one or both parents failed to provide a strong, positive role model during childhood) accompanied by the natal Saturn falling in either the 5th or 7th house. For women in particular, one tends to find this combination of factors will include a personal history of a father who deserted the child or, at least, was harsh, unfeeling and remote. If a woman's natal Sun receives squares or oppositions from the outer planets and there are some weakening aspects from Neptune to her Venus or Mars, a history of abuse or molestation by adult males during the woman's childhood is sadly rather common. The pattern then is of early exploitive sexual experience and a developing sense in the young female that such relationships are not only "normal" but likely the only ones for which she is "fated."

It is important to understand, with this particular combination of natal factors, that it is *not* the early sexual experiences with adult males which *cause* a life-long pattern of relationships with much older men. It is the 5th or 7th house placement of Saturn and the absence of a strong, positive relationship with the father which "cause" the young girl to seek relationships with much older men. Precocious sexuality and early affairs with older men seem to be based on an inability to form peer relationships with contemporaries and a need to play out a childlike and protected role within the context of a relationship with a mature and parental male. The dominant theme of these natal characteristics is that such May/December match-ups do not require of the junior partner a full acceptance of responsibility for the success of the relationship, but rather allow the junior partner to enjoy the benefits of a safe, undemanding male "sponsor" without being asked to function as a full contributing partner. It is this manifestation which causes us to describe Saturn natal house placements in the 5th and particularly the 7th as suggesting "difficulty in establishing and maintaining relationships." The "difficulty" is simply that the girl believes unconsciously that, if asked to function as full partner in a peer relationship with a man, she would almost certainly fail. The easiest course of action then is to enter into relationships where such demands are not made by the senior male partner who is typically quite content with a limited sexual relationship and does not seek a true partnership.

With men, such combinations of difficult parental experiences and a 5th or 7th house natal Saturn placement are more likely to produce withdrawal from relationships in general and a life pattern of hermit-like, crusty bachelor behavior rather than May/

December relationships. Much more commonly, the male counter-player in May/ December relationships will show natal chart factors which (1) involve the strong sexually oriented signs of Taurus, Scorpio and Capricorn, (2) Sun or Mars in the 8th house, and (3) not uncommonly, Neptune in the 5th or 7th, suggesting a recurring discontent with and romantic fantasizing about relationships.

In general then, May/December relationships (some of which are surprisingly durable) occur between (A) women who, because of hard aspects to Sun from the outer planets had an unfulfilling father/daughter relationship and did not mature with a positive and confident attitude toward men *and* have the 5th or 7th house placement of Saturn which causes the seeking of undemanding and limited forms of relationships with men and (B) men who seek relationships primarily for sexual gratification (as suggested by the prominence of the 8th house) and have an inability to accept the more mundane qualities of a peer relationship with a woman because of the pervasive romantic discontent engendered by the Neptune placement. Other factors, of course, modify and give a particular flavor to such relationships (e.g., a strong presence of the parental Cancerian qualities in the male or the dreamy romanticism of Pisces in the woman), but the general predictors seem to be those cited above.

Of course, May/December match-ups with the woman as the senior partner have always existed, and in today's more tolerant social environment, such relationships are becoming more evident if not more common. The same general predictors apply with the young male showing the same natal characteristics as the young female (i.e. Saturn in the 7th with hard aspects to the Moon from the outer planets) and the senior female partner revealing a natal predisposition for a sex-centered relationship (prominent presence of Taurus, Scorpio and Capricorn) and the weakening influence of Neptune on the woman's view of partnerships. Even more commonly, the prominent qualities of Cardinal signs and the "parenting" tones of Cancer or Capricorn will occur in the senior female natal chart, strengthening any predisposition to play out the maternal side of the relationship. As with the junior female, the young male often has experienced an unsatisfactory mother/son relationship and doubts his capacity to meet the demands of a peer relationship with a contemporary woman. Again, it is important to stress that in such May/December match-ups of either combination, the junior partners are heterosexual by preference and enjoy their biologic role; they just do not have confidence in their ability to perform it to the satisfaction of a peer. This is clearly different than the homosexual rejection of the biologic role and the preference for the traditional role of the biologically opposite sex.

In analyzing a synastric problem then, we should look for these predictors as part of developing an understanding for what kind of relationships are most natural and comfortable for the individual. Perhaps the most serious error we might make is to allow any pre-formed attitudes about the "appropriateness" or motives of the individuals in such May/December match-ups to influence our analysis. While such match-ups are atypical and unconventional, for the individuals involved they are *not* abnormal; they are their most natural and fulfilling method of filling the relationship needs. Let he/she who has never had an off-center fantasy cast the first stone.

Roles to Fit the Personality in Relationships

One of the more rewarding experiences in astrology comes when, through an analysis of an individual's birth gifts and potentials, we can help that individual come to terms with and make peace with the true inner qualities of their personality. These qualities which be sufficiently divergent from social norms that the individual has suffered greatly in trying to force themselves to conform to the "standard" roles imposed by society. In synastry, it is not uncommon to find that a pattern of failed or unsatisfactory relationships derives from this stress between the demands and conventions of society and the essential qualities of the personality. Even in an era of feminism and a more fluid general attitude about what activities are "appropriate" for the sexes, there remains a strong cultural bias toward seeing certain attitudes, values and activities as "feminine" or "masculine" and, of course, this carries over to the roles individuals feel compelled to play in a relationship. Despite the more strident complaints of the feminists, these generalities about the sexes are nothing more than the aggregated observations over thousands of generations of the fundamental proclivities of the sexes (rather than any nasty male conspiracy). Cultural anthropologists have quite thoroughly demonstrated that these general personality qualities were a necessary survival mechanism for the human race through all but the last few centuries of its several million year history. The generalities about "masculine" and "feminine" behavior, temperaments, strengths and weaknesses, etc., are, as with most generalities, generally valid. The problem arises when an individual, because of unique personal qualities, cannot comfortably conform to the social norms which grow out of these valid generalities. With astrology in general and synastry in particular, we can identify these exceptions to the generalities and aid the individual in both being more comfortable with their natural potentials and, in relationships, understanding a bit better what kind of partnership is most likely to work well for them.

The uncommon but still existent problem of a heterosexual person with marked personality qualities which run cross-grain to the social norms of their biological roles presents a special problem for us. Women with a dominant presence of Fire, Cardinal and masculine signs, angular houses and strong, energizing aspects or a man with a dominance of Water, Mutable and feminine signs and cadent houses will have almost unavoidably suffered difficult early years struggling to meet the social demands of their youth sub-cultures. These "pushy tomboys" or "nerds" come out of their early years shy, socially uncertain and often embittered, yet will still try to play out their assigned gender roles in relationships, usually with sad and discouraging results. Again, we must stress that these are heterosexual persons by preference and are not rejecting their biological roles. They are only persons whose personal qualities contain an androgenous combination of traits; a delicate balance of so-called "masculine" and "feminine" qualities, talents and interests. Their problem is two-fold: the society around them presses them to sublimate the personality elements which do not match their biological roles; and, because they do represent a rather small percentage of the population, they have greater difficulty locating partners whose personalities blend with their own. It is not surprising that these people often become deeply discouraged about relationships and, in their late 20's or early 30's, withdraw into a bitter, insular life style, walling off even the potential of finding a harmonious mate.

With application of general astrological analysis, we can help these persons to understand and be comfortable with their androgenous qualities and overcome unspoken fears that they are "strange" or latently homosexual or failures as human beings. With synastric techniques, we can help them understand that their natural partners are also androgenous sorts, happily heterosexual but atypical and just as discouraged and discontent. Obviously, synastric techniques can compare the personalities of specific individuals and suggest whether particular individuals of this group can come together and meet each other's uncommon, but entirely healthy and honest, needs. If we can, with compassion and insight, help these unusual people make peace with themselves, reinvigorate their openness to potential relationships and satisfy them that there is no cosmic and immutable law which requires the female to be the passive and domestic partner and the male to thump his chest and carry a war club, we have done a small but valuable service.

Relationships as a Form of Self-Punishment

Why, we ask, do some people continually and serially involve themselves with relationships which result in their abuse, mistreatment and distress? Why do they tolerate partners who are insensitive, greedy, dishonest and even sometimes violent with seemingly endless patience and self-abnegation? The conventional wisdom (which is probably generally valid) is that this pattern of behavior grows out of a seriously diminished self-esteem and an inability to believe that they are intrinsically valuable enough to warrant the true affection and regard of a partner, that they are destined to eventually "fail" as humans under the close scrutiny of a continuing relationship. The strategy used by such persons then is to allow themselves to become involved only with other humans whose incapacities are as great or greater than their own real or imagined ones. Women in particular who suffer with this personality pattern are vulnerable to partners who seem so utterly needful of their womanly attributes and so wholly at the mercy of these needs that no "failure" on the part of the woman would dislodge the man from the relationship. Nothing seems more seductive to such personalities than the hysterical declaration that "If you leave me I'll (a) die, (b) commit suicide, or (c) kill you": an abject confession (seemingly) of the unbreakable hold the person has on the hysterical partner.

Tragically, the result of all this is usually exactly the opposite of what was hoped for: the emotionally crippled and unstable partners exaggerate each other's worst qualities and the partnership deteriorates into the messiest and most self-defeating situations. Even more tragic is that a series of such experiences only reinforces the doubt and anxiety of the individuals over their own capacities to perform satisfactorily within a relationship and create a balanced and successful partnership. Eventually they will give up and sink into escapism of drugs or alcohol, promiscuity or retreat.

With general astrological techniques, we can identify those factors which diminish the person's sense of their own value and help them understand that they have an especially difficult task of developing a sense of personal worth. They particularly need to seek circumstances and partnerships which can provide strong, positive and reinforcing feedback and to avoid situations which become self-fulfilling negative prophesies. Hard aspects to Moon from Saturn (including the seldom used, but in this case, significant biquintile 144°) and Neptune weaken the self-esteem. Coupled with squares or oppositions to Venus from these same planets, the individual will have great difficulty developing any confidence in themselves as lovers and sex partners. Women will often come to believe that all they have to offer a man is abject sexual submission, while men with such difficult aspects will unconsciously tell themselves that money, power or status is all they can offer to interest a woman. Neither person believes that they intrinsically have anything of value to offer simply as friends, companions or colleagues.

In looking at composites involving such personalities, we must be particularly alert to hard aspects in the composite from Neptune or Pluto to Moon or Venus. Neptune squares or oppositions would suggest the partnership will aggravate the already weak self-images of the individuals. Squares or oppositions from Pluto deepen any tendency toward a polarization of the individual personalities, reaching out to extreme expressions of dominance/passivity, bondage and sado-masochism which are often latently present in personalities with fragile self-esteem. In extreme situations, it is these sorts of composite horrors which produce the pimp/prostitute connection or equally unpleasant results.

While one of the most difficult tasks for an astrologer, we can do our best to help the person understand that their history of disastrous relationships is mostly a result of these destructive natal factors which make their sense of self-worth fragile and uncertain and to help them see what motivated them to enter into these doomed partnerships. With composites we can see some of the impact on the self-esteem of the individual which a constant exposure to the other partner might generate, whether it will be a reassuring and supportive interplay or whether it further diminishes the self-image. At the least, we can try to alert the person to their tendencies and hope their own intelligence and insight will make it less likely in the future that they will be seduced into poor match-ups by the abject need of an equally uncertain and unstable partner.

Caveat Astrologea Finitum *(DON'T OVERINTERPRET!)*

In these appended, somewhat wandering observations and speculations, I have deliberately not offered any precise equations of signs, aspects and houses which then should be interpreted to certainly produce some of the behavior described. Some of the primary natal chart ingredients are suggested but only the primaries, not the many subtle and contributory lesser factors. Aside from my desire to stimulate the reader to find their own unique and personal answers to these intriguing astrological puzzles, we must always remind ourselves of the most reliable axiom of the art: no single factor will produce a visible behavioral result. It is the *convergence* of many factors all pointing in a parallel direction which results in distinct and obvious behavior patterns. Charts must be interpreted holistically. The typical chart will have many factors pulling in many directions with the result that the behavior patterns of the individual will wind up somewhere in the quite ordinary and conventional "middle," following a relatively tranquil life pattern without extremes. It is only in the arithmetical uncommon situation where all or most of the dominant elements of the chart pile up on one side of the ledger do we then see such out-of-the-ordinary behavior in relationships as May/December match-ups, role reversals, self-defeating partnerships and the like. Every serious astrologer should have this axiom pasted on the inside of their skull as a reminder to avoid over-interpreting the significance of a few strong elements in charts and to keep from scaring the hell out of the poor person whose chart is being analyzed. Even when a chart does indicate a potent pull toward such atypical behavior, never underestimate the power of social convention, fear, guilt or, in many cases, the certain conviction that God is watching and would certainly send down a lightning bolt if the person gave in to their inner drives. Charts are only birth *potentials*. We should constantly thank the deities of the cosmos that, along with those potentials, they included a large measure of free will in giving expression to our particular package of hereditary gifts and burdens.

CHARTS AND GRIDS FOR SYNASTRY

	☉	☽	☿	♀	♂	♃	♄	♅	♆	♇	NATAL °	SIGN	HOUSE	SOLAR °	SIGN	HOUSE
☉																
☽																
☿																
♀																
♂																
♃																
♄																
♅																
♆																
♇																
A																

Figure A: Natal and Solar Chart Work Sheet

Worksheets, like much else in astrology, ultimately must be adapted to particular needs of the practitioner. For the beginner in synastry, the worksheet in Figure A is a good, multi-purpose starting point in laying out the natal and solar charts of an individual. Since only the signs and houses change from the natal to solar chart while the aspects remain constant, this compact sheet allows the astrologer to see on one sheet the relationship between the two charts. The same format, or course, can be used for the construction of the composite chart.

Figure B: Synastric Overlay Grid

This is a simple grid in which any combination of notal or solar planetary positions can be arrayed for analysis of the aspect relationships between charts. The reader may wish to add columns to display the overlay house positions (i.e. the houses of one subject in which the planets of another subject fall). The same format may be used for comparison of mid-points of one chart to the natal positions of another.

SUBJECT # 1

	☉	☽	☿	♀	♂	♃	♄	♅	♆	♇	A
☉	•										
☽		•									
☿			•								
♀				•							
♂					•						
♃						•					
♄							•				
♅								•			
♆									•		
♇										•	
A											•

SUBJECT # 2

"Sally" and "John"
A Case Study in the use of synastric grids and analytic techniques

To illustrate the use of the charts and grids of synastry and, within the limits of the case study method, point up some of the analytic conclusions which can be derived from synastric techniques, I have chosen a case which first came to me in the early 1970's and one in which I had the unusual opportunity to track the lives of the individuals for more than fifteen years thereafter. The case involved "Sally," a very pretty 19 year old working as a technician and showing promise of a fine career and "John," then 42 years old and a successful executive. They had met in the course of their work and fell almost immediately into a very intense romantic and sexual relationship. At the time Sally brought her questions to me, the relationship had been functioning about four months. Sally, of course, wanted most of all to know whether this overwhelmingly romantic and intense affair would lead to a permanent relationship and marriage, an outcome she was persuaded would be the answer to her prayers. On the following page are the natal and solar charts of Sally and John.

At first look, these charts would not seem to have much in common despite the fact that their natal Suns are in compatible signs. Sally's chart is dominated by the 1st, 2nd and 3rd houses with Gemini in key positions. Her basic inclinations would be rather self-oriented with a concern for creating a personal environment which conformed to her 19-year-old paradigm of "the good life." The tell-tale 7th house position of Saturn suggested that she would rationalize fulfilling this need by looking to much older, established men (although the basic dynamic remained an unconscious doubt that she could meet the requirements of true peer relationship with a contemporary male). In addition, her 7th house placement of Neptune created a rather over-romanticized image of male/female relationships and made her vulnerable to blurring the line between fantasy and reality in one-to-one relationships.

John, despite his sturdy and conservative sun sign, had a chart dominated by the highly emotionally responsive water signs. With his stellium in the parental and Cardinal sign of Cancer and his intensely sexual Scorpio placement of Venus, he would have been a very enthusiastic lover. With Saturn in the 11th house, he tended to find more compatibility with persons either much older or much younger than himself, especially in terms of his social values and world view. The 8th house Sun placement not only caused him to look primarily to sexual fulfillment in a relationship, but also added to his general sensuality of style. The Venus/Mars trine in water signs made the role of lover an easy and comfortable one. For Sally, with her much afflicted Venus causing difficulty for her in moving easily into intimacy, his casual confidence and emotional responsiveness was magnetic.

Sally (natal)

	☉	☽	☿	♀	♂	♃	♄	♅	♆	♇	NATAL °	SIGN	HOUSE	SOLAR °	SIGN	HOUSE
☉		•	•	•	•	♂	⊼		⊼	□	23	♉	2	27	♓	11
☽			•	•	♂	•	•	•	•	•	10	♊	3	14	♈	11
☿				•	•	♂	•	•	•	•	12	♉	3	16	♓	11
♀					•	•	☍	□	☍	△	16	♈	1	20	♒	9
♂						•	•	•	•	•	9	♊	3	13	♈	11
♃							•	•	•	•	29	♉	3	3	♈	11
♄								□	♂	✶	21	♎	7	25	♌	5
♅									□	•	15	♋	4	19	♉	12
♆										✶	21	♎	7	25	♌	5
♇				Asc. ♓ 27°							20	♌	5	24	♊	2
A	✶	•	✶	•	•	✶	•	•	•	•						

John (natal)

	☉	☽	☿	♀	♂	♃	♄	♅	♆	♇	NATAL °	SIGN	HOUSE	SOLAR °	SIGN	HOUSE
☉		✶	♂	∠	•	•	•	•	•	✶	24	♍	8	7	♒	5
☽			•	•	•	♂	•	•	•	♂	22	♋	6	5	♐	3
☿				•	•	•	□	•	•	•	2	♎	8	15	♒	5
♀					△	△	✶	•	✶	•	10	♏	9	15	♓	6
♂						♂	☍	□	•	♂	12	♋	6	25	♏	3
♃							•	□	•	♂	16	♋	6	29	♏	3
♄								•	△	•	5	♑	11	18	♉	8
♅									•	□	14	♈	3	27	♌	12
♆											4	♍	7	17	♑	4
♇				Asc. ♒ 7°							20	♋	6	3	♐	3
A	•	•	△	□	•	•	•	•	•	•						

This was a coming together almost classic in its ingredients: a pretty 19 year old with a head full of romantic fantasy and a preference for older men and an attractive, emotionally response and sexual man whose maturity only gave an extra polish to his natural aptitudes as a lover. It was no wonder at this time that they saw themselves as *star-crossed lovers.*

The following overlay grids which compare the *solar* projected qualities of each of these persons, as they acted on each other's natal charts and generated the early attraction, draw a fairly clear picture of what each believed to be the "personality" of the others, sadly almost entirely in error. With John's Virgo Sun and dominance of Water signs, Sally's solar-projected Pisces "Sun" (her natal Ascendant) and her solar-projected Aquarius "Venus" matching his Ascendant had persuaded him initially that Sally would fill his need for a sweet, romantic companion. Even the close square formed between his natal Mars and Sally's solar-projected "Moon" only heightened the emotional and sexual intensity of his response, a response mirrored in Sally's response to the close opposition of her natal Sun and John's solar-projected "Mars."

Sally "saw" in John his projected Aquarius and Sagittarius qualities and found these warmly compatible with her Gemini Moon and Mars and Aries Venus. In addition, each managed to "capture" critical planets in the 5th and 7th houses, further invigorating the

Comparison of Sally (solar) and John (natal)		27 ♓ ☉	14 ♈ ☽	16 ♓ ☿	20 ♒ ♀	13 ♈ ♂	3 ♈ ♃	25 ♌ ♄	19 ♉ ♅	25 ♌ ♆	24 ♊ ♇	23 ♉ A
24 ♍	☉	☍		☍	•		•	•	△	•	□	△
22 ♋	☽	△	•	△	⊼	•	•	•	✶	□	•	✶
2 ♎	☿	•	•	•	•	•	✶	•	•	•	•	•
10 ♏	♀	•	•	△	•	•	•	•	☍	•	•	•
12 ♋	♂	•	□	△	•	□	•	•	•	•	•	
16 ♋	♃	•	□	△	•	□	•	•	✶	•		
5 ♑	♄	•	•	•	•		□	•				
14 ♈	♅	•	☌	•	•	☌	•	•	•	•		
4 ♍	♆	•	•	•	•	•	⊼	•	•	•	•	•
20 ♋	♇	△	•	△	•	•	•	•	✶	•	•	✶
7 ♒	A	•	•	•		•	✶					•

Comparison of John (solar) and Sally (natal)

		23 ♉ ☉	10 ♊ ☽	12 ♉ ☿	16 ♈ ♀	9 ♊ ♂	29 ♉ ♃	21 ♎ ♄	15 ♋ ♅	21 ♎ ♆	20 ♌ ♇	27 ♓ A
7 ♒	☉	•	△	□	•	△	•	•	•	•	•	•
5 ♐	☽	•	△	•	•	△	☍	•	•	•	•	•
15 ♒	☿	•	△	•	•	△	•	△	⊼	△	☍	•
23 ♓	♀	✶	•	•	•	•	✶	⊼	•	⊼	•	☌
25 ♏	♂	☍	•	•	•	•	☍	•	•	•	□	△
29 ♏	♃	☍	•	•	•	•	☍	•	•	•	•	△
18 ♉	♄	☌	•	☌	•	•	•	•	✶	•	•	•
27 ♌	♅	□	•	•	•	•	□	•	•	•	☌	•
17 ♑	♆	△	•	△	•	•	•	□	☍	□		
3 ♐	♇		☍	•	•	☍	☍	•	•	•	•	•
24 ♍	A	△	•	•	•	•	△	•	•	•	•	☍

early contacts. At the time Sally brought this problem to me, the real personalities of each were beginning to break through the solar chart illusions and create doubts about the true content of the relationship.

It is quite apparent, in responding to the "attraction" of each other's solar charts, the trines and oppositions dominated the important interactions between the inner planets. This pattern initially had suggested to each that there was a great deal of both compatibility between them and, in the case of the opposition, that a "natural" partnership quality was built into the relationship. Even where an occasional square entered the responses, it tended only to heighten the emotionalism of the attraction.

The following overlay of the two natal charts, however, revealed a much different picture. Much of the apparent compatibility (the trines) have disappeared and there is little to suggest any capacity for functioning as partners. Instead, a pattern of strong (but not necessarily happy) aspects between the Venuses and the Uranuses indicates the only real link between the natal personalities was to impulsively persist in a limited romantic/sexual interaction. Despite the powerful initial attraction, Sally and John appeared to be making love to fantasies which existed almost entirely in their own imaginations rather to the real individuals revealed by the charts. Sally's predisposition to self-gratification and affairs with older men and her less than realistic visions about relationships coupled with John's intense emotionalism, sexual priorities and shared discontent and illusions about relationships had permitted them to continue this romantic illusion for some time, but it would be inevitable that the underlying natal personalities would eventually break through this dreamy scenario and confront the two with the fact that they were not, in truth, compatible personalities.

Comparison of Sally and John Natal Charts

		23 ♉ ☉	10 ♊ ☽	12 ♉ ☿	16 ♈ ♀	9 ♊ ♂	29 ♉ ♃	21 ♎ ♄	15 ♋ ♅	21 ♎ ♆	20 ♌ ♇	27 ♓ A
24 ♍	☉	△	•	•	•	•	△	•	•	•	•	☍
22 ♋	☽	✶	•	•	□	•	•	□	☌	□	•	✶
2 ♎	☿	•	•	•	•	•	△	•	•	•	•	☍
10 ♏	♀	•	⊼	☍	•	•	•	•	△	•	•	•
12 ♋	♂	•	•	✶	□	•	•	•	☌	•	•	•
16 ♋	♃	•	•	✶	□	•	•	•	☌	•	•	•
5 ♑	♄	•	•	•	•	•	•	•	•	•	•	•
14 ♈	♅	•	•	•	☌	•	•	•	•	•	•	
4 ♍	♆	△	•	△	•	•	•	□	☍	□		
20 ♋	♇	✶	•	•	□	•	•	□	☌	□	•	•
7 ♒	A	•	△	•	•	△	•	•	•	•	•	•

In the final step of constructing the composite chart below for Sally and John to attempt to analyze the probable outcome should they attempt to establish a continuing and more committed partnership, the essential character of the interaction is quite clear. Despite their essentially incompatible personalities, they probably could, if they chose, sustain a partnership for a time. Nonetheless, the composite chart rather clearly shows that the heart of the partnership would be a 5th house interaction: a form of relating much more suitable for persons who see each other occasionally, but do not attempt to live together or create a true blending of the personalities. This is a "fun and games" house, ideal for frequent dating and "getting married for the weekend," but seldom a sound basis for a 24 hours a day, seven days a week relationship. The placement of Mars in the 4th house would probably make any attempt to share a home fraught with confrontation and irritability, exposing the underlying incompatibilities. Perhaps most unpromising is the heavy afflictions from Neptune in the composite, suggesting that the relationship would

Composite chart: Sally and John

	☉	☽	☿	♀	♂	♃	♄	♅	♆	♇	NATAL °	SIGN	HOUSE
☉		☌	•	•	☌	•	•	•	□	•	4	♋	5
☽			•	•	☌	☌	•	•	□	•	1	♋	5
☿				•	•	•	•	✶	✶	☌	1	♌	6
♀					•	•	△	✶	✶	☌	28	♋	5
♂						☌	•	•	□	•	26	♊	4
♃							•	•	□	•	23	♊	4
♄								☍	✶	•	28	♏	9
♅									△	✶	0	♊	3
♆										•	28	♍	7
♇											5	♌	6
A	△	△	•	•	△	△	□	□	•	•			

endlessly suffer not only from illusion and misunderstanding, but also from the fact that neither person would ever be secure in their feelings about either the purpose or the long-term future of the relationship.

This analysis was not, of course, what Sally wanted to hear. She nodded her head in seeming understanding, but it was evident that she was not prepared to accept my half-whimsical prescription that they rent adjacent apartments and enjoy each other as frequent visitors, but not as roomies or marriage partners. As is often the case, there was no opportunity to discuss this matter with the other partner at the time, a person I felt might be able to deal more realistically with the situation.

It would be nice to report here that all this brilliant analysis and sage advice saved Sally and John from much grief and sadness. It did not and, for the umpteenth time, the astrologer failed to deflect the individuals from what seemed an obviously dead-end course. One of the hard lessons an astrologer learns is that no matter how good the advice and insight, individuals still steer their own lives and run off of cliffs despite our best efforts. It was with mixed feelings that I watched the lives of Sally and John unfold over the following fifteen years.

About two months later, John, with the advantage of more life experience and perhaps a more rational approach to life, arrived at the same general conclusions revealed by the synastric analysis. He suggested that they not spend so much time together, enjoy each other at a less involved level and, especially, not have great expectations that the relationship would lead to marriage. Sally was predictably deeply disappointed and hurt by this sensible but still devastating decision of John's. She broke off the relationship entirely and, full of anger and hurt, leaped into an ill-advised marriage to a wealthy businessman within a few months of the break-up, a marriage which ended rather un-pleasantly within a year. Fifteen years later, Sally (now in her mid-30's and still quite beautiful) is making a fourth try at marriage. The three preceding unsuccessful tries all involved men at least 20 years her senior: successful, established and affluent. When I last spoke with her, she had great hopes for the fourth partnership because it involved a man nearer her own age and of modest circumstances. Time, it seems, had been more successful than I had been in teaching her something of herself.

John continued amiably through the fifteen years, attracting a rather consistent flow of young women and revelling in these romantically and sexually exciting escapades, but successfully withdrawing from them before they became permanent commitments. He claims that he would, as he nears the end of his sixth decade, like to find some nice lady and get married, but I rather doubt this will occur. He still maintains the best and warmest relationships with all the ladies he has known, shepherding them through their subse-quent marriages and children. It is difficult to know whether he would characterize himself as "happy," but the life mode he follows seems to be a not entirely unrewarding reconciliation of his persistent inability to find a satisfactory enduring relationship (Neptune in the 7th) and his highly activated Venus and Mars. On balance, he seems to have made a more tranquil peace with his own natal chart personality than has Sally.

This case study then is a fair exercise in several basic themes in synastry. Persons can be mightily attracted, be largely incompatible, yet can form some sort of functioning partnership: enough of one at least to persuade the individuals to continue to try to make the relationship work long after they should. It illustrates some of the dynamics of May/ December atypical relationships with all the pitfalls contained therein. Perhaps most of all, it illustrates the limits and frustrations of the practicing astrologer. To see and understand a problem, and even to communicate it clearly to the subjects is still no guarantee that the subjects will use their free will in a positive way. All we can do is try.

The Whitford Planet Series

Among the most important astrology books being published today

E.W. Neville continues a long and highly respected tradition: The Whitford Planet Series. These books, by some of America's foremost astrologers, represent the most current thinking about the art and science of Astrology available today. They are essential tools for anyone who is a serious student or practitioner, bringing them the information and ideas they need in an accurate, clear, straightforward manner.

The books on the following pages may be purchased from the publisher or your bookstore.. To order or request a free catalogue write to Whitford Press, 1469 Morstein Road, West Chester, Pennsylvania 19380. Please include $2.00 for postage with your book order.

**Planets in Aspect:
Understanding Your
Inner Dynamics**
Robert Pelletier.
Explores aspects–the
planetary relationships that
describe our individual
energy patterns–and shows
how we can integrate them
into our lives. Every major
aspect is covered.
Size: 6 1/2" x 9 1/4"
363 pp.   paperbound
ISBN: 0-914918-20-6
$19.95

**Planets in Composite:
Analyzing Human
Relationships**
Robert Hand.
Shows how to use and
interpret the composite chart
to understand relationships.
Includes delineations of
composite Sun, Moon, and
planets in all houses and
major aspects.
Size: 6 1/2" x 9 1/4"
paperbound   372 pp.
ISBN: 0-914918-22-2
$19.95

Planets in Houses: Experiencing Your Environment

Robert Pelletier. Delineates the meaning of each planet according to its house position. Also interpreted is the relationship of the occupied house to the other houses.
Size: 6 1/2" x 9 1/4"
paperbound   372 pp.
ISBN: 0-914918-27-3
$19.95

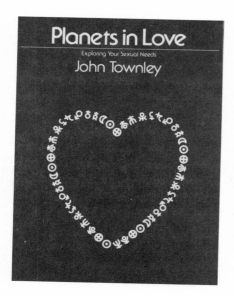

Planets in Love: Exploring Your Emotional and Sexual Needs

John Townley.
An intimate astrological analysis of sex and love, with 550 interpretations of each planet in every sign, house, and major aspect.
Size: 6 1/2" x 9 1/4"
372 pp.   paperbound
ISBN: 0-914918-21-4
$18.95

Planets in Signs
Skye Alexander.
The complete picture of the Sun, the Moon and planets through the twelve signs of the zodiac. Includes elements and modalities, and the meaning of dominance or weakness of one of these important energies. Examples of famous people are included for illustration. A complete and in-depth study of the planets operation through the astrological signs.
Size: 6 1/2" x 9 1/4"
paperbound   272 pp.
ISBN: 0-914918-79-6
$18.95

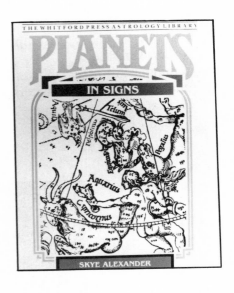

Planets in Transit:
Life Cycles for Living
Robert Hand.
Delineations of the Sun, Moon, and each planet transiting each natal house and forming each aspect to the natal Sun, Moon, planets, Ascendant, and Midheaven.
Size: 6 1/2" x 9 1/4"
532 pp.   paperbound
ISBN: 0-914918-24-9
$22.95

Planets in Youth:
Patterns of Early Development
Robert Hand.
A major astrological thinker looks at children and childhood. All important horoscope factors are delineated.

Size: 6 1/2" x 9 1/4"   paperbound   372 pp.
ISBN: 0-914918-26-5 $18.95

Also by E.W. Neville

Tarot for Lovers Love may make the world go 'round, but it also causes lots of confusion for many of us. In this enlightening, easy-to-use book, E. W. Neville helps you understand yourself and your relationships through the timeless and beautiful medium of Tarot. (Whitford)

Size: 6 1/4" x 9 1/4"   188 pp.
ISBN:0-914918-75-3   paperbound $14.95

Other Books from the Whitford Astrological Library

Asteroid Goddesses: Ceres, Pallas, Juno & Vesta with Ephemeris Demetra George with Douglas Bloch.
A comprehensive guide to utilizing these four asteroids in astrology. Includes delineations by sign, house and aspects.
Size: 5 3/8" x 8 3/8"
367 pp.   paperbound
ISBN: 0-917086-75-9
$14.95

Astrology Inside Out
Bruce Nevin.
This original rethinking of astrology uses visualization and meditation exercises to help beginners and experienced astrologers strengthen their intuitive grasp of astrological patterning.
Size: 6 1/2" x 9 1/4"
300 pp.   paperbound
ISBN: 0-914918-19-2
$18.95

Astrology, Nutrition and Health Robert Carl Jansky.
Demonstrates in non-technical language how astrology can help the reader understand the components of metabolism and health.
Size: 6 1/2" x 9 1/4"
180 pp.   paperbound
ISBN: 0-914918-08-7
$12.95

Astrology & Past Lives
Mary Devlin.
This unique and original book is the first to examine birth charts for previous incarnations. Devlin shows you how to interpret past-life charts and compare them to your present one.
Size: 6 1/2" x 9 1/4"
287 pp.   paperbound
ISBN: 0-914918-71-0
$18.95

Astrology & Relationships
Mary Devlin.
More people consult astrologers about relationship problems than any other single issue. The author of *Astrology & Past Lives* helps you understand your relationships from a variety of astrological perspectives. First, she considers the relationship needs of the individual, as revealed by the natal chart. Next, she analyzes parent/child relationships–where it all begins. Finally, she examines love, romance, sex, marriage, and friendship in depth. Devlin includes synastry delineations, case histories, and past-life interpretations in this thorough study of interpersonal relationships.
Size: 6 1/2" x 9 1/4"
288 pp.   paperbound
ISBN: 0-914918-77-X
$16.95

Birth Pattern Psychology
Tamise Van Pelt.
Utilizing a synthesis of major personality theories, Van Pelt establishes a context in which to understand human communication and behavior. Illustrated.
Size: 6 1/2" x 9 1/4"
351 pp.   paperbound
ISBN: 0-914918-33-8
$14.95

Compendium of Astrology
Rose Lineman and Jan Popelka.
The *Compendium* contains the basic information needed to build a horoscope. A detailed reference text for practicing astrologers and students.
Size: 8" x 9 1/4"
304 pp.   paperbound
ISBN: 0-914918-43-5
$14.95

Essays on Astrology
Robert Hand.
Essays on Astrology is an invaluable reference book. Provides fresh insight into the latest thinking of this very significant astrologer.
Size: 6 1/2" x 9 1/4"
176 pp.   paperbound
ISBN: 0-914918-42-7
$14.95

Essential Dignities
J. Lee Lehman, Ph.D.
In this exciting new book, Dr. Lehman recovers an important ancient aspect of astrology which has become misunderstood and diluted: rulerships. By attempting to simplify astrology, contemporary sources have completely obscured the essential differences between planet, sign, and house. While the novice may benefit from this simplification, much of the old logic of the rulership system is covered up. What was nearly lost is given new power and the potential for understanding. A wealth of information is presented in a clear and concise way with many accurate charts.
Size: 6 1/4" x 9 1/4"
256 pp.   paperbound
ISBN: 0-924608-03-X
$14.95

Horary Astrology Rediscovered
Olivia Barclay.
Exploring a branch of astrology that is concerned with answering questions pertaining to life and life events. Ms. Barclay's book is a captivating and beautifully written survey of horary astrology and its relationship with other forms of the science. More than 25 charts and graphs illustrate planetary rulerships, planetary movements, fortitudes and debilities of planets, and answers to questions. A fascinating look at this little-studied branch of astrology.
Size: 6 1/4" x 9 1/4"
340 pp.   paperbound
ISBN:0-914918-99-0
$18.95

Horoscope Symbols
Robert Hand.
Explains the basics with insight, wisdom and perspective. Explores midpoints, harmonics, retrograde planets and more. (Whitford)
Size: 6 1/2"x 9 1/4"
385 pp.   paperbound
ISBN: 0-914918-16-8
$19.95

A Look at Tomorrow Today
Leonard Cataldo and Robert Pelletier.
In this compelling and fascinating study readers are invited to find and utilize the vast riches within. They will discover that they are constituents of one of the twelve zodiacal signs, what that means, and how it influences his life and behavior.
Size: 6 1/4" x 9 1/4"
500 pp.   paperbound
ISBN:0-914918-94-X
$18.95

Marriage Made in Heaven:
An Astrological Guide to Relationships
Alexandra Mark, Ph.D.
Beginning with the construction of a solar chart and birth time chart, this concise, easy-to-read, book takes the reader through the complexities of love and marriage. For the novice astrologer or the experienced, Dr. Mark brings new insight and understanding to how our relationships are influenced by the heavens.
Size: 6" x 9"
256 pages   paperbound
ISBN: 0-914918-90-7 $14.95

Our Stars of Destiny
Faith Javane.
This study focuses on one specific advance in Esoteric Astrology--the introduction and study of the Pentacle (Star of Destiny) and the Pentacle Aspects of the Horoscope. These tools, both old and new, will aid the reader through the symbols they reveal in the Quest for Higher Consciousness.
Size: 6" x 9"
256 pages   paperbound
ISBN: 0-9149189-92-3
$14.95

Quintiles and Tredeciles
Dusty Bunker.
Explores the little-known 72-degree and 108-degree aspects and explains their cosmic significance in the individual chart. The numerological and astrological relevance of quintiles and tredeciles unfolds in four chapters and a wealth of diagrams and charts. Historical details on the meanings of numbers--taken from numerology; sacred geometry; masonic, religious, and Egyptian symbology; and astrology--transport the reader to times when numbers were an "extreme reduction of philosophic thought."

Size 6 1/4" x 9 1/4"
182 pp.   paperbound
ISBN: 0-914918-69-6
$12.95

The Ultimate Asteroid Book
J. Lee Lehman, Ph.D.
The most complete book to date on asteroids. More than seventy of these fascinating heavenly bodies are covered in this book by one of the world's foremost authorities on asteroids. Lehman groups the asteroids according to their areas of influence--business, power, intellect, sex, escapism, and more--and shows you how to interpret their positions to fine-tune your understanding of the birth chart. Lehman also looks at the asteroids from a mythological and historical perspective.
Size: 6 1/4" x 9 1/4"
352 pp.   paperbound
ISBN: 0-914918-78-8
$18.95

World Ephemeris: 20th Century, Midnight Edition.
World Ephemeris: 20th Century, Noon Edition
The *World Ephemeris for the 20th Century* by Para Research is the first computer-calculated and computer-typeset ephemeris with letter quality printing. Sun's position accurate to one second of arc; planetary positions given to one minute of arc. Please specify edition desired.
Size: 8" x 9 1/4"
524 pp.   paperbound
ISBN: 0-914918-60-5 (Midnight edition)
$13.95
ISBN: 0-914918-61-3 (Noon edition)
$13.95